Mrs. J. Sadlier

**The old house by the Boyne**

Recollections of an Irish borough

Mrs. J. Sadlier

**The old house by the Boyne**
*Recollections of an Irish borough*

ISBN/EAN: 9783744740746

Printed in Europe, USA, Canada, Australia, Japan

Cover: Foto ©ninafisch / pixelio.de

More available books at **www.hansebooks.com**

# THE
# OLD HOUSE BY THE BOYNE;

OR,

## RECOLLECTIONS OF AN IRISH BOROUGH.

By MRS. J. SADLIER,

AUTHORESS OF "BLAKES AND FLANAGANS;" "WILLIE BURKE;" "NEW
LIGHTS;" "THE CONFEDERATE CHIEFTAINS;" "ELINOR PRESTON"
"BESSY CONWAY;" "THE CONFESSIONS OF AN APOSTATE;" "CON
O'REGAN;" "OLD AND NEW;" "THE HERMIT OF THE ROCK."

NEW YORK:
P. J. KENEDY,
EXCELSIOR CATHOLIC PUBLISHING HOUSE,
5 BARCLAY ST.

1899.

Copyright,
D. & J. SADLIER & CO.
1885.

# DEDICATION.

To those of my many Drogheda friends whom the reaper Death, and the vicissitudes of fifty years have left remaining amid the historic scenes I have here faintly sketched—and also to the memory of those others who have long since passed to the unseen world—in token of my undying remembrance of the pleasant days, and weeks, and months spent amongst them in the sunny years of my life's spring-time, these few "Reminiscences" of their ancient and honored borough are cordially and gratefully dedicated.

M. A. SADLIER.

# THE OLD HOUSE BY THE BOYNE;

### OR,

## RECOLLECTIONS OF AN IRISH BOROUGH.

### CHAPTER I.

LET people say what they will of modern improvements, and the advantages of modern progress, there are few amongst us who do not love to contemplate the relics of past ages, monuments of a time, or times long anterior to the rise of "modern progress," and boasting none of the "modern improvements." Few American-born readers can realize to themselves the antique character of an old European town dating from the medieval times, the quaint, queer, yet simple and substantial edifices of the older parts contrasting oddly with the newer and more ornamentative portions. the growth of later years. Comparatively few of these old fortified boroughs are now to be seen in the British islands, at least, in anything like their original aspect. Of those which still arrest the traveller's attention in journeying through Ireland, one of the old-

grandeur over the steep and narrow street which bears its name, guarding the approach to the Tholsel or Town Hall, which stands near the junction of Lawrence street and West street with Shop street and Peter street; the latter two forming the line from the bridge to the North Barracks and St. Peter's Church, ever memorable as the scene of the burning of over two thousand of the first citizens of Drogheda (who had taken shelter within it) by order of Oliver Cromwell. The West Gate at the opposite extremity of the town has all but disappeared in the lapse of time, and so, too, with Sunday Gate, the northern approach to the old borough in the days of its primeval strength.

Here and there within the ancient boundaries may still be seen the remains of many civil, ecclesiastical and monastic buildings of the old time, such as Mary's Abbey, a Carmelite foundation near the modern church of that name already mentioned, appropriated to Protestant worship,—Magdalen's Steeple, the time-honored remains of a stately Dominican Church, of old connected with an Abbey of the same order. Then, just within the West Gate, stand the ruins of an old Observantine friary, called "The Old Abbey." The dilapidated remains of the Grey Friary form a picturesque object on the high ground in the northeastern part of the town, and on the south side, but a short distance from the river, some faint traces may still be seen of what was once a Priory and Hospital of the Knights of St. John. Other relics of the mon astic institutions of long-past ages are still to be seen in various parts of the town, but in a state of such utter dilapidation as only to be distinguished on a near approach. One of these is the old friary of St Lawrence, a little way outside Lawrence's Gate, surrounded by a very ancient burying-ground called "The Cord"—a singular designation, the origin of which is now lost in the night of time.*

The Tholsel itself, a gloomy, dark-faced building, situate in West street, near the corner of Shop street, is a curious, but by no means attractive specimen of the civil architecture of the Middle Ages, and no one can look on its massive stone walls, and deeply-set windows, without reverting in thought to the stormy strife of those by-past times, and the sturdy burgesses who of old assembled for "law and justice" within its walls.

Antiquity is, indeed, stamped on the town and all around it, but there is scarcely any locality, any nook or corner within or without the walls where modern buildings, civil, military, commercial and ecclesiastical, are not to be seen rising up in strange contrast to the hoary monuments around them, striking illustra-

* One of our earliest recollections of Drogheda was the perilous ascent, from an adjoining tombstone, of the jagged fragment of wall which alone remains of the old friary, in order to procure a branch of the ivy that festoons its top, to bear back in triumph to our home away north in "green vallied Breffny," as a momento of our first visit to the old historic borough. The sunshine was bright that summer morning, clothing even the old gray ruin and its ivy crown with solemn beauty.

tions, one and the other, of the busy, active, progressive Present, and the calm, sluggish, stern, mysterious Past. So to-day, and even twenty years ago, when last we looked on the well-remembered scene, the banks of the Boyne, where it threads its way between two counties, through the heart of Drogheda, were thickly studded with spinning-mills, corn-mills, and all the other huge fabrics in which modern progress has encased the complicated machinery that does her mighty will in catering for man's use and comfort. Barracks of spacious dimensions adorn the northern and southern extremities of the town; the northern at the head of Peter street as already indicated, the southern on the lofty eminence known as Mill-Mount, commanding from a massive circular tower on the fort, a magnificent view of the river, the town, and the adjoining country, rich in Irish fertility. Through all this motley assemblage of the old and the new, the civil, the military, the secular, and the ecclesiastical, flows on the silvery Boyne, dividing the northern from the southern portions of "the County of the Town of Drogheda," as the old records have it, and as the natives of the place are still proud to call it. Fraught with a thousand historic associations, and a wealth of poetry all its own, the beautiful "bride of Lough Ramor" winds her way through the heart of the old borough to swell the waters of the Irish Sea over the white strand of Bettystown and Mornington.

The town of Drogheda is decidedly an old town, and all is old about it. Its people are old—old in their lineage, to a great extent Norman,—and old in their contempt for what is new and showy, and pretentious. Passing through the streets, you will recognize above the shop-doors, and on door-plates, the names of the knightly Norman families who were actors in the earliest authentic history of Drogheda— the De Verdons (minus only the *d*), the Gernons, the Pentlands, the Whites, the Dardises, the Faulkners, the Simcocks, and many other ancient families are still represented in the old borough, and the Norman is still the staple and dominant element in the population. Then, again, the simple, old-time faith of the townspeople has happily lost none of its positive, straightforward Catholicity, and Drogheda, the Gate of the North, is to-day what it has been ever since the Reformation crossed the Channel, one of the most thoroughly Catholic towns in Ireland. When the ceremonies of religion were proscribed by law in the northern province, and the poverty to which Ulster Catholics were reduced left them only thatched cabins wherein to worship God, the ritual of the Church was still carried out within the walls of Drogheda, and thither, as on pilgrimage, went the northern Catholics, year by year at Paschal time, to witness the religious solemnities they might never see at home. Drogheda was in those days, even but two generations back, the Rome of Ulster, and happy were they who from Cavan, Monaghan, Fermanagh, or Armagh, could go to spend Holy Week in Drogheda. There the religious communities always maintained their ground, and even now the old borough has a sort of monastic character shared by few in Ireland, and by none north of itself.

Though stripped of the wealth and power they once enjoyed, and thrown for support on the charity and piety of the townspeople, the Franciscans, the Dominicans, and the Augustinians still haunted the vicinity of their ancient Abbeys in and around the borough, assisting the secular clergy in ministering to the spiritual wants of the people, and in return for the shelter and protection afforded them, within the strong old town, and the pious offerings of the faithful which supplied their humble wants, "the friars" gave their benison to the place, and whilst edifying the people by their simple and useful lives and the practice of all virtue, they perpetuated amongst them that spirit of piety, and those genuine Catholic instincts which made Drogheda the good old Catholic town that we have described it.

Amongst such a people, and in such a place, it may well be supposed that old social customs, too, would survive the lapse of time, in defiance of modern innovation. Such is really the case, and, perhaps, with the single exception of Galway, no other city or town in Ireland retains so many of the old-time customs, or so much of the good old cheerful spirit in which they had their origin. With some of these peculiarities the reader will make acquaintance in the course of our simple story, to which we must now address ourselves, having sufficiently (as we hope) indicated the manner of place where its scene is laid.

Some fifty years ago there stood (and may still, for aught we know) on the steep shore of the Boyne, just over the Bettystown road which winds close by the river side, an old gray house whose venerable front was thinly shaded by a few spreading trees, chiefly ash and sycamore, whose growth appeared to have been coeval with the house itself, judging by their brown gnarled branches and the grotesque forms their trunks had assumed in the lapse of years. A long flight of narrow stone steps led from the low porch with its two rustic benches to the road and the river, by a wicket gate opening on the green margined footpath that skirts "the dusty highway." A somewhat dilapidated stone wall ran along the base of the almost precipitous slope in front of the house, and a sort of straggling fence of flowering shrubs ran up the steep ascent in parallel lines on either side the steps. Here and there from amid the sparse herbage rose a stunted white-thorn, a prickly furze, or a laurel—the shining green of the latter contrasting well in summer's brief day with the delicate white blossoms of the one and the rich yellow of the other, and in winter giving life to the bleak hill side where only the hardy evergreen could live. The house that crowned the steep was as old and as weather-beaten as house could be, and be inhabited with comfort. It consisted of two stories, surmounted by a high pitched roof of slates, which might, from their appearance, have dated from that very indefinite period " the Wars of Ireland," yet whole and sound withal, as though neglect, at least, had not aided the work of time in defacing and disfiguring the old fabric. The windows were few high, and narrow, with the quaintest of old architraves, and leaden casements with small lozenge-shaped panes that seemed as if meant to exclude as much of the sunlight as possible from the interior of the mansion—for mansion it was, though not a large one. The hall-door was of dark oak curiously panelled, and, like the windows, deeply set in the massive stone wall. It was a gloomy dwelling, as one would say on a first glance, and yet there was that about it which invited a closer examination, and suggested a certain degree of curiosity as to who might be its inmates. People are apt to associate mystery and romance with old houses, if only they look like having " a history," and this one did, though the building and all about it had little claim to beauty, and not much to taste or elegance. Sombre and somewhat stately, it looked, in its dark decay, like what it was, the ancestral home of a family that had once held high place amongst the old Norman settlers on the Boyne side, impoverished now and of small account amongst the thriving, money-making burghers of the new age.

It is late autumn; the short day is drawing to a close, and the lights are coming out in the town and along the river, the wind is blowing from the sea, and dark masses of clouds are drifting over the firmament, whose blue is still seen at intervals far up in the zenith. Dim through the gray light that was fast changing into darkness, might be seen a solitary female figure ascending the steps to our old house, with the quick elastic foot of youth, her figure wrapped in a gray cloak, the hood of which was thrown over her head and drawn closely around her face. Reaching the door, she paused a moment, as though arranging something in her mind, then raised her hand to the grim black knocker representing a grotesque human face, and knocked as one who should be speedily admitted, smiling at some quaint conceit as the sound reverberated in hollow echoes through the old mansion.

"Thank God!" said, in a subdued voice, the old woman, who, with candle in hand, came to the door. "Thank God you're come back safe, Miss Rose! Dear me! if there isn't the candle gone out!"

"Safe! why should I not come back safe? What did you suppose was going to happen to me?"

"Oh! then, it's hard to say, Miss, hard to say! it's ill walkin' at nightfall out of doors, and Baltray is a wild place, at the best. But wait a minute, Miss, till I go and light the candle."

A merry laugh was the lady's answer as she tripped along the flagged hall, and opened a door at the further end, from which a warm cheerful glow streamed out for a moment on the dark walls.

"The Lord save us!" muttered old Nancy, as she groped her way through a smaller passage branching off from the hall to the rear portion of the building,

" long as I'm in the place, I never can get over the fear of it. An' to see Miss Rose there, how little she minds it. Dark an' light, night an' day, all's one to her!"

The room that Rose Ackland entered was a sort of parlor, large, though not lofty, and scantly, but comfortably furnished; the furniture being of that antiquated style which might be expected in such a place, some of it showing but too plainly the many, many years it had been in use. There was no carpet on the dark oaken floor, with the exception of a piece some eight or ten feet square in front of the wide, grateless fireplace, in which some logs of wood were burning on brazen dogs, shedding that ruddy glow over the nearer parts of the old room which painters love to catch in their home-pictures. There was no other light in the room. Two persons sat by the fire; one a gentleman advanced in years, the other a lady many years younger, yet no longer young, whose pale, subdued features looked wan in the firelight, yet fair and sweet withal. Her eyes were on her knitting, but not her thoughts, and every moment the shadow was growing deeper on her brow, when Rose's entrance dispelled the cloud and drew an exclamation of pleasure even from the silent old man whose look had been moodily fixed on the flickering blaze before him. A large, portly looking cat which had been dozing in luxurious ease on the arm of his chair roused herself, too, and bounded from her perch to welcome the new arrival.

"How long you staid, Rose!" said the elder lady reproachfully; "we began to fear that something must be wrong, and I could scarcely persuade your grandpapa from going to meet you. Indeed, my child, you ought to be more careful!"

"Careful, Aunt Lydia! careful of what?" said Rose, as, having kissed her grandfather, and laid aside her cloak and bonnet, she sat down by her matronly aunt, and stooped to fondle the dignified tabby who was rubbing against her skirts, purring her welcome home.

"Why, careful of your life,—of your health, my dear,—not to speak of propriety."

"No *need* to speak of propriety, I should hope, my sage aunt!" and Rose's dark eyes twinkled mirthfully. "They are all very *proper* people at Baltray, and I hope you consider *me* both proper and sedate." She tried hard to look sedate, at which her aunt smiled, and tapped her cheek, whilst her grandfather laughed, a low, quiet laugh peculiar to himself.

"You may as well let her alone, Lydia; you see she grows wilder and more wilful as she grows older. But what news from Baltray, Rosey? How did you find old Mabel?"

"Much better in body, grandpa, but sorely troubled in mind."

"Indeed? why, what's the matter with her?"

"Anything wrong with Barney?"

"No, aunt, Barney is doing very well, indeed. But you will laugh when you hear the cause of Mabel's trouble. She has been dreaming of late about us here, and is quite sure that something is going to happen. She bid me tell you, aunt, in particular, that she heard the Banshee *keening* every night for the last three———."

"Nonsense, Rosey!" said Miss Ackland, lowering her voice with an anxious look at her father, who was somewhat deaf, "how can you rattle on so?—I wonder at you to repeat such silly stuff."

"Well, but, aunt! she told me to tell you, and I'm sure I didn't think it was any harm. And she gave me another message for you," she added, pouting, "but I suppose I must not tell it."

The aunt smiled, a shade of something like curiosity appearing on her calm face. "You may as well finish when once you began, only speak lower. What was Mabel's other message for me?"

"That last night, as she lay between sleeping and waking, one that *you* used to know came and stood beside her bed, and a smile on his face for all the world as if he was alive and well."

"Child, child, what have you been saying?" cried the old man, pointing to his daughter, and Rose, turning quickly, saw that her aunt had fallen back in her chair pale and trembling. Rose, in great trepidation, began to apologize, but her aunt, recovering her composure, rose with a forced smile, and saying it was almost time for tea, kissed the rosy cheek of the wondering girl, and left the room. In vain did Rose look to her grandfather for explanation; he had fallen into one of his musing fits, and seemed wholly unconscious of her presence. There was a comical look of bewilderment on Rose's face, as she stood gazing on the door by which her aunt had retreated. "Message, indeed!" said she, half aloud, "well, I'm sure Mabel may deliver her own messages for me, for the time to come! But, dear me! who'd have thought that my stately Aunt Lydia should be so overcome by the 'silly stuff' she blamed poor me for repeating! Well! miracles will never cease!"

When the little family met at tea half an hour later, there was not a trace of emotion on Miss Ackland's face; a shade paler than her wont she might have been, but her manner was just the same as usual, calm, self-possessed, and what some might consider, cold—the very opposite of Rose's bright, gushing, superabundant vivacity. Rose, with her black eyes round, full, sparkling, her rosy cheeks, and wavy brown hair, her rounded girlish figure, somewhat inclining to the "plump," and the careless buoyancy of spirit which defied all rules of conventional mannerism, was the very personification of life's blithe springtime, whilst her aunt, tall, shapely, dignified, though rather handsome not particularly so, and sad-browed withal, was like autumn,—early autumn,—her smile, when she did smile, bright and cheering as the sun that lights October woods and makes a glory of their gorgeous beauty. As for the old gentleman, the father of one and the grandfather of the other, he seemed to have reached that, perhaps, enviable stage of existence when life's cares are but half felt, and life's pleasures but half enjoyed—the dimness of age was settling down on his senses, and although his face, once strikingly handsome, still retained traces of superior intelligence, and his tall figure had lost but little of its original height, Mr. Ackland looked the old man he was, with the weight of threescore years and ten bowing down his once stalwart frame. His long hair, "silver'd o'er with age," and parted in the middle, hung down on either side his head, giving to his strongly-marked Norman features that venerable aspect so becoming in age. Beside the old gentleman, on a high chair that had probably been Rose's when a baby, and regularly set at table for the purpose, sat Tib the cat, watching demurely the progress of the meal of which she always had her due apportionment, for Mr. Ackland would by no means trust the feeding of his favorite to old Nancy, who was known to regard her with no friendly feelings, for reasons known to herself, and not altogether unknown to others.

There was comfort within the quiet dwelling, and around the plain but neatly-served tea-table of the Acklands. The room which served them as a general *salle-a-manger*, was smaller than the one in which we first saw them, with an old-fashioned grate and a coal fire in the fireplace, and directly opposite an arched recess, in which stood a heavy mahogany sideboard, as old apparently as itself. Red moreen curtains were drawn down over the one window of the room, shutting out the dark night and the howling winds that were abroad on land and water.

"How snug it is in here,' said Rose, glancing around with that sense of comfort which belongs of right and by force of contrast to the winter evening, " but it is a wild night on sea, and I fear we shall hear of shipwrecks to-morrow. Do you know, aunt, I have never got over the fear of high wind since the night of the great storm."

"I wonder you remember it so well, Rosey," said her aunt, speaking with apparent effort, for some sad memory seemed uppermost in her mind at the moment; "you were but a little child at the time; it was the year before your poor mamma's death."

"Oh! *don't* I remember it for all that? Indeed I do!"

"What do you remember, Rose?' inquired Mr. Ackland, who had caught but the one word. Unlike most deaf persons he never raised his voice in speaking; his tones were, if anything, lower and more subdued than in former years, before that first symptom of advancing age had come upon him. "What did you say you remembered?"

"The night of the great storm, grandpapa, a night like this always makes me think of it."

"Ah! that *was* an awful night," said the old man dreamily, as though endeavoring to recall the time and the scene; "yes, I, too, remember it well. But"— and his eye shone with something of its former fire, " tremendous as the storm was our Fair Trader weathered it. Wasn't it great of the little captain and his saucy craft to keep afloat in such weather, when the sea was covered with wrecks, and the noblest ships that sailed the channel went down head foremost? ha! and she the only Drogheda vessel out that night! eh, Lydia?"

"It was certainly something to boast of, papa," said Miss Ackland, pleased to see her father's interest excited, and desirous of keeping it up. "I don't wonder that the merchants of Drogheda presented Captain B—— with such a substantial testimonial in token of their admiration."

"*I* was one of the first to move in getting it up," said Mr. Ackland, and he drew himself up with the harmless vanity of an old man.

"So I have often heard, papa, and, indeed, I remember it well myself. The Trader was popular before, but it was that night that made her reputation and that of her active, spirited little captain, of whom I have heard you speak many a time."

Nancy now appeared to "remove the tea-things," in answer to Miss Ackland's ring, and Rose could not help laughing at the scowling look she cast on the cat, and the muttered comments on her being allowed at the table all as one as a Christian, which she knew could not reach "the master's" ears.

"God grant he mayn't be sorry for it when it's too late!" said she, half to the ladies, half to herself, as she made her exit with the tea-tray, after darting another angry look at the unconscious object of her singular aversion.

## CHAPTER II.

THE old house was somewhat dull at times for Rose Ackland's liking; not but what she was happy —happy in the love and gentle companionship of her aunt, and the doting fondness of her grandfather whose darling she was, as may well be supposed; moreover, she had never known a gayer life than that she led with them, and she knew no reason, therefore, why she should desire a change. She was happy, too, in the regular routine of her daily life, and in its unbroken peace forgot its dullness and monotony. Hers was not a nature wherein there lie depths unseen of mortal eye, depths which, like the pool of Bethesda, await their time to be troubled, stirred into good or evil; bright, cheerful, transparent, she was born to make joy around her, and to be made glad and joyous; gloom and discontent were alike unknown to her, and care she had never known, so could not realize. Brought up by her aunt in the sweet and soothing regularity of a Christian life, surrounded only by the good and the refined, she had never seen the dark side of life, or of human nature, and passion she knew not even by name. Yet bright, calm, and peaceful as her life was, and little as she knew of the world without, there were times, as we have said, when the gloom and the silence of the old house chilled her buoyant spirit, and she started at the echo of her own footfall, through the tenantless rooms and along the narrow, dimly-lighted corridors, that ran around the winding staircase ascending from the centre of the hall to the topmost story. When of an evening her aunt lapsed into thoughtful silence, as often happened, and her grandpapa dozed in his arm-chair, Rose would have recourse for a while to her piano, but she soon tired of playing when no one listened, and then she was fain to go to the kitchen, and have a chat with old Nancy, who having been in the family since long, long before she was born, knew all about her mother, and the good old days when Mr. Ackland was Mayor of Drogheda, and his house "great for company." In the altered circumstances of the family, Nancy was the only one that remained of a goodly retinue of servants, and although the old woman never lost sight of what the Acklands had been, and never presumed, to any great extent, on her long and faithful service, still it was natural that she should feel herself, and be treated by the family, as something more than an ordinary domestic.

That old kitchen of Nancy's, though large and stone-floored, was the cleanest and cheeriest of kitchens, a very picture of domestic comfort, and so Rose thought when, leaving her grandfather and aunt at their chess or backgammon, she stole off to the kitchen, and took a chair placed by Nancy near the fire, that bleak winter's night after her visit to Baltray. She was scarcely seated when the cat made her appearance, and took her station in the chimney corner opposite, not, however, without an energetic protest on the part of Nancy, who could with difficulty be persuaded to let her remain there.

"She's as wise as any Christian," said she, "the Lord forgive me for evenin' a Christian to a cat—but, sure, it's no wonder," and she lowered her voice to a whisper, "it's the devil's own wit she has, the Lord save us!"

"Why, Nancy," cried Rose with her merry laugh, "how hard you are upon poor Tab! What in the world makes you hate her so?"

"Oh! I'll tell you that another time—when she's not to the fore. It isn't safe ta'kin about the likes of her an' them listenin.' You were down at Baltray, Miss Rosey—what way is Mabel?"

"Pretty well—for her, you know—but fretting herself to death on account of a dream she had."

"A drame!" cried Nancy, much excited; she was given to dreaming herself; "ah then, what was the drame about!"

"Well, that is more than *I* can tell you; she bid me tell Aunt Lydia that she had dreamed of somebody *she* used to know, and the best of it was, that as soon as I told my aunt, thinking, to be sure, that she would laugh at the old creature's sending *her* such a message, she got as pale as death, and came near fainting, I believe. I declare she frightened me almost out of my wits."

"Was it a man or a woman she seen in the drame— that's Mabel, I mane?"

"A man, for I noticed she said '*he*.' But, my goodness! what of that? I'm sure *I* dream about all sorts of things, and people, too, and it never troubles me in the least."

Ah! God help your wit, poor child!" said Nancy in a very serious tone, shaking her head the while, "it's little *you* know about trouble in drames or out o' them. Your time's to come yit,—*astore*, it's all before you."

"What's before me?" said Rose, turning quickly, her curiosity somewhat excited by the old woman's manner still more than her words. "What do you mean, Nancy?"

"I mane, dear, that when you have lived as long, an' come through as much as your aunt,—but God forbid you'd ever do that!" she muttered in an under tone—"you'd maybe be as feard of the drames that come by night as she is now."

"As *she* is?" cried Rose, much surprised; "why, you don't mean to speak so of my aunt, do you? Has *she* had so much trouble in her life? I know all about grandpapa's losses in trade, and all that, and how my poor papa and mamma died within a year of each other. I have often heard my aunt speak of those things, but in a quiet, gentle way,—I never saw her so overcome as she was to-night when I gave her

Mabel's message. What can it mean?" And a shade of thought, all unusual, flitted over the bright girlish face. She was silent a moment, so was Nancy, but when Rose at last lifted her eyes to the old woman standing by her side, she was struck by the look of conscious intelligence that was in her keen gray eyes. "Nancy!" she said, laying hold of her arm, "*you* know it all—you can tell me. I never thought of that. You have known my aunt so long!"

"Ah! God's blessin' be about her, sure I seen her a weeny little thing not so high as the table! Ay!" she added, as if to herself, "I knew her when she was as merry as a kid, an' as happy as the day was long. An' no wonder she would—ah! no wonder. Well! it's a quare world, anyhow!—och! didn't I know them all—all—didn't I know *him*, too,—an' many's the bright silver crown he gave me! Oh sure, sure, it was a pity they didn't come together, for there never was a couple better matched, a'1' so every one said!"

"But you talk of *him*, Nancy? Now, I want to know who *he* was, and all about him. Tell me—there's a good Nancy."

Nancy could never resist the young lady's coaxing—no, never, and she made up her mind to tell her all she knew herself of Miss Ackland's early life; with that intention, she squatted beside her on the floor in that attitude so familiar to an old Irishwoman of her class when she sets herself for a *shanachus*, her hands clasped tightly round her knees.

"Miss Rose," she began, "your aunt wasn't always the same as you see her now. Well! now, only look at that cat," dropping her voice very low, "see how she watches me; I'll engage, now, she understands every word I'm sayin'."

"Oh, dear me, Nancy, don't mind the cat—do go on with your story!"

"Well! Miss, as I was goin' to tell you, your aunt was a fine darlin' young lady about twenty years agone, not so full of fun, or fond of divarsion as you are, but still brisk an' lively, an' as purty a crature as you'd wish to look at—ay! a deal purtier than you are now, Miss Rose, for you see she had skin as white as milk, an' hair as black as a sloe, an' eyes like the blue sky of a bright summer's day when the sun is shinin' through it, An' then she was so tall an' straight, an' you could a'most span her waist, an' she had a step like a queen—well! it's a folly to talk, she *was* a beauty—so *I* thought, anyhow."

"My goodness, Nancy! never mind telling me what Aunt Lydia was then—I can well imagine what she must have been, from what I see her now! But what about the gentleman—for I suppose he *was* a gentleman?"

"'Deed, then, he was, Miss, an' the heart's blood of a gentleman, too, none of your pinked out, dandified sham genteels, but a rale off-handed, good-natured, dashing fellow, with the sperit of a prince, an' the heart of a lion, as I often hard the ould master say—ochone! it's little he thought, then, of all that was to happen in the long run! Tall an' handsome he was, too, with his beautiful head of light-colored hair, an' a light complexion, too, an' the purtiest smile you ever seen on a man's face. An' the voice he had—why, you'd love to hear him talkin', Miss Rose, even if you didn't know him, at all. Well! well! it's a quare way things goes on in this wicked world, when the likes of him 'id be trated in the way he was."

"What way was he treated, Nancy? Or who was he, at all?"

"That's what I'm goin' to tell you, Miss Rose, if you'll only have patience."

"What are you going to tell her, Nancy?"

Both started, and looked round in blank dismay; it was Miss Ackland who spoke, and the icy coldness of her tone, and the stony severity of her look somehow reminded Rose, disconcerted as she was, of the handsome, fair-haired, dashing cavalier to whose praises she had been so eagerly listening, and made her sympathize with that unknown individual in the "treatment" he might possibly have received. Nancy was on her feet in a moment, but somehow she forgot to answer the question put to her.

Miss Ackland looked from one to the other, and she smiled a bitter, inward smile, all unlike her own. Then she laid her hand kindly on her niece's head— "Rose, my dear, go to your grandpapa, he is rather low in spirits to-night, so try and make him laugh, as I know you can."

"Yes, Aunt Lydia!" and Rose tripped away, taking Tab in her arms.

It was not till the parlor door was heard closing after admitting her niece, that Miss Ackland spoke to Nancy; then she said—"Nancy, what were you telling Miss Rose, just now?"

"Nothing at all only—only—now, don't look at me that way, Miss Ackland, and I'll tell you the truth. The dear child wanted to know who it was that Mabel had been dramin' about, that her message troubled *you* so much——"

"Troubled *me* so much?—Nancy, you forget yourself!"

"Well! I didn't mane to say that, Miss Ackland, but now that it's out, let it go. I'm sure its no wondher it would trouble you to hear of *him* that's——"

"Nancy, I have one thing to tell you, once for all," interrupted Miss Ackland more sternly than her old domestic had ever heard her speak—"I do not wish you to speak to Miss Rose of—of," her lip trembled, and her voice faltered—"of the person you allude to. When I deem it proper that she should know the sad story of my life, I will tell her myself. To hear it now would only throw a cloud over her young life, without serving any good purpose. Some day I may tell her all, but not now—oh! not now—and, remember, Nancy! what I say to you—never breathe a word of anything relating to *him*—to me—

in those long-past days. But, tell me, how much *does* she know?"

"Nothing, Miss, nothing worth speaking of—only that there *was* such a person."

"Not his name?"

"No, Miss Ackland; nothing at all only what I tell you."

"It is well; see that it continue so."

The lady then went on to speak of some household matters on which she had come to consult Nancy, and no further allusion was made to the forbidden topic. When Miss Ackland left the kitchen, the old woman stood a moment looking after her, then shook her head, and muttered to herself—"That's the world all over!—Out o' sight, out o' mind!" Simple, soft-hearted old Nancy! much you knew about it!

Miss Ackland thought it a strange coincidence that for the first time in years long her father had that evening reverted to the same period of her life which had been the subject of Nancy's gossip. The stranger it was, too, because it was tacitly avoided by both father and daughter in their most private and confidential intercourse. The allusion was slight and casual, it is true, but even so it had stirred the depths of a lonely and widowed heart. "Oh, Ralph!" she murmured, as on her way back from the kitchen she passed the parlor door, and turned into a dark room adjoining, the window of which in daylight commanded a view of the river's course down to Morn lngton, and a glimpse of the more distant sea—" oh, Ralph! Ralph Melville! why does your memory haunt me still? cruel! you pursue me even from the grave!—The grave!" and she shuddered,—as leaning against the side of the deep recess of the window she looked out on the gloomy night, and the troubled waters far below, revealed ever and anon by the forked lightning's lurid glare,—" The grave! ah! my poor Ralph! not even the mournful comfort is mine to know that you sleep in hallowed earth! But why, why can I not forget the dismal past? Why does that mournful voice echo forever in my heart— why is ever before my eyes that last sad, reproachful look?—Oh my God! why can I not forget?"

She was aroused from her painful reverie by the blithe cheery voice of Rose singing in the parlor a song, that her grandfather loved—"The Canadian Boat-Song." Silently Lydia listened, the tears streaming down her cheeks. It was *his* song, the first she had heard him sing, and the scene rose vividly before her, so vividly that all the long lapse of years, the weariness, the pain that lay between was forgotten, that happy evening was back again, and the sea for the while gave up its dead to live and love as of old, in the prime of youth and health.

Suddenly a dull heavy sound reached Lydia's ear, amid the roar of winds and the surging of waters. It was the signal gun of some ship in distress,—out at sea, but near the coast. Forgetting the life-long sorrows which a moment before had absorbed her every thought and feeling, Miss Ackland started at the ominous sound, and opening the window, leaned out; again, over the increasing storm, boomed forth the signal gun, nearer and more distinct than before, awaking the sullen echoes of rock and river, and rolling by on the wintry blast. Hastily closing the window, Miss Ackland hurried to the parlor, at the door of which she was met by Rose pale and trembling. The old man, too, had left his seat, and stood in a listening attitude, a troubled, anxious look on his aged countenance.

"Oh! Aunt Lydia, where can it be?" cried Rose, grasping her aunt's arm. Mr. Ackland looked the same question.

"I fear, papa, it is bearing down on the rocks near Clogher."

"Clogher, did you say, Lydia?—Now, God forbid!"

"It is somewhere near there, I very much fear, papa!"

"Oh! grandpapa, there it is again, that awful sound! nearer, nearer still!"

"Can nothing be done, papa?" said Miss Ackland anxiously.

"God knows, child, God knows. Get me my hat, Rosey, I must have a look at the night, and the lie of that vessel."

The hat and cloak were brought, and Mr. Ackland sallied forth, followed by all his "womankind," for Nancy, too, had heard the signals of distress, and, terrified, rose from her prayers by the fireside to join the family group on the esplanade in front of the house. Shot after shot was now booming through the air in quick succession, denoting the increasing peril of the mariners.

"Well, papa?" inquired Miss Ackland, when they had all stood a moment silent whilst the old man's practised eye scanned the dismal scene.

"You were right, Lydia, the sound comes from the direction of Clogher, and wo betide any vessel that is driving before the wind to-night off that rocky ridge, for the gale is a fierce northeaster."

"But, papa, don't you think some boats will put off to try and save the crew?"

"I much fear that no boat could live to-night in such a sea as that which sweeps round the Head. Still, they're a hardy set of fellows those Clogher fishermen, and I'm sure they'll do it, if men can."

"God grant it!" was the fervent prayer of all the hearts in that group of anxious watchers.

"If they could only make the Tower,* now, and get over the bar," said Mr. Ackland, "the Baltray men wouldn't have such a sea to breast, and *they* might save some lives. God bless us all, it's a fearful night! Many a stout craft will go down in the storm, if it be not the mercy of God! See the fiery glare that shines through the darkness out on the deep! Lydia! do you still hear the gun? My old ears are so dull of hearing!"

\* Maiden Tower, which stands on the beach at Mornington, near the mouth of the Boyne.

"Yes, there it is again—but the intervals are longer—perhaps—perhaps efforts are being made to save the crew!"

"Ah! my child, I fear little can be done—but let us go in," added the old man sadly, "*we* can do nothing, anyhow!"

"We can pray, papa, and that will still be something."

"Indeed," said Rose, "I have been praying ever since we came out, and so has Nancy." It was true enough, for the latter was telling her beads with great devotion. So the little family adjourned to the lighted parlor, and they all knelt to supplicate Mary the Star of the Sea to assist all distressed mariners that night, and more especially those who were in danger of perishing, almost within their sight.

"If it be not Thy holy will that they should be saved, O Lord!" prayed Miss Ackland with bowed head and clasped hands, "have mercy, at least, on their poor souls, and prepare them for eternity

Long they all knelt and prayed, while the storm raged without, but in vain they listened for the signal-gun; it reached their ears no more.

Next morning the family were all astir early; the storm had subsided, and the pale wintry sun was rising from the blue sea-wave in the golden east. Not slow was the news in reaching the old house on the hill. A foreign merchantman had gone to pieces on the rocks near Clogher Head.

And the crew? what of them?"

"Most of them were saved, partly by the efforts of the Clogher fishermen, partly by swimming, and clambering up the rocks."

"Thank God for that, anyhow!" said old Nancy with pious fervor, as she hastened with the welcome tidings to the room where the family were just sitting down to breakfast. Rose clapped her hands joyfully.

"Oh dear! I'm so glad! I thought they were all drowned, and that would have been such a pity!—oh! I'm sure the Blessed Virgin heard our prayers! I know she did!"

"What is that, Lydia?" inquired Mr. Ackland, "any news from the coast?"

"Yes, papa," Miss Ackland said, in that slightly elevated tone which her father's infirmity required, "the ship went to pieces on the rocks this side of Clogher Head, but nearly all the crew were saved."

"Thank God, child, thank God! there is nothing bad, they say, but might be worse. I shall walk into town by and by to try and find out what became of the poor fellows."

"And I think, papa, if you'll send us out a car, Rose and I will drive down to Clogher and see how matters are there. I am most anxious to know all about the shipwreck, and see if anything is being done for those of her crew who were saved."

"Very well, my dear, I will send Connor"—(the car-driver usually employed by the family). A little while after, the tall thin form of old George Ack'an l—

familiar enough to the good people of Drogheda—might be seen walking, gold-headed cane in hand, through Lawrence's Gate, and down Lawrence street and Shop street, on his way to the office of an old friend and former partner on the Quay, where he expected to get the desired information. Long before he reached his destination, he knew all that was known in Drogheda, for every one he passed in the streets was talking of the wreck of the good ship *San Pietro* of Leghorn, near Clogher Head, that the crew were all saved except a few, and that the captain was already in town making arrangements for the temporary accommodation of his men. Some of the townspeople had been already to the scene of the disaster, bringing with them ample supplies of everything necessary for the immediate relief of the survivors.

When Mr. Ackland returned home to his three o'clock dinner, he was met in the hall by his granddaughter, all a-glow with life and health, and brimful of intelligence. "God bless the child!" was the old man's inward ejaculation as the cheering vision burst on his age-dimmed eyes.

"Well, Rosey, my pet, what news have you for me? What of the *San Pietro?*"

"Oh! grandpapa, we saw all the poor sailors. Almost every house in Clogher has some of them for the present, but you know what poor accommodations they have for anybody there."

"I know, my child, but they will not be long left

to the Clogher people's care; I believe they will be brought into town this afternoon."

By this time the old gentleman had laid aside, with Rose's assistance, his overcoat, hat, and stick, and had ensconced himself snugly in his arm-chair in front of the parlor fire. Rose drew a *tabouret* and placed herself at his side.

"Grandpapa," said she, "do you know there was one passenger on board the San Pietro?"

"Yes?—A supercargo, I suppose, or some friend of the captain?"

"No, grandpapa, the sailors didn't know anything about him; but he is a gentleman, that's certain, by his appearance—Aunt Lydia said she was sure he was."

"Well, and what then?"

"Why nothing, grandpapa, only Aunt Lydia said she couldn't think of leaving him in such a place, and he quite ill, too, so she got Tom Madigan to put a bed in a cart and take him up here."

"Oh! that's how it is, is it? So your aunt has brought him home?"

"Yes, papa," said Miss Ackland, who now entered to announce dinner, "I knew you would not object to my doing so, and I know when you see the poor young man you will be glad I did. He was quite insensible when I found him in Madigan's cottage, and might have died there soon for want of proper care."

The old man's lip quivered, and a tear moistened his eyelids—"Humph, that's so like you, Lydia, you never calculate cost or trouble when any one requires your assistance. No, my daughter, I do *not* object to what you have done, so long as *you* are willing to undertake this new responsibility. Come, let us go to dinner." Kind, benevolent old man, type of patriarchal age, and of all the broad sympathy with his kind which marks the true gentleman. Rich was George Ackland in the midst of that poverty to which honor and honesty had voluntarily consigned him. Rich in the esteem and respect of the community in which he lived, and of which he had once been a leading and prominent member. He belonged to an old Protestant family, but had become a Catholic a little before his marriage with the daughter of another old Norman family, the Chesters, then and now occupying a high position amongst the Catholic gentry of Louth. Like most converts to the faith Mr. Ackland was a practical, zealous Catholic, illustrating faithfully in his life the beautiful precepts of the religion he had embraced, and whilst looked up to by Catholics with proud affection, commanded even from Protestants the respect due to an honorable and high-minded gentleman, never so high amongst them as since the repeated failures of large mercantile houses with whom he was connected had involved his affairs in irretrievable ruin. Such was old George Ackland.

## CHAPTER III.

Two weeks had passed before the young stranger was pronounced out of danger, and another week before he was permitted to leave his bed. His life had been in imminent danger from concussion of the brain, the effect of his having been dashed by a wave against a jutting fragment of rock on the night of the shipwreck. His perilous position on the ledge where he was thrown had been fortunately discovered by one of the sailors in time to rescue him before the returning wave should carry him to certain death. During his illness, he had been assiduously tended by Miss Ackland and old Nancy, the former, especially, spending great part of her time in the sick-room. The most perfect quiet being declared necessary for the patient's recovery, neither Mr. Ackland nor Rose was admitted to the room until after the object of the family's charitable care had been pronounced out of danger, and was sitting up. It had been a source of some anxiety to Miss Ackland how she was to communicate with her patient when once his reason began to return; she had naturally supposed that he could speak no English, and her knowledge of foreign lan guages was unluckily limited to French. Her pleasure, then, was equal to her surprise when, in the delirium which supervened on the lethargic stupor of the first twenty-four or thirty hours, the disjointed sentences that reached her ears from his parched lips were as often English as Italian—though sometimes a mixture of both. Her mind once made easy on that score, she devoted herself with renewed assiduity to the duties of her self-imposed charge, and looked hopefully forward to the satisfaction of seeing her cares rewarded by the perfect recovery of her interesting patient, for such he really was.

As for the young stranger himself, his first return to consciousness was like that of a person awaking from a dream. Near a window within sight of where he lay sat Miss Ackland knitting, her graceful head bent forward, and her delicate profile clearly marked against the dark wall beyond. The sweet face was already familiar to him, for all through that long feverish dream, he had seen it by his bed, and bending over him with loving kindness like that of a pitying angel, or a fond mother, as he murmured now softly to himself. From the lady's face, the young man's eyes wandered round the room; it was old and dark, at least so it seemed to him in the subdued light which struggled through the half-closed window. A few pictures, religious pictures, he could see, hung on the walls, and opposite the foot of his bed, a crucifix, under which was a holy-water font. The sight of these familiar objects drew tears of tender remembrance from the young man's eyes, and raised his heart for a moment to the Divine Power who had, he felt, preserved him from a great danger though as yet he knew not how. A cursory glance at the furniture of the room, old and plain and well worn, revealed to him clearly the fact that the dwelling was not the abode of wealth or luxury, though it as evidently was, of religion and charity. So he lay musing a little while, unwilling to disturb the delicious languor that follows the departure of pain, and marks the first stage of convalescence. He turned his eyes again on the lady at the window, wondering who and what she might be, and watched as in a pleasant tranquil dream, the motion of her fingers, and the glinting of the needles in the dim light. From the present his thoughts wandered to the past, and in the half conscious state of his mind, he could fancy that he saw again the mother who was no longer amongst the living, sitting by her window in that far-off southern city by the blue waters of the Mediterranean. At last the lady rose, laid down her knitting and approached his bed, softly, noiselessly; the spell was broken, but the reality was still pleasant, and romantic enough to excite interest and curiosity in a youthful mind.

Great and very agreeable was Miss Ackland's surprise when on bending, as usual, over her patient, she saw him fully awake, the light of reason shining in his eyes, and in the faint smile that brightened the wan, wasted features.

"'Thank God!" was Miss Ackland's first fervent ejaculation.

"God and you, lady!" the youth replied in his faint low accents. "I owe you much—very, very much gratitude. It seems as though I had been long asleep and dreaming. But pray tell me where I am?"

"You are in Drogheda, or, at least, very near it, and we of this house"—she paused, then smiling added—" we are honest people, I assure you. You left the brigands behind you in Italy So rest content for the present, and in due time you shall know all. I must go now and get you some little nourishment. The fever being gone, we must try and build you up again."

The little delicacies which Miss Ackland wished to prepare for her patient, were not so easily procured as one might expect. The item of expense was one of the points on which Nancy and her mistress oftenest disagreed. She thought Miss Ackland too generous by half, considering the altered circumstances of the family, and it was her practice to remind her on all manner of occasions that "charity begins at home." The old woman had grumbled audibly enough at the bringing of the young stranger to the house. "That's always the way with Miss Ackland—she never thinks of the expense. Now here'll be docthor's bills to be paid, an' other expenses to the back o' that, an' I suppose it must all come out of the poor masther's pocket, an' God he knows, there's too much to come out of it already. Well! some people 'ill never be wise !"

To do Nancy justice, however, she soon began to take an interest in the poor young stranger, and was quite willing to sit up with him in her turn, no matter how hard she had worked all day. Anything that depended on herself to do for him, or that did not imply expense to the family, was all right in Nancy's estimation, but when most inclined to pity the young gentleman " lyin' on the broad of his back in a strange country, far away from his own," she still never went to the length of approving of Miss Ackland's " layin' out money in handfuls on one who wasn't a drop's blood to her or hers,—an' sure what matter, if they could only afford it?"

On the present occasion, however, Nancy was so rejoiced to hear of the change for the better in their patient, that she made no very strenuous objection to the wine-whey which her mistress came to prepare, consoling herself with the comfortable assurance that the worst was over, and the tax on the family resources would, in all probability, soon cease.

During the few days that elapsed before the young stranger was allowed to leave his bed, he was left oftener alone, the necessity for constant attendance no longer existing. Mr. Ackland was now a regular visitor to the sick-room, and although Rose had not yet been permitted formally to make his acquaintance, he was not unaware that such a person belonged to the household Through the half-open door he had sometimes caught glimpses of a female figure which he knew was not that of his kind lady-nurse; he had heard, too, the distant sound of a clear voice trolling some merry lay as only youth's lightsome heart can, and once when he lay " between waking and sleeping," thinking of nothing in particular, but listening dreamily to the winds that whistled shrilly round the old mansion, the room-door was softly opened, and a bright, girlish face appeared for a moment regarding him with a look half arch, half inquisitive. He had barely time to look his surprise when the face vanished, and the door closed, much to his chagrin, for he began to feel the *ennui* of convalescence, and to long for some other society than that of the grave and thoughtful Miss Ackland, and her venerable parent. Some days after, when he was up and sitting in an arm-chair near the fire which was now every day made in his room, he was roused from a fit of abstraction by the stealthy opening of the door, and a suppressed giggling laugh outside, followed by the entrance into the room of a large cat oddly enough attired in an old woman's deep-bordered cap with a ruffle round her neck, the rest of her goodly bulk in the dress which nature gave her. The ludicrous sight, all the more so from the dignified gravity with which the animal stopped short and surveyed him from under her strange head-gear, made the youth burst into an uncontrollable fit of laughter, the first he had had since he left Leghorn. His merriment was evidently shared by some one outside, and he was tempted to try his strength in a journey to the door, when a face was thrust in very different from that which he expected to see. It was, in fact, that of old Nancy, his assistant-nurse, and evidently in no good humor was she then, as, calling the cat to her, she darted out of the room, without so much as looking in his direction. In the passage outside he heard her voice in no gentle tone calling after some one.

"Ah, then, wait till I catch you, Miss Rosey!—if I don't be up to you for puttin' my cap an' frill on that unlucky cat! Ay! you may laugh, but it's no laughin' matther to me, for a stitch o' them things 'ill never go on me. As sure as I'm a livin' woman I'll tell your aunt! now!"

It was only when the voice had died away in the distance that the young man ventured to laugh at the droll scene, the first part of which had evidently been intended for his special amusement, while Nancy's inopportune appearance, he shrewdly suspected, was not purely accidental, her anger at the base use to which her finery was applied, being decidedly the best part of the entertainment. One thing he had learned from old Nancy's vehement objurgation, to wit, that the young lady's name was Rosey—"Miss Rosey she called her," he said to himself, and he kept repeating the name over and over as a sort of vocal link between him and the world outside the quaint, yet snug chamber which was, for the present, virtually his prison. A sort of indirect acquaintance had thus sprung up between the two young people that was undoubtedly very piquant and pleasing to one perhaps to both; for it was something new to Rose Ackland to have one of her own age, of either sex, to play off her pranks on, or to share in her almost childish amusements.

Still, when a few days after, Giacomo, as Miss Ackland and her father had learned to call the young stranger, made his first appearance in the parlor, a little before the usual hour for the family dinner, Rose, introduced by her aunt, curtsied as demurely as though she had never made him laugh, or laughed with him. Giacomo, of course, followed her example, and bowed politely as to a person then met for the first time.

"My niece has had little experience in tending the sick," observed Miss Ackland, "and, being none of the most sedate, I kept her away from you, Giacomo, fearing her intrusion might seriously interfere with the doctor's orders regarding quiet. I believe you have not made her acquaintance before?"

Giacomo replied in the negative,—Rose must have her word, too: "No, Aunt Lydia, he didn't make *my* acquaintance, but he made Tab's."

"How is that, child?"

"Why, she paid him a visit the other day *en grande toilette!*—ask Nancy if she didn't."

The old woman was in the room, at the moment, putting fresh wood on the fire. She shook her head, and then her fist, at her young mistress, but declined further answer, and left the room laughing; **Nancy's** anger was never of long duration, least of all with "Miss Rosey."

That sprightly damsel, now called on for an explanation, gave it right willingly, to the no small amusement of her grandpapa, for whose benefit it was told over again. Such trifles amuse youth and age,—the young and the very old! Miss Ackland smiled,—she seldom laughed—and gently rebuked her niece for such childish folly.

"Yet, after all," she added, in a low voice, when Rose's back was turned, "yet, after all, Giacomo, I like to see young people enjoying themselves in their own way, and I am often thankful to see how well our Rose manages to amuse herself even in this lonely old house of ours, with no other society than that of her old grandpapa and her elderly maiden aunt."

"Elderly!" the youth could not help repeating, as he caught the arch smile that flitted over the fair features of the speaker.

"Yes, elderly," she replied, catching his meaning, and she gently shook her head, "elderly, there's no denying. But there is papa moving his chair towards you. Talk to him while I go and see if dinner is ready. Be sure you raise your voice a little—a very little will do—so that he can hear you. I suppose you are aware that dear papa's hearing is not so good as it has been?" Giacomo replied in the affirmative, and Miss Ackland left the room.

Now Mr. Ackland was by no means inquisitive, he seldom or never manifested any of that curiosity in the affairs of others which is supposed to be characteristic of old people. But it was very natural, and, indeed, very prudent that he should wish to know something of the connections and antecedents of the youth whom circumstances had thus introduced into the small circle which was his world. In the course of a ten minutes' conversation he had learned quite sufficient of the young man's position in life and his uneventful history to satisfy him that he might safely extend to him the rites of hospitality so long as his health required. It was not so much the nature or extent of Giacomo's revelations concerning himself or his family that satisfied the old gentleman's natural anxiety, as the frank ingenuousness of his manner, the honest truthfulness stamped on his features, dark and Italian-like as they were. It was impossible not to feel that truth and all sincerity looked from his eyes, and spoke in his voice; and Mr. Ackland feeling and believing it, shook hands cordially with Giacomo, and hoped he would continue to make his house his home so long as he found it necessary to remain in Drogheda.

Giacomo's thanks were interrupted by the entrance of Rose to summon her grandfather and their guest to dinner. The young Italian, mindful of the duties of politeness, stepped forward to offer his arm to the young lady, but she darted off like a lapwing shaking her saucy curls, and laughing, as she afterwards told Giacomo, at the thought of him offering his arm to her, and he scarcely able to walk himself. "I am sure," said she, "you look more like needing support than I do."

Before the little party sat down to dinner, Mr. Ackland, with the formal politeness of his day and generation, introduced their guest to his daughter and granddaughter as Signor Giacomo Malvili, of Leghorn, Italy.

"No—no, not *Signor*, Mr. Ackland!" protested Giacomo; "nobody ever called me '*Signor*' at home —only Giacomo."

"Well! well! my dear boy, so be it. Pray, take your seat, and let us see how far you have recovered your appetite."

The dinner over, and the weather being fine for the season, Mr. Ackland invited his guest to sit with him in the porch, where, on one or other of the stone benches, with a cushion under him, he was wont to spend, even at that season, the hour immediately after dinner,—in summer longer time, for the place commanded a noble view of river, sea, and land—the silvery Boyne below, and the rich plains of Meath beyond, dotted with the straggling suburbs of the borough and many private dwellings, the ancient and venerable town stretching westward, its forts, and walls, and church towers, and broken arches and steeples full in sight.

"This must be all new and strange to you," observed Mr. Ackland. "Everything you see here is so different from your own country."

"New it is, but not strange," said the youth, casting his eyes half listlessly, half curiously over the varied scene, fair to look upon even in the bleakness of winter. "I have so often heard of Drogheda, and had its peculiarities described to me, that it seems as though I had long known it. I have heard my father say that it is very different from most Irish or British towns of the present day !"

"And that is true, Giacomo, ours is in many respects an interesting town, which I hope you will find out before you leave us." The youth bowed his thanks. "But you spoke of your father—he has often visited Drogheda, then, since he knows it so well ?"

A cloud passed over the young man's face. "Yes, I believe so," he replied somewhat coldly, then abruptly asked if Mr. Ackland knew whether the Captain of the *San Pietro* had yet returned to Italy. The captain, a rough but kind-hearted sailor, had been once or twice to see Giacomo during his illness, and the latter had, as Mr. Ackland knew, given him money for the relief of his distressed crew ; he himself having some trading connections in Drogheda, was like Giacomo himself, the guest of a private family.

"He told me when I last saw him that a few of the Drogheda merchants had subscribed enough amongst themselves to defray the expenses of his crew back to Leghorn, and that he would likely go home at the same time."

"I believe he is gone," said Mr. Ackland; "I heard

in town yesterday, that he and his crew were to sail to-day in the Lady Hamilton."

"I am sorry I did not see him," said Giacomo, " perhaps I might have been able to go with him, and I know my father will be so anxious—however, I gave the captain a few lines for him, telling him that I am almost well now, and exceedingly well cared for, so that he need not fear on my account."

"But, tell me, Giacomo," said Mr. Ackland, "how is it that you speak English so well, you being born and brought up in Leghorn. You have only the very slightest foreign accent!"

"Oh! that is nothing strange. I have been speaking English all my life. Your language is a good deal spoken in Leghorn, as in some other ports on our western coast. Pray, Mr. Ackland, in what direction from here are those rocks which proved fatal to the *San Pietro?*"

Mr. Ackland pointed in the direction of Clogher. "There they lie," said he, "a portion of the mighty barrier which guards our little island from the sea's incursions. You cannot see them, however, but the place is well worthy of a visit, and the ladies shall take you down some day when you are well enough, to see the bold promontory which there juts far into the Irish Sea."

"And the cave, grandpapa," said Rose from the doorway behind, "he must see the cave, you know, above all things, and we shall have him go down into it, just to try his nerves."

"You are very kind, Miss Rose," said Giacomo, gravely; "only wait till I have full command of my feet again, and you shall see that my nerves will not fail me."

"Don't be too sure of that, Signor," for so Rose persisted in calling him, "wait till you have clambered down over the side-face of Clogher Head into the cave."

"What sort of cave may it be?"

"Oh! as for that, you must wait till you see it. I can't take the trouble of describing it. But it's a pirate's cave, you understand, where those sea-rovers used to hide their booty long ago. The sailors and fishermen about here tell all manner of strange, and some of them frightful, stories about it. It is easy seen that you are a stranger here, or you'd be sure to have heard of the Pirate's Cave at Clogher."

"You have quite excited my curiosity, Miss Rose. I must visit the cave, by all means, before I leave the neighborhood."

"Oh! we have more than that to show you about Drogheda. Have we not, grandpapa?"

"What did you say, Rosey?"

"I was telling the Signor, grandpapa, about the Pirate's Cave at Clogher, and I asked you if we hadn't many other places of interest to show him as well as that."

'Of course we have, Rosey, and I must speak to your aunt about taking Giacomo to see our Drogheda lions as soon as he is able."

"Oh! that reminds me, grandpapa," said the volatile Rose, taking hold of his arm, "Aunt Lydia thinks it is time for you and the Signor to come in. It is almost dark, you see, and the evening is damp and chill."

"It is well you thought of your message even now, you little chattering magpie," said the fond parent, stroking her hair with his large hand, as he rose, and, motioning his guest to go before, proceeded along the hall to that "room of the household," a sort of back-parlor, where most of his in-door hours were spent. The contrast between the warm, cheerful room within, and the cold, hazy twilight without, was very pleasant, and as Giacomo took the place pointed out to him at one side of the fireplace, while Mr. Ackland occupied the other in his arm-chair, he looked around with an exquisite feeling of comfort almost unknown before. Fireside enjoyments are little known in sunny Italy.

After tea, Mr. Ackland proposed a game of chess; Giacomo did not play chess; backgammon, then, or draughts? No, but he would like to learn, if any one were kind enough to take the trouble of teaching him. Whether intentionally or not, he looked at Rose, but Rose answering the look said very curtly—

"Not I, anyhow; I hate chess, draughts, backgammon and the whole tribe of 'games;' they are all so prosy and so tiresome. I wonder at you, Signor, to think of learning such old-fashioned games at your time of life. Pray, how old are you, Signor Giacomo?"

"Some months over twenty," said Giacomo, smiling at the odd *brusquerie* of the girl's manner. "I shall soon be twenty-one."

"Dear me! how old you are! Why, I thought you were no older than I am!—well, after all, I wish *I* was twenty!"

"My dear Rose," said her aunt, "how you do rattle on! Suppose you *were* twenty, it is very possible you might wish yourself back at rosy eighteen, or younger still. Go bring the backgammon-box; since you will not undertake to teach Giacomo, I will."

"Very well, then, I'll play ball with pussy," producing a woollen ball she had made for the purpose. "Signor Giacomo, are you fond of cats?"

"Not very," and Giacomo tried to maintain his gravity; "I see you have a very fine specimen of the tribe here," glancing at Tab where she sat on the arm of the old gentleman's chair.

"I only wish you could convince old Nancy of that. Do you know she has got a notion into her head that our poor old Tab is an enchanted Dane, or something of the kind?"

"An enchanted Dane! how would she make that out?"

"Oh! I forgot that you weren't brought up in this country. You have read, though, of how the Danes used to invade Ireland every once in a while, and stay in it, in full possession, as long as the kings and chiefs would let them?" Giacomo assented.

"Well! it's a common belief in many parts of the

country—that is amongst the peasantry, and so forth—that there are Danish treasures hidden away in ever so many places, and guarded by magic spells."

"Is it possible that such things are believed in Ireland?"

"Possible! yes, indeed, it is, very possible and very true, and, moreover, certain of the *cats* are supposed to be enchanted Danes. Oh! here comes Nancy—you shall hear her opinion of Tab. Now, pray attend." Then raising her voice she went on—"You must know, Signor, that Nancy believes our Tab to be an enchanted Dane."

"An' worse than that, Miss Rosey," said the old woman, laying down some wood on the hearth.

"Indeed, Nancy, and pray what worse *can* she be?" asked Giacomo, at a sign from Rose.

"Well! that's what I wouldn't care to tell you, sir, and herself to the fore. Some other time," and she was moving away.

"No, no, Nancy, that won't do—tell it now!" cried Rose, "I'll soon put Tab out of hearing!" and she hastened to put the cat, poor harmless creature, outside the door.

"How is this, Rosey? what are you about?" asked her grandpapa, surprised at this unceremonious treatment of his favorite.

Rose explained the matter to his satisfaction, and he closed his eyes for a comfortable nap during Nancy's recital. He always closed his ears against her malicious insinuations in regard to Tabby.

So Nancy crouching beside Miss Rose in her favorite attitude, with her elbow resting on one knee, and her chin on her hand, began to tell how " a student was travellin' in foreign parts, in Jarmany or somewhere there, an' bein' benighted in a forest, he wandhered on ever till at last he came to a fine grand house, an' when he rang the bell, an' tould his story, they recaved him kindly, an' made him welcome to stay over night, an' take share of the best they had. How, when supper-time came, he was brought to table with the rest, and the first thing he seen was a great big cat, sittin' in a chair beside the fine dacent ould gentleman that was in it, the father of the family. Well, the student watched the cat, all the time the supper was going on, and saw that her master gave her the first of everything he put on his plate, and that if he forgot it any time, she would slap his arm with her paw, and grind her teeth, her eyes blazin' like live coals. So the student asked how long the cat had been in the house, and why the ould gentleman had made such a pet of her, and was told that she was there in his father's and grandfather's time, and was just as great a pet with every one of them. With that the student told them that it wasn't a cat, at all, that was in it, but an evil sperit, and that if they'd give him leave he'd prove it to them that very night. Well, to be sure, the ould gentleman, in particular, was very angry that such a thing should be said of his cat, and the student had hard work to get him persuaded; but at last he bid him look at the cat, and, sure enough, she was ragin' mad, and looked as if she would tear the stranger to pieces, gettin' closer and closer to the ould gentleman. So, at long last, he gave in, and the student made them bring some holy water, an' took the ould gentleman an' the rest of the family with him in a round ring he made with it on the floor, and then he pulled out his book and began a-readin', an' after he had read a good while, till the sweat was runnin' down his face, *the thing*—for, of coorse, it wasn't a cat—went off in a flame of fire, an' took part of the side-wall with it. How the student told them then that it was an evil sperit that had haunted the house for ever so many years, and that he got the souls of the father and grandfather, and would have had the grandson, too, if God hadn't sent *him* that way with power to deliver him. And, finally, how the ould gentleman and his family didn't know what on earth to make of the student, they were so thankful, but they couldn't get him to stay past the one night, and he left them in the mornin', after givin' them all his blessin', an' tellin' them they'd never be troubled any more with the evil sperit." "So now," added **Nancy**, " you may all see that it isn't a lucky thing to be makin' so much of a brute baste—it's against nature, so it is, an' God grant the master may never be sorry for doin' it! But the quality must see their hobby out, let it be what it may."

A becoming degree of horror was expressed by **Giacomo**, much to **Nancy's** satisfaction, and she was leaving the room in a state of comfortable complacency, when Rose, having slily opened the door, and brought in the cat from the hall where she found her as if waiting for re-admission, managed to get in the rear of Nancy, and placed Tab on the old woman's back, with her paws round her neck. Little expecting such a salute, Nancy screamed, trying in vain to shake off the cat, whose claws stuck fast in her woollen kerchief, and it was not till Miss Ackland came to her assistance that she succeeded in her desperate efforts to release herself from the strange embrace; Rose had made her escape laughing, and poor Nancy was left under the impression that the cat had come back purposely to hear the story, and had thus shown her anger for the liberty taken with the feline race.

## CHAPTER IV.

**November** was drawing to a close by the time Giacomo was able to walk abroad, and although he naturally felt anxious to return home, and was, moreover, conscious that he had trespassed too long on the kind hospitality of his new friends, he found it no so easy matter to get away. In the first place, the weather was not favorable, as he was duly and frequently informed by Mr. Ackland or his daughter, in a tone of mock condolence that was sufficiently amusing. As for Rose, she did not appear to trouble herself much about the matter. In the next place, he was constantly reminded that he had, as yet, seen nothing of the old borough, its people, or its ways, and see it he must and should. So said Miss Ackland, in her gentle but decided way, and Giacomo was fain to obey.

"Well," said Mr. Ackland one morning at breakfast, "now that our young friend has consented to remain with us over Christmas, and see the sights, what is your programme for the exhibition, Lydia?"

"For the churches, papa, and other objects of religious interest I mean to place Giacomo in the hands of Jemmy Nulty, who undoubtedly belongs, himself, to the same category."

"Very true, Lydia, very true; and what then?"

"Oh! as for the rest we shall ourselves do the honors—that is Rose and I."

"You are really very good, Aunt Lydia," pouted Rose, "you do me a great deal of honor, but I don't think I should make a good *ciccrona*."

"And why, pray?"

"Why, because I hate playing the guide, that's all, and I know that if I went with you, I should have to do most of the talking."

"Dear me, Rose," said her aunt with a smile, "when did you begin to dislike talking? Still, I don't wonder, for, I suppose, even tongues will tire, and you have been chattering so much of late that yours must need a little rest."

The individual selected by Miss Ackland as Giacomo's guide to the churches was a character not to be met with outside of Ireland, perhaps, we might say, outside of Drogheda. He was by profession *a pilgrim*, which, in the Irish acceptation, means a lay person, whether man or woman, who devotes his or her life to works of piety, including, of course, frequent "journeys" to Lough Derg and other famous pilgrimages. Some of these "pilgrims" are not sincere in their prof.ssions of extraordinary piety, but such was not the case with Jemmy Nulty, for Jemmy was "an Israelite, indeed, in whom there *was* no guile," and, although the simplicity of the dove was his, not a particle had he of the cunning of the serpent. A man full of faith and full of charity was our Drogheda "pilgrim," believing all things that religion teaches, and thinking no evil of man, woman, or child; to Jemmy Nulty all the world presented itself through the silver veil of charity, and, knowing no evil in himself, he could not see it in others, or, seeing, beheld it afar off as in a mirror, something dim and undefined to his simple, upright mind. For the rest, Jemmy had no very great temptation to make a trade of hypocrisy, for he and a brother, as pious and unworldly as himself, who lived with him, and was, we believe, his only relative, were the joint owners of a small cottage in the suburbs " out West Gate," with some other resources, which, though trifling in themselves, were amply sufficient for the few wants of this primitive pair. A little before the time of which we speak, Jemmy had become the sole proprietor of the little domicile, the mortal part of his brother Phil having gone to rest in the shadow of the old Dominican Abbey in The Cord " out Lawrence's Gate;" his spirit being taken to heaven by the blessed angels, as certain of the neighbors had seen " with their own eyes" one clear summer night, when the moon was high, and the winds were asleep, and the river and the sea, and the slumbering earth reflected the beauty and the light of heaven. All that was earthly in Jemmy Nulty's heart died out with Phil's gentle life, and ever after the old man lived more with the blessed inhabitants of the world beyond the stars than his fellow-mortals on earth. All that he loved here below were the good friars who ministered at the altars of the chapels he most frequented, and "the dear nuns," that is to say, the Sisters of the Presentation and Dominican Orders, who greatly favored the old man by supplying him with scapulars and other religious objects, not only for his own private and personal use, but to distribute to the piously-disposed friends and patrons by whom he was lodged and kindly entertained during his pilgrimages hither and thither.* The few families in his native town who were habitually visited by Jemmy regarded themselves as highly honored, and the Acklands were so fortunate as to be of the number.

Such, in his general character, was Jemmy Nulty, when he came at Miss Ackland's bidding one morning a day or two after the conversation just mentioned. But the distinctive individuality of the man struck our young Italian with surprise when he walked with only a "God save all here!" into the front parlor where, as being the most cheerful room on the ground-floor, such of the family as were indoors usually spent their mornings. Jemmy's attire was a long dark-colored surtout, not much the worse

*Amongst the most pleasing recollections of the author's childish days was the summer-visit of this identical "pilgrim," on his way to "Lough Dhar-rog," as he was wont to pronounce Lough Derg. Few visitors were so warmly welcomed by young or old in that "old house at home."

for wear, but hanging loosely about his tall, and somewhat heavy frame, for Jemmy was a man of large proportions; this garment, with a long waistcoat, or vest to match, knee-breeches, also of a dark color, worsted stockings, and the national "brogues" of the Irish peasantry, constituted Jemmy's apparel all the year round, Sunday and holiday, winter and summer. The happy smile that was on his face was peculiar to himself; it was the light from within shining out on features that, wanting it, would have been stolid and unmeaning. Jemmy was smiling, then, and Giacomo thought it was only for the occasion, but he soon found that the smile never left the good man's face, being, indeed, its habitual expression.

"God save all here!" said Jemmy, opening the parlor-door, and Miss Ackland responded with the fitting "God save you kindly, Jemmy!" as naturally as though she had been born and bred amongst the lowly. With perfect ease and self-possession, the old man saluted Mr. Ackland, raising his voice to just the pitch that was adapted to his hearing.

"I met Miss Rose abroad in the garden, as I came in the back way," said Jemmy; "the dear young lady is as fresh as a rose this mornin'."

"Yes, Jemmy, she spends good part of her time out doors." said Miss Ackland. "I am glad you came so early, Jemmy, for I want you very particularly."

"Ah, then, I'd have been here sooner, Miss," said Jemmy, "only that I happened to meet Father Dardis jist as I came out Lawrence's Gate, and the dear gentleman asked me to go before him to a house where he was goin' on a sick-call, to see that things were a little bit dacent for what he was bringin' with him. So, of coorse, I had to go."

"Of course, Jemmy, of course; but now I must tell you why I sent for you. This young gentleman whom you see here is an Italian, and a Catholic—a good one, too, Jemmy,—and as he has seen none of the chapels (except the High Lane where he has been at Mass once or twice with us) I want you to take him round them all, and be sure you show him everything about them and the convents that is worth seeing."

"Oh! indeed, an' I'll do that, Miss," and Jemmy turned his benign smile on Giacomo; "it was only yesterday that a fisherman from Clogher below was tellin' me in the priest's house at the Low Lane all about the dear young gentleman, an' what a power o' money he gave the Madigans an' the rest when he went down with you an' Miss Rose the other day to see them. He has goodness in his face whoever he is. Dear knows, Miss, but he puts me in mind of the fine gentleman that came with you an' your sister-in-law that's dead an' gone—the heavens be her bed!— that was Miss Rose's mother—to see me one time when I was sick."

Miss Ackland changed color, as she replied in a tremulous voice—"You entirely mistake, Jemmy, the gentleman you mean was tall, with light hair, and this young gentleman is much smaller, and of dark complexion."

"Well! I suppose it's on my eyes it is; they're not so good as they used to be. I'm gettin' old, thanks an' praise be to God for the fine long day He's givin' me."

Jemmy had a way of speaking that was entirely his own; with his eyes half closed, he let the words flow, as it were, from his mouth, with a sort of hissing sound, in the full, rich round accents of the Louth peasantry, generally with great rapidity, sometimes with great unction and fervor, his hands the while lightly joined, not clasped, over his capacious chest, which was, indeed, his habitual attitude, whether sitting, or standing.

"Will the dear young gentleman come now, or would he rayther wait for another day?" said Jemmy, standing up.

"Oh! certainly, I will go to-day," said Giacomo; "I couldn't think of troubling you to come again on my account."

"Oh! my dear, it's no trouble in life to me—sure, it's proud and happy I am to show the chapels an' things, for the glory of God an' His blessed Mother, an' all the holy Saints."

"Jemmy," said Mr. Ackland, whilst Giacomo was gone to prepare for going out, "what about that neighbor of yours whose cow broke into your little garden and eat your cabbages? I hope you are going to prosecute him?"

"Is it me, your honor?" said Jemmy, and for a moment the smile left his face, so great was his dismay at the bare idea of "going to law"—"is it me take the law of the poor dear man bekase his cow broke into the little garden I have!—No, dear sir, I wouldn't do it if she ate every green leaf that was in it. Sure it wasn't the dear man's fault, any way."

"But they say it was his fault, Jemmy, for that you asked him once or twice to repair the fence between his yard and your garden, and the lazy, worthless fellow couldn't be got to do it. Come, now, Jemmy, did you, or did you not ask him to repair the fence?"

Jemmy was fairly cornered, but his charity was not to be overcome. "Och! well, I suppose I did, for the poor thing used to be comin' in very often, you see, lookin' for the bit to ate, but sure he hadn't time, Mr. Ackland, if he had he'd have done it, I'll go bail. He has to work hard, sir, to keep so many mouths fed. Well! I'll be biddin' you good mornin', Mr. Ackland, an' you, too, dear lady," turning to Miss Ackland, who had listened much amused to Jemmy's ingenious defence of the neighbor and his trespassing cow.

As Giacomo and his guide emerged from the hall-door, they beheld Rose in shawl and bonnet tripping down the steps before them. "What a strange girl she is," thought the young Italian, "can she mean to go with us after all?"

But she meant no such thing; having reached the gate below she stopped a moment, turned, and smil ing waved her hand, then turned off down the Boyne road, in the opposite direction to that which the others were to take, and was quickly lost to view. "I wish she had come," was the young man's next thought; 'after all, I fear it will be dull work this visiting the churches—or chapels as they call them—with this good man for all company."

It was not so dull as Giacomo expected, for Jemmy Nulty grew eloquent when expatiating on anything appertaining to religion or religious worship, and although the chapels of Drogheda were not then what other ages had seen there, being plain, and, for the most part, little indebted to art for style or beauty, yet to Jemmy's enthusiastic imagination they were worthy of all praise, and where no grace or beauty was visible to other eyes, he saw, and glowingly described it. They visited in turn the Franciscan Chapel in the High Lane, off St. Lawrence street, the Augustinian Chapel in the Low Lane, off Shop street, and the Dominican Chapel in a court adjoining Linenhall street. Giacomo, accustomed to the richly adorned churches of Italy, saw little to admire in these, but he could not bear to say so to his simple-hearted guide, who having never seen finer, or so fine anywhere else, could hardly realize that finer were to be seen even in foreign parts, " barrin' it might be in Roome." The parish chapel in West street, being larger, impressed Giacomo more, and he said—"This is a nice little church."

"You mane *chapel*," said Jemmy, with unwonted

eagerness, "it's the Prodestants that has the *chu.ches*,— it's chapels we call ours. Don't say 'church,' dear, nekase that's a Prodestant word, you see."

Corrected, but not instructed, Giacomo smiled as he turned to take a look at the pictures, and then, kneeling a moment before the altar where Jemmy was bowing down in rapt devotion, the young man thanked God for that blessed unity of faith by which the Catholic sees everywhere through life the same objects of pious veneration, the same sacred images of saints and martyrs, of the Virgin Mother and her Divine Child, and the pictured story of the sublime tragedy of man's redemption which earliest fixed his gaze, and stamped the mysteries of faith on his infant mind. Softened even to tears, he bowed his head in lowly reverence before a picture of the Divine Mother, and breathed a prayer for the soul of the earthly mother who had taught him to love that heavenly queen. "Now, dear," said Jemmy, when, leaving the parish chapel, they turned up Peter street, " now we'll go an' take a look at the Presentation Convent in Fair street, an', after that, we'll go to the Sienna Convent, out La'rence's Gate there, where you'll see the skull of the blessed an' holy martyr, Oliver Plunket. You know who he was, I suppose?"

Unluckily, Giacomo did not know, but he shrank from saying so, and Jemmy went on: "That was the holy Archbishop of Armagh that was hung in Lun'- nun beyant on account of his religion."

"What wicked people those must have been who put him to death, and such a death as that!"

"Oh! poor things, poor things, it's blind they were, not wicked. Maybe it's jist as bad we'd be ourselves if we hadn't the light of faith to guide us. Wasn't it what Our dear Lord said on the cross when He prayed for His enemies—'Father, forgive them for they know not what they do?' An' sure it was the same with the poor things that hung the blessed an' holy archbishop? Oh! God help us all, it's poor, poor cratures we'd be if we were left to ourselves, anyway!"

It was with a strange feeling of awe and reverence that Giacomo gazed on the ghastly object, so carefully preserved by the Dominican nuns of Drogheda, in a rich and elegant case. "There," thought he, "is the casket that once contained God's noblest work, the thoughtful mind of man, and of a great and good man—a man who had the courage to die for his faith." Long he stood, lost in thought, his eyes fixed on the vacant "throne of the mind," still bearing in its conformation visible traces of the inflexible will, the indomitable energy, the intellectual superiority which distinguished the martyred primate of Ireland in the ill-omened reign of Charles the Second.

At length Jemmy touched his arm, and whispered that they had other places to go yet, and the night would soon be closing in, if they didn't hurry. So, thanking the polite and affable religious, who, in her capacious habit of white serge, had been patiently standing by, after "showing the house" to the strange gentleman,—more from courtesy than necessity, when Jemmy was with him—Giacomo followed his guide to The Cord to examine the little that remains of the old Dominican Abbey; it was only a stretch of gray, or rather blackened wall—

"The ruin that Time and the tempest had spared,"

but it impressed the reverential mind of our young Italian with deep solemnity, being the first that he had seen of those numerous remains of ancient piety for which he had heard Ireland was famous.

Turning, at length, to make some remark to his companion, he was surprised to find that he had vanished from his side, and it was some time before he discovered him kneeling on a grave at the other side of the Abbey-wall.

"Some relative of yours, I suppose, Jemmy?" inquired Giacomo.

"My brother, sir,—poor Phil, that was—he was all I had on earth, but, thank God! he's gone home before me. Well! dear sir, have you seen enough for this day, or will you go any farther?

"I think not, Jemmy, for," looking at his watch, "I find it is almost three o'clock, and that is dinner-hour at Mr. Ackland's. But what church is that?" pointing to a tower and steeple which occupied a commanding position in the northern part of the town.

"That?" said Jemmy, looking at the object as usual with half-closed eyes, "oh! that's St. Peter's

Church, a Prodestan' church, sir, an' more's the pity for it to have a saint's name, an' St. Peter's above all, in regard to him bein' the first Pope, an' the rock the true Church is built on! Well! well! it's a quare world, anyhow! But I suppose you often hard tell of Oliver Crummel that put thousands an' thousands of poor cratures to death for no other rason but bekase they were Catholics?" Yes, Giacomo had heard and read of him. "Well! dear, when he brought his sojers an' his guns an' his whole army here to take Drogheda, an' got in, afther a hard fight an' a long siege of it, there below at St. Mary's Church—Prodestant too, you see, like St. Peter's!—didn't he burn up hundreds an' thousands of poor Christians in the steeple of that very church where the cratures went up thinkin' to hide themselves. Well! well! that *was* a bad deed!"

"A bad deed," said Giacomo, the hot blood rushing to his cheek and brow!—"Why it was a devilish deed, and the man that did it must have been more devil than man!"

"God knows, dear, God knows *what* he was, but, anyway, he's dead an' judged long ago, an' it's no use speakin' hard of him now." Poor Jemmy Nulty! rare specimen of primitive charity and meekness! even for Oliver Cromwell he had no harsh words, admirable Christian philosopher that he was in his lowly simplicity of heart!

The two had now reached the road, the same that led to Mr. Ackland's back-gate, and, after pointing to the house, not very far distant, Jemmy took his leave, with a kind and paternal benediction, gently but firmly refusing the silver crown that Giacomo would have placed in his hand.

Rose was in the parlor feeding her linnet when Giacomo entered; she said without turning her head—"So you've got back. You should have been where I was this forenoon."

"And where was that, may I ask?"

"Down at Baltray, a fishing village not far from here; there's one there wants badly to see you."

"To see *me*? You surely are not in earnest, Miss Rose?"

"Yes, I am, Signor Giacomo!—there's an old woman there, Mabel by name, who having heard of your adventure has a great curiosity to see you, and see you she must."

"She does me honor," said Giacomo drily. "I had no idea that any one about here could waste a wish on seeing *me*—least of all, the lady you mention."

"Come now, Signor, don't be ironical; Mabel is a much more important person with us here than you may imagine, and though she be the widow of a fisherman, and the mother of another, she is more of a lady by nature than many who ride in their carriage. She was an old servant of my mother's, and I believe of my grandmother's, and is as much devoted to the family still, as though she had no other ties on earth."

"Why, really, you excite my curiosity, Miss Rose!" said Giacomo in all earnestness; "I should like to see your old woman,—of course none the less so for her desiring to see *me*."

"Very well, you shall go to Baltray the first fine day that comes."

During dinner, and the hour or so that followed, Giacomo's account of his ramble through the town, and of Jemmy Nulty's glowing archeological and hagiological descriptions, passed the time pleasantly. Seated around the fire in the large back parlor, " the room of the household," the little circle was just prepared for the enjoyment of a deliciously quiet evening, each being precisely in that mood when thought finds ready expression, and memory, waking in the genial ray, sets the old a-story-telling, and the young a-dreaming while they listen to "the tales of other days." Miss Ackland sat in the deep shadow at one corner of the wide fireplace,—poor Lydia, her life was in the shadow!—opposite her was Rose, half leaning against her grandfather's chair, the old gentleman and Giacomo occupying the centre, in the full light of the cheerful blaze. Rose had been petitioning her grandfather for a story.

"Well! I will tell you a story, Rose," said the old man out of a pensive but not painful reverie; "I will tell you a story, if your aunt will sing us a song. It's long since I heard my Lydia sing."

Miss Ackland smiled, and went at once to the piano; her father's wish had all her life been law to her—the law of the heart. Running over such a prelude as one is apt to play when they are undecided

what to sing, she turned a smiling look on her father, then commenced that most exquisite song of Moore's —" I wish I was by that dim lake," adapted to one of the sweetest of Irish melodies—" Shule Aroon."*
How touchingly mournful the words are, and how fully they embodied the secret sorrow that preyed forever on Miss Ackland's heart, the reader may judge, as also the tender pathos with which she sang them:

> " I wish I was by that dim lake,
>   Where sinful souls their farewell take
>   Of this vain world, and half-way lie
>   In the cold shadow, ere they die.
>   There, there, far from thee,
>   Deceitful world! my home should be;
>   Where come what might of gloom and **pain**,
>   False hope should ne'er deceive again.
>
> " The lifeless sky, the mournful sound
>   Of unseen waters falling round;
>   The dry leaves quiv'ring o'er my head,
>   Like man, unquiet e'en when dead!
>   These, ay! these shall wean
>   My soul from life's deluding scene,
>   And turn each thought, o'ercharged with gloom,
>   Like willows, downward towards the tomb.

* How much Moore admired this fine air may be judged from the fact of his having written two songs to it, one of which, that mentioned in the text, is of Sir John Stephenson's arrangement; the other, "Alone in crowds I wander on," may be found in the supplement to the Irish Melodies arranged by Sir Henry Bishop. Gerald Griffin has immortalized it by his beautiful song " My Mary of the curling hair!"

'As they who to their couch at night
Would win repose, first quench the light,
So must the hopes that keep this breast
Awake, be quench'd, ere it can rest.
Cold, cold this heart must grow,
Unmoved by either joy or woe,
Like freezing founts, where all that's thrown
Within their current turns to stone."

It seemed as though the petrifying process referred to in the last stanza had been going in Miss Ackland's exterior, at least, while she sang, for by the time she had finished the song, her face was pale and rigid as that of a marble statue, and nor tear nor smile gave token of inward emotion as she passed in silence to her seat. A spell seemed even to have fallen on her hearers, the spell of human sympathy, evoked by the saddest, sweetest sounds that Giacomo at least, had ever heard. Mr. Ackland leaned back in his chair, one hand shading his eyes, and so he long remained, his mind wandering, doubtless, in the dim regions of the past where the dead do dwell. It was Rose who first broke the silence, which she did with a mock sigh that was anything but sympathetic.

"Dear me! Aunt Lydia, what a doleful song that was! I protest I feel as though I were like Niobe turning into stone. How do *you* feel, Signor?"

The question was so ludicrous that it made every one smile, and then, the gloomy spell broken, sunshine came again, and, to make sure of it, Rose said, "I'll sing a song myself. What shall it be, grandpa?— oh! I know just what will suit!" And, without leaving her seat, she trolled her merry lay—it was "Life let us cherish," then deservedly popular in Drogheda society.

"Why are we fond of toil and care?—
Why choose the rankling thorn to wear,
And heedless by the lily stray
That blossoms in our way?"

repeated Rose, after singing the song; "now that is what I call sensible, and I mean to practice it all my life long! What say you, Signor? Do *you* believe in people making mopes of themselves because they come upon some dark days in life, or meet with some disappointment?"

Giacomo did not answer; he looked at Miss Ackland, and saw that, although she tried to force a smile, the effort cost her more than she would wish to have noticed.

"Rose, my dear," said she, in a voice as firm as she could make it, "I sincerely hope that your philosophy may never be put to any very hard ordeal. Happy are they who *have* no 'rankling thorn to wear.' But, papa, you forget the story you were to tell us."

"The story I meant to tell, my dear, will only interest our young friend here; it is not new to you or Rose."

"Oh! no matter for that, grandpapa," cried Rose, eagerly, "I do love to hear you tell a story, whether I heard it before or not."

"Well! Giacomo," said the old gentleman, "the story I am about to tell you is a true story, and occurred within my own memory to a family here in Drogheda with whom I was well acquainted." He paused a moment, and a melancholy smile flitted over his face, as memory retraced the scenes he was about to describe.

## CHAPTER V.

"THERE is a family here in Drogheda," said Mr. Ackland, "with whom mine lived on very intimate terms in my young days. Their name is Hilton." "Oh! I know now, grandpapa!" cried Rose; her grandfather smiled and went on: "There were several brothers and sisters of these Hiltons when I was a young man, and as generally happens in such cases, theirs was a pleasant home, and many a happy evening I spent amongst them with my poor sister who is long since dead. The Hiltons were then, and what remains of them, are still, Protestants, Episcopalians of the old school, that is to say, as near being Catholics as any who are not Catholics could be, with those genial, old-fashioned ways, which you oftenest find in old Catholic families. They were not to say wealthy, yet had property sufficient to maintain them comfortably, and to some extent elegantly, without embarking in trade, of the fluctuations and vicissitudes of which the old gentleman had a hereditary horror, while the younger members were rather disposed to look down on commercial pursuits and 'people in business' with that unaccountable contempt only to be found amongst the 'gentry' of Ireland and the 'lairds' of Scotland."

"Yes, to be sure!" said Rose—

"'The Laird o' Cockpen he's proud an' he's great'—but pray go on, grandpapa, I never heard so much about the Hiltons before."

"I have said there was a large family of them in those early days of mine, and many of my pleasantest recollections are of boating parties, rural excursions, and social gatherings in winter evenings, for which we and others were mainly indebted to them, old and young as they were,—for the elders of the family were just as fond of social enjoyment as the youngest amongst us. But time passed on, and the family circle at The Grange (as their place was, and is still, called) began to break up; the young people married and scattered away hither and thither; two of them died unmarried, and my dear old friends were left in age with only their eldest son, William, who had married early in life, and when his parents were at length left to the solitude of their then lonely dwelling, brought his wife and three little children to live with them at The Grange. Fortunately, William Hilton and his wife were both of a cheerful and lively disposition, and they so managed matters that the old couple had, to the last, as much social enjoyment as their age permitted; the house was as pleasant for visitors as ever, and at times the surviving members of the family came together again from their homes, more or less distant, under the old paternal roof.

But the time came at last when the parent stem was broken; first the father, then, a year or two after, the mother, went to sleep in the old family-vault, and William Hilton was master of The Grange. By this time I had married, and your mother, Lydia, was quite a favorite with Mrs. Hilton, as my poor sister Rhoda had been with her dear old mother-in-law some fifteen years before. After the death of the old people, The Grange did seem somewhat lonely, and my wife and I spent as much of our time there as we could spare from home, where we had two little ones yourself, Lydia, and your brother Alexander, Rose's father, claiming the mother's attention. But it was not in William's nature, or Susan's either, to be long dull or despondent, and in the course of a year or so the old house began to look like itself again, and the intimate friends of the family began to drop in, as of old, for an evening's entertainment, which was cheerfully and kindly given; then others came, until the gloom of death was gradually banished, and the Hilton homestead was blithe and happy as ever. It was just then—when the sunshine had, at length, prevailed over the dark clouds of mourning, and the world was again bright for the Hiltons, that a strange circumstance occurred, which has made their name famous in our old borough."

Here the old man stopped to stir up the fire which had been going down somewhat; Giacomo drew a long breath, as one whose attention had been overstrained, and all of the little circle, as if by one common impulse, drew their seats closer around the hearth. "First," said Mr. Ackland, "let us have some more wood on the fire—Lydia, my dear, be so good as to ring!" The wood was brought, the fire burned cheerily, and the story was resumed.

"It was one night in mid-winter that Mrs. Hilton was taken with some sudden illness of an alarming nature; the whole household was quickly astir, and James, the man-servant, was sent into town for the family doctor. He had scarcely arrived, and examined his patient, when James was again dispatched for another physician, the most eminent in the town, and all night long the two remained, watching the symptoms of the strange disease, which baffled their skill, and defeated all their efforts to arrest its progress. Towards morning the fatal truth was announced to the afflicted husband, and the four young children were brought to the bedside of their dying mother to receive her blessing and last farewell. The doctors left soon after, having done all that their art could suggest, and all in vain, for as they told Mr. Hilton, death was there, and all the doctors in the world could do nothing for the patient. The gray winter's dawn revealed a mournful scene; the wife and mother had just departed, the voice of mourning filled the house, and the pall of death had fallen again on the so-lately cheerful household of The Grange. A little while after, my wife and I were there, word having been sent us of the sad catastrophe, and never shall I forget the expression of poor Hilton's face as, meeting us at the door of the death-room, he said—'She is gone—Susan is dead!' What could I say what could any one say? So I wrung his hand in silence and followed him to the bed where his wife lay—not yet 'laid out.'

"Two mournful days, and as many dreary nights passed away, and then Susan Hilton was laid in the family-vault, by the side of her mother-in-law who had died little more than a year before.

"The evening succeeding the funeral, which had taken place early in the day, Fanny and I went to keep poor William Hilton company in his now lonely dwelling. Cheerful we could not be ourselves, and we did not try to feign what would have been unnatural, and painful to the heart-stricken mourner. So after the children were gone to bed, my wife herself going up to see them comfortably settled for the night, we three sat together by the fireside in the parlor where so many happy hours had been spent, talking of her who was taken so suddenly from our midst— recalling her fine and amiable qualities, and dwelling with mournful tenderness on the loveable traits of her character. Sad at heart we all were to think that we should see her no more on earth.

"All at once a ring came to the front-door, and William Hilton started, then said with a sad smile, turning to us—'If poor Susan were not dead, I should say that was her ring.'

"Again the bell rang, louder, sharper than before

and the two female servants rushed into the room pale with terror.

"'Why do you not open the door?' said their master in surprise.

"'The Lord save us, sir,' cried one of them, 'it's so like the mistress' ring that—that—oh sir, there it is again!'

"Mr. Hilton did not take time to chide them for their folly, but rising from his seat, he went himself to open the door; as if by a mechanical impulse my wife and I followed—the door was opened, into the hall glided a spectral figure, and on into the parlor it passed. We all followed, the servants shrieked, and hid their face—so did my wife—it was Mrs. Hilton in her winding-sheet!

"'Great God, Susan, is it you?' said Mr. Hilton approaching the figure.

"'Yes, William, it is I—oh! I am cold—cold!'

"'William, are you afraid of me?'"

"The next moment the wife was clasped to her husband's heart, and we knew that Susan Hilton was before us, not in the spirit only, but in the flesh! No time was lost, you may be assured, in putting her to bed, and administering such restoratives as her half-frozen state required. When thoroughly warmed, the poor lady fell into a heavy, unbroken sleep, from which she did not awake till the morning was far advanced.

"When Mrs. Hilton opened her eyes, and looked around, her first word was—'James, where is James?'

"'Why do you ask, my love?' said Mr. Hilton, 'do you want him?'"

"Mrs. Hilton only repeated the question, when it was ascertained that James had left the house the previous evening, and had not yet returned. Hearing this, Mrs. Hilton raised her left hand, and fixed her eyes on the ring finger, on which a fresh wound was plainly discernible, the finger, moreover, being much swollen.

"'Then it was *not* a dream,' said she, and she shuddered.

"'What do you mean, Susan?' inquired her husband.

"'I *was* buried then—that is, I was placed in the vault—and James *did* cut my finger. Tell me how it all happened—was I dead?'

"'It seemed so, darling,' said her husband, in a soothing tone; we were all alarmed by the wildness of her look. 'Do you not remember taking leave of us all?'

"'Yes, yes, I remember.'

"'Well! you died, as we thought, a short time after.'

"'Oh! I see it all, now,—Almighty God be praised! I was dead and buried, yet now live and breathe above ground again. Oh William! oh my friends, help me to thank our merciful God, unworthy as I am of His so great goodness! But, under God, I owe my escape to James!'

"'Why, how is that, Susan? what *can* you mean?'

"'I mean that James saved my life, though quite unintentionally, I have no doubt. I remember now perfectly the sensations I experienced at the moment when I thought myself dying—the mortal terror that, as it were, froze my blood, and benumbed every faculty of my soul at the thought that I was passing into the dread presence of the Supreme Judge; the next thing I was conscious of was a deathly coldness through all my frame, as if of a person who had lain all night on the ground in the open air; then I felt that one of my fingers was cut and bleeding, I opened my eyes and looked up; there was James bending over me, a knife in his hand, his face plainly seen in the light from a dark lanthorn placed on my breast as I lay in the coffin. He was as pale as death, and I could see that his hands trembled. "Oh James!" said I, and immediately he dropped the knife and ran away, fortunately leaving the lanthorn behind him, and the door unlocked, so that I was able to get out, and make my way home. My greatest difficulty was the churchyard gate, which being locked, I was forced to clamber over it; you know it is not high, and being of open iron work, I had sufficient resting-place on either side for my poor frozen feet.'

"It was all clear now: Mrs. Hilton had been only in a kind of trance when she seemed to be dead; her marriage ring and a valuable guard-ring had been left on, the finger being too much swollen to remove them, and this circumstance having come to James' knowledge, he possessed himself of the key of the vault, and went to secure the prize before decomposition should have set in. Finding that he could not take off the rings, the man was proceeding to cut off the finger, when the lady recovered from her death-like trance, and the robber of the tomb fled in dismay."

"But what became of him?" asked Giacomo; "was he ever seen again?"

"Oh! indeed he was," said Rose, answering for her grandfather; "I often heard it told how Mrs. Hilton prevailed on her husband to hunt him out, and settle a small pension on him. For himself he could never forgive the fellow, but Mrs. Hilton would always have it that he was the means of saving her life."

"And did the lady live long after?"

"Yes," said Mr. Ackland, "she lived for full fourteen years, and had several children after her wonderful resuscitation. Some of her children and grandchildren are still living in the old manor-house, though she and her husband have been many, many years tenants of the tomb where she once lay a living corpse for nigh twenty-four hours."*

"It is a strange story," said Giacomo thoughtfully, "but I heard another of a somewhat similar kind said to have occurred in Cologne on the Rhine."

"Yes," said Miss Ackland, "I remember reading the story to which you allude: I believe it is com-

---

* This story is true in all its principal details. The name of the family is changed, however, for obvious reasons.

memorated by a monument in that city, called the Monument of the Dead-Alive."

"Dear me!" exclaimed Rose with a shudder, "what a position to find one's self in on awaking from a trance!—lying in a coffin in a dismal vault with the dead all around, and in Mrs. Hilton's case, a robber before one in the ungracious act of sawing off one's finger! Only fancy!—I wonder she didn't lose her senses, or die in reality of pure fright. I'm sure *I* should!"

"You don't know, my dear, you don't know," said her grandfather, stroking her dark tresses with his hand. "But it grows late, had we not better say our night-prayers, Lydia, and retire? I know not how you youngsters may feel, but I feel disposed to sleep."

Nancy being summoned, the Rosary and other prayers were said, and the little household was soon at rest within, while the snow fell, and wind blew without.

Two or three days had passed before the roads were in such condition as to permit the visit to Baltray. Even then the walking was not very good, so Connor was sent for, and one clear bright morning Miss Ackland, Rose, and Giacomo started on their visit to Mabel. They found the old woman cowering over the hearth, alone in the cottage, her son and grandson being out in their boat and her daughter-in-law gone "into town" to dispose of the last "take." The children, she said, were "about the doors somewhere, divartin' themselves."

"And how do you find yourself to-day, Mabel?" said Miss Ackland stooping over her.

"Middlin', dear, m'ddlin'—but better that than worse. How is all with you at the house?"

"Quite well, Mabe', thank you."

"Is any one with you, Miss Lyddy?" For the old woman's sight was wearing dim.

"Yes, Mabel, *I'm* with her," said Rose in her merry girlish way, "and there's somebody else with her, too!—Guess, now, who it is!" And Rose placed herself between Giacomo and the old woman.

"Och! don't I know well enough who it is, Miss Rose, agra! didn't I tell you to bring the young gentleman till I'd see him!"

Reaching her hand to Miss Ackland to help her up, Mabel raised herself from her crouching position on the hearth, and turned slowly round, fixing her black eyes, still keen and sharp though somewhat dim with age, on the face of the young stranger, who smiled at the earnestness with which she scrutinized him.

"It's a good face," said she, turning at length to Miss Ackland, "it's strange to me, though," and she shook her head, then peering again into the young man's face—"there's nothing in it I ever seen before, barrin' the smile, an' I'd know that anywhere, however he came by it. God mark you with grace, child!" And with a suddenness which surprised even Miss Ackland and Rose, accustomed as they were to her strange ways, the crone laid her yellow wrinkled hand on Giacomo's head, the while her failing memory seemed to search in the past for the broken link of some familiar association. "The dark grave and the deep say keeps ever their own," she muttered, "but there's quare things happens sometimes,—an' Him above can do more than that. Still it's all dark—dark—I never seen him in my drames—I'm glad to see you, young gentleman!" she added in a louder voice, with the incoherence of a failing mind.

"I thank you, good Mabel!" said Giacomo, impressed in a way he could not understand, by the old woman's singular manner, her tall figure only slightly stooped, her old-fashioned apparel neat and clean, though poor, and the keen intelligence that flashed at times from the eyes that gleamed in the weather-browned face under the red kerchief which formed the woman's head-gear.

"Why, he spakes English," Mabel said with a start, once more addressing Miss Ackland. The latter explained by saying that the young gentleman had been early sent to school to learn English, his family, though Italians, being much engaged in trade with English and Irish seaports.

"To be sure, honey, to be sure," said Mabel, turning her eyes again on the young Italian—"it's aisy seen that he's a foreigner, he's so yallow, though comely enough, sure! Well! well! I thought—God help me! I don't know what I thought. Ah! Miss Lyddy, dear an' darlin', I do be thinkin' quare things —quare things, alanna, when I'm sittin' here all alone by myself. An' then, when night comes, I see it all over again in my dramcs. Livin' an' dead are about me then, an' I see everything—everything. You wouldn't b'lieve, Miss Lyddy, what things comes nto this ould head o' mine when I'm lyin' broad awake even, in the dead o' night. If I'd tell you I'm sure you'd laugh at me—but anyway I couldn't tell you— it's best not. But there—see how forgetful I'm growin'—I hadn't the manners to ax one o' you to sit down." And with instinctive politeness she tried to wipe a seat, a three-legged stool, it was—and push it over to where Miss Ackland stood. Before she could offer another to Rose, Miss Ackland told her not to trouble herself.

"I see you have your little black tea-pot by the fire," she said smiling, "and I know of old you don't like tea that is too long drawing,—so we'll leave you, Mabel, as Connor is waiting outside with the car, and I intend to drive our young friend here as far as the Tower. So, you see we have no time to lose, for the days are short, and papa would be anxious, too, if we staid out over long."

"He would, asthore, he would," said Mabel, following them to the door. "But listen hither, Miss Lyddy," and she lowered her voice to a whisper, and bent her head close to the lady—" don't go too near the say wid *him*—don't, now, honey! you don't know what fate might be on him, an', no matther who he is, there's something in him that one's heart warms to Ah! God's blessin' be about you," as Miss Ackland lingering a moment behind, placed something in her hand, "sure you're always givin' me, one way an' another. Well! more's the pity," she soliloquized, looking after her, "more's the pity that she was crossed in her young days, an' that heavy grief came upon her. An' the heavy, heavy grief it was, an' will be, too, till the earth covers her. None but God Himself can give *her* comfort now, for all she looks the same as ever!"

"Where are we going now, Aunt Lydia?" Rose asked, when they were again seated on the car, the two ladies one side, Giacomo the other, Connor on his elevated seat between,—"Did I hear you speak of the Tower?"

"Yes, my dear, I am going to show Giacomo one of our sights, so long as we are in the vicinity."

A short drive along the river edge brought them to the mouth of the Boyne, and in sight of a tall, square tower of a whitish, or rather a dull yellowish color, standing on the beach, rising lone amid the gray sands and pebbles that fringed the river and the sea. It was a lonely place, voiceless ever, save the sound of the waters and the scream of the curlew; dreary as solitude could make it, and with no beauty to cheer the eye, except what it borrowed from the sea-wave's glancing sheen,—the landward view was dull and monotonous. Yet the scene, wild and lonely as it was, struck Giacomo with a feeling new and strange. The solitude of the place weighed upon his senses, and yet the hushed repose of all around had a soothing effect on his mind.

"What a wild place!" he said at length; "is this the Tower we came to see, Miss Ackland?"

"Yes, Giacomo, this is Maiden Tower."

"Maiden Tower!" he repeated; "and why is it so called?"

"The story is too long to tell you now," the lady smiling replied; "Connor and his horse would have little reason to thank me were I to keep them here on a December day while I related an old-time legend. Mark the place well, however, and this evening you shall hear what tradition says of the lone tower on the beach. There is a good sea-view from the top, but it is too cold to go up to-day."

"But the Lady's Finger, Aunt Lydia," said Rose, laughing, "you forget that," pointing out to Giacomo a sort of obelisk not a third as high as the tower, standing at a little distance landward; "is not that a delicate finger for a lady to point with?"

"Yours is, at any rate," thought Giacomo, as he marked, perhaps for the first time, the rare beauty of the little outstretched hand.

"Does tradition say anything of the Finger, Aunt Lydia? I really forget, but I suppose it does,—and if it does not, we can say it ourselves, for the Lady of the Finger must be the Maiden of the Tower."

"It would seem so, Rose," said her aunt, "but I regret to say that tradition is silent with regard to the obelisk. Come, let us go, we shall be late for dinner, and you know your grandpapa does not like to be kept waiting."

None there could read the sorrowful meaning that was in Miss Ackland's look as she cast her eyes around before leaving the place. She was thinking of a time long years before when in the bright summer-time she had wandered on the beach by Maiden Tower with one who shared her every thought and feeling—one whom she should see never more on earth. Other friends were then around, dear and valued, some of whom were now also with the dead, but what were they all to that sorrowing heart filled with one beloved image? His deep voice murmured in the sea, and whispered in the wind that sighed around the tower.

That evening when her father dosed in his arm-chair, and Rose was engaged with a volume of Scott's poetry, Giacomo ventured to remind Miss Ackland of the promised legend.

"It is both short and simple," she replied, "but sufficiently tinged with the marvellous—and the improbable," she added smiling—"to keep its hold on the popular imagination. Mind I do not vouch for the truth of what I am going to relate,

"'I tell the tale as 'twas told to me.'

The story goes that in very ancient times, probably those of the Crusades, a lady of this vicinity had the grief to see her lover go off to fight in foreign parts, promising, however, to return in a year and a day—the charmed period of old stories It was agreed on by this sorrowful pair of lovers that if the knight—for such, it appears, was his dignity—succeeded to his wishes abroad, and came home safe to his lady-love, he should hoist a white flag when his vessel neared the Boyne's mouth, but if, on the contrary, any mishap had befallen him, and that the vessel returned without him, a black flag, streaming from the mast-head, should give notice of the sad event. The knight departed on glory bent, and his lady-love, partly to beguile the first months of absence, and to provide a lofty place whence she might watch the more constantly when the time of his return came near, and catch the first sight of his well-known bark, built the tower you saw to-day. The year and a day had just elapsed when a sail, which her heart told her was *his*, hove in sight on the far horizon; near and more near it came, and already the lone watcher began to anticipate the rapturous joy of the meeting, now so close at hand, when, woe of woes! her straining eyes beheld the sable ensign of death slowly unfurled, and floating from the mast-head; the sight was more than she could bear, and she cast herself from the height of her tower into the sea, and perished in sight of her wretched lover, whose shriek of despair echoed far over the waters, and perhaps reached even her dying ear; he had only hoisted the black flag to try the strength and sincerity of her affection. Such, Giacomo, is the legend of Maiden Tower. Local history, to be sure, gives a different account of its origin, but, you know, I have only to deal with the more romantic version told by the fishermen of the coast, and the peasantry of the adjoining country. You smile: I see you are somewhat skeptical in such matters."

"Perhaps I am," he replied; "at all events, one cannot help thinking that there must have been some very silly people in those days, of which such wild tales are told. If there never had been damsels foolish enough to throw themselves into the sea in a fit of disappointment, I am sure people would never have imagined such things when telling old stories."

"Very true," said Miss Ackland, the deep shadow gathering over her fair brow; "but, although we may justly despise the folly, not to say wickedness, of any one professing the Christian faith who would allow passion to run away with their reason, or induce them to shrink as cowards from the stern battle of life, I would not have you think or speak lightly of that love which, under proper control, is capable of producing great results. There *is* a love, Giacomo, that is stronger than death, and over which time has no power. Oh! believe me there is!"

There was something in Miss Ackland's voice when she said this, that even more than the words themselves made Giacomo start; he looked at her, but her eyes were fixed on vacancy, and a strange smile, as of exultation, was playing about her parted lips, giving a new and more spiritual expression to her features. All at once the smile vanished, and Miss Ackland looking up perceived that she had been the object of Giacomo's keen scrutiny; she colored and with a sort of impatient gesture called Rose to bring over her book and read aloud. "I see papa is just waking up," said she, "but, never mind, read a little louder, so that he may hear you. I know he likes Marmion.'"

The poem was new to the young Italian, and its beauties lost nothing by Rose's reading. Her voice was musical and well modulated, and it was like a dream, Giacomo thought, to sit and look on her bright young face, and hear her tell over in sweet ringing numbers, that story of love and chivalry and old romance.

## CHAPTER VI.

Next day brought Giacomo letters from home there was one from his young sister Maddalena, full of the tenderest affection, and all the exuberant joy of an almost childish heart, at the complete recovery of a beloved brother, with the enthusiastic gratitude of early youth for those already dear, though unknown friends, who had supplied to him in his utmost need, the place of "the loved ones at home." The letter was in Italian, but when read in English to Miss Ackland, that lady failed not to discover, in addition to the amiable feelings already mentioned, a dreamy, pensive character in the writer, very unlike the idea she had formed of Giacomo's sister. Not that the young man was himself either prosy or commonplace, and there was in him poetry enough for all purposes of ordinary life, but the poetry lay very far down in his heart, under divers strata of common sense, sound judgment, and other such qualities whereof the lords of creation are wont to take the full merit to themselves. Now with Maddalena it was easy to see that the case was entirely different; she was evidently a creature of feeling and sentiment, and Miss Ackland somehow felt attracted towards her as people seldom are to those whom they have never seen.

There was also a letter from his father, which seemed to disconcert the young man more than a little. He had only read a few lines when he rose from his feet, and taking the letter to the window, stood there while he finished its perusal. Even then he did not return immediately to his seat, and at last Miss Ackland expressed her hope that there was no bal news in the letter.

"Well! I know not whether *you* may consider it bad news or good," he said, turning with a smile that was not cheerful, "my father insists on my going 1ome immediately."

"Is it possible? why I thought you were to remain with us over Christmas."

"I thought so, too, but it seems my father will not have it so."

"Well! I am really sorry," said Miss Ackland, "but, after all, it is nothing more than might be expected. It is natural, you know, that your father should wish to have you at that festive season—the more so as your poor mother is dead, and only your sister now at home. But, indeed, it is far from being good news to me—or to any of us, I am sure."

Giacomo did not tell Miss Ackland that his father had given him peremptory orders to return by the very first opportunity that offered, and not to remain one hour longer than he could possibly avoid. His thanks to the Acklands, too, were so cold, so measured, that the young man could not repeat them in the same way, and he felt mortified and distressed to think that his father should show so little gratitude where so much was due. For himself, though naturally anxious to see his father and sister again, he felt half reluctant to leave a place where a new era of existence had dawned on him—a place that had so many agreeable associations, and where such an indescribable charm hung around every object. Nestling, as it were, in that quiet nook of the busy world, with only a few companions, each interesting in their own degree, and their ways so different from any he had ever seen before, so simple, so natural, so refined, and in one, at least, so piquant, that his sojourn there was more a pleasant dream than one of life's realities. That short period had, he felt, thrown his thoughts into a different channel, and given him hopes and aspirations new and undefined, but none the less sensible. Now that the dream was suddenly broken, and the visions it had brought melting away in the cold vapors of every-day life, he felt how very sweet it had been. With the poet he sadly thought—

"It is all but a dream at the best,"
And when happiest soonest o'er,"—

but there was no help for it now, and Giacomo Malvili was not the one to indulge in idle or vain regrets, when life's duties called him hence. He endeavored to turn his thoughts on home, and look forward with the unmixed joy he used to feel to a return thither after even a short absence; he thought of the father of whom he was so proud, and of the gentle, graceful sister of whom he was so fond, but, do as he would, with those dear home-images would come the gay, laughing face of Rose, looking arch and mischievous through her brown curls, and the sweet, thoughtful look of Miss Ackland, with her winning smile, and her kind motherly accents, sweet as music to his ear. Mr. Ackland had his full share in Giacomo's regret, and even old Nancy was not forgotten, for he had won his way to the old woman's heart, and had latterly been admitted to the special privilege of a seat at evening by the kitchen fire when it pleased him to stroll in. This was a flattering compliment, as Giacomo was made to feel, for it placed him directly on a family footing in the house, and gave him the benefit of Nancy's songs and stories, in common with Rose, who much affected the good woman's company, as before indicated. Even the snug, cozy kitchen, with its bright turf fire and well-swept hearth, had, then, its share of pleasant associations, and, perhaps, fully as many as the parlor, for reasons which the younger portion of our readers will be at no loss to understand.

When the family met at dinner, Giacomo's approaching departure was, of course, the first and most important topic. Miss Ackland looked graver because of it, and her father still more so, but it was no little mortifying to Giacomo's vanity, if vanity he had, to see the careless indifference of Rose, who was, indeed, gayer, if possible, than usual, and seemed little disposed to trouble herself about who went or who stayed, so long as her aunt and grandpapa remained, and Nancy and the cat! That such was the case, she made Giacomo sensible in various ways, and he felt humbled and not a little annoyed by the girl's total indifference. "She has no heart!" was the thought that fixed itself in his mind, and he came, accordingly, to the wise conclusion that he, too, would be gay, and cheerful, just to let Miss Rose see that he cared as little about her as she did about him.

In the evening, Mr. Ackland would have Giacomo play backgammon with him. "probably," he said, "for the last time." Whilst the men were being arranged on the board, the old man chatted on. "Giacomo," said he, "what would you think of seeing a blind man play backgammon?"

"Well! I cannot say what I would think, Mr. Ackland,—but, at all events, it is a sight I do not expect to see."

"Yet I saw it, Giacomo, and that many a time."

Giacomo's surprise was not greater than that of Miss Ackland. "Why, papa, are you serious?" she asked.

"Perfectly serious, Lydia! You have often heard me speak of Arthur O'Neil, the blind harper, who was, in my young days, an occasional visitor at our house?" Of course Miss Ackland had, and she looked much interested. Rose's curiosity was also excited, and aying down Mary Howitt's Poems which she had been reading, she leaned over the back of her grandpapa's chair to hear "all about the blind harper," whose fame was not unknown even to her.

"All I mean to tell now, Rosey, is not much," said Mr. Ackland, "for the men are arranged, and we must go on with our game."

"But do you mean to say, grandpapa, that O'Neil could play backgammon and he blind?"

"Yes, my dear, and draughts, too;*—I have seen my father and he play at backgammon or draughts for hours at a time.

"Then he was admitted to the society of gentlemen?" said Giacomo.

"Indeed he was, and not by courtesy, but by right, for he was a gentleman himself in every sense of the word, and a most agreeable, entertaining companion, apart from his music. The first houses in the province of Ulster, and as far beyond its limits as he chose to go, were at all times open to him. Amongst his friends and patrons was that venerable historian and scholar, Charles O'Connor of Ballinagar. Indeed, the noblest in the land welcomed him to their social board. He was proud of his ancestry, and had the crest of the O'Neils engraved on his silver coat-buttons."

"I believe, papa," said Miss Ackland, "O'Neil was

---

* For a particular account of this celebrated man, see Hunting's valuable work on the Ancient Music of Ireland.

not addicted to those low vices which disgraced so many of the itenerant harpers of these latter days."

"No, my dear, he was not. On the contrary, his habits were those of a high-bred gentleman, and although formed himself to shine in society, he was not fond of large or mixed companies, and never indulged in any excess. He was, indeed, very exclusive in his choice of company, and only relished what was really good. Blind though he was, he was scrupulously neat, too, in his personal appearance."

"But how did he manage to dress himself, grandpapa?" asked Rose, girl-like.

"My dear child, he never had it to do; he always had his body-servant with him, besides another to carry his harp. But oh! that harp! when I think of the music he used to draw from it, my old ears tingle even now, and my heart thrills with something of the delight with which I used to hear him. Poor O'Neil! last of our national minstrels! how often your magic strains echoed through this very room!"

The tears came into the old man's eyes, and he leaned back in his chair, evidently oppressed by the weight of rushing memories that

"Lock'd in the countless chambers of the brain"

came with the one awaked. For a moment all were silent, even Rose, but that mercurial young lady was never long in that condition of being,—"What!" she cried, "here in this room?—So that dear, delightful old harper used to play in this very room?"

"Yes, my dear, and in various other rooms of our old domicile," said her grandpapa smiling at her childish eagerness.

"Well! now, that *is* charming," and Rose clapped her hands, "I am so glad to know it!"

"And why?" said her aunt.

"Oh! because, it is such a nice new—no, *old* picture for my memory's cabinet. I had many images there already of the old people and young people, that used to be here in old times, and I have such pleasure when I'm all alone sometimes, or when we're all sitting here of an evening, imagining what they used to say and do, but now I have got one better than all, and he fills up the picture so nicely! I'm sure I shall often dream of that heavenly music grandpapa describes, and the blind old harper playing backgammon!"

"By the bye, that reminds me of our game, Giacomo," said Mr. Ackland, "I was forgetting all about it."

"An astonishing coincidence, papa, Mr. Brodigan would call that."

"Talking of Brodigan, Lydia," said her father, "he has not been here for a long time. Take care, Giacomo, or I shall take that man on your *deux* point. Aces! upon my word! now, I have you!"

"Talk of *somebody* and he will appear," said Miss Ackland, as a loud knock was heard at the hall-door; "now I shouldn't wonder if that were Mr. Brodigan."

It was Mr. Brodigan, and his fine, full, manly voice was soon heard in the hall, good-humoredly calling

Nancy to account for having allowed him to knock
wice. Nancy said something in reply.

"Oh! yes, that's always the way with you women,"
said the voice, as Rose opened the parlor door, "I
never knew one of you yet that hadn't her excuse
ready. Ah! there you are, Miss Rose, as blooming
as your namesake—a December rose, ha! ha!—and
my old friend, looking as well—as well as can be—
and Miss Lydia—handsome as ever—how are you
all?—eh! who's this?" seeing Giacomo, after he
had shaken hands with all the rest, and was placing
his large, portly figure in an arm-chair by the fire.

Giacomo was formally introduced, with the additional circumstance of his recent escape from shipwreck.

"Oh! the San Pietro! So this is the young gentleman whom you took home—ahem! invited here,
after the wreck?—A fine fellow, upon my honor!—
That reminds me of that dashing Captain Melville
whom I used to meet here, and who was lost at sea,
afterwards. Quite a coincidence, eh?"

Miss Ackland rose and walked with an unsteady
step to the table where her work lay; her father
coughed and fidgetted in his chair, then offered his
snuff-box to Mr. Brodigan, drew the blazing faggots
together on the brazen dogs on the hearth, and finally
asked what sort of weather it was out of doors.

"Splendid weather for Christmas, Mr. Ackland, if
it only lasts. Keen frost above, and white crisp snow
under foot. Fine bracing weather, sir!"

This worthy gentleman, a corn-merchant of the town, and a fair sample of its burghers, was a new manifestation of character to the young Italian, and he listened with pleasure to his round mellow voice, as he talked over the various local topics of the day, with Mr. Ackland. It was the old gentleman's custom to take one glass of punch every night, before he retired, and Mr. Brodigan, of course, joined him on that evening, declaring, upon his word, that there was nothing better after a smart walk of a cold winter night than a good "tumbler of punch." But although Mr. Brodigan admitted the efficacy of the punch as a specific for cold, he was by no means addicted to its use, and seldom went beyond "a tumbler or so," saying that "enough was as good as a feast." But he waxed mellow under the genial influence of the fire, and the glass of punch, and asked the ladies if they wouldn't favor him with some music. Of course they would; Miss Ackland played, Rose sang "Gaily the Troubadour touched his Guitar," Mr. Brodigan beating time on the table with his fingers, and humming the air at the same time in a way that made Giacomo wish to hear him sing. His wish was gratified, for Rose, having finished her song, said—"Now, Mr. Brodigan, it is your turn. You will favor us with a song, will you not?"

"Of course I will, Miss Rose!—you know it is an old saying that it is bad enough to be a bad singer, and not be bad about it. You know all my songs, Ladies,—now tell me what I shall sing?"

"Oh! you know my favorite," said Miss Ackland.

"And mine, Mr. Brodigan," added Rose.

"Well! now, ladies, I declare I'd like to oblige you both," he said laughing, "and I don't see how I can do it, except to sing for both."

"A happy thought!" said Mr. Ackland.

So Mr. Brodigan, clearing his throat in the most approved fashion, sang for Miss Ackland "The Light of other Days," then new and much in favor, and for Rose "The Haunted Spring," one of Lover's most beautiful Songs of Ireland, and he sang both well, and with true feeling of expression; music both vocal and instrumental was much cared for in Drogheda society, and if men or women (we mean, of course, ladies and gentlemen) had ever so little voice, they cultivated it as a sort of duty they owed their neighbors and friends.

"I'm sorry Mrs. Brodigan and the girls didn't come," said Miss Ackland; "we could have had a set of quadrilles, if they had!"

"So am I, Miss Lydia," said the worthy merchant, "and I assure you it isn't my fault, for I tried hard to prevail upon them, but they were all afraid of the cold, and Mrs. Brodigan had a touch of a sore throat, so they stayed at home. I dropped in for a moment at Gernon's on my way up, and what do you think but Mrs. G. has another 'touch of a sore throat.' Quite a coincidence, isn't it? But that reminds me of my message, which I was near forgetting. There's Grand Benediction in the afternoon, you know, at

West street Chapel,—of course, we'll all meet there, and Mrs. Brodigan wants you to come home with us afterwards to dinner. And our young Leghorner here," turning to Giacomo, "will consider himself very particularly invited."

"You are very kind, Mr. Brodigan, and I should be most happy to accept your invitation," said Giacomo, "but I shall be on my way home by Sunday—that is, if I can find a vessel going."

Mr. Brodigan expressed his regret, and hoped to have the pleasure of seeing him at his table at some future time. The other promised to go, and Mr. Brodigan took his departure, stoutly refusing "another glass of punch."—"No, no, thank you, one's enough at a time. Good-night, all."

After the worthy merchant had left, and the family prayers were said, the little circle in Mr. Ackland's old parlor drew closer round the fire; long they sat and talked, unmindful of the swiftly-passing hours. till Mr. Ackland, at length, looking at his watch, surprised them all by the startling announcement that it was past twelve o'clock.

"In that case," said Miss Ackland, "we must dissolve the meeting, and I hereby formally dismiss you all to the land of dreams."

"And I shall be glad to go," said Rose, quoting N. P. Willis, "provided I may dream of grandpapa's dear old gentlemanly harper, and hear his entrancing music, which would then, you know, be literally 'the music of the spheres.'

Would not that be a coincidence?" and so saying, having reached the room-door, she laughingly kissed her hand to those she was leaving behind, and tripped away with her night-light, humming "I'd be a butterfly." Giacomo thought of the figures of Hebe he had seen in his own country, and wondered if any of those grand old sculptors had had such models as Rose Ackland.

He had gone to bed and fallen asleep, after the pious preparation carefully taught him by his mother in his early childhood, and had slept he knew not how long, when he was awoke by a strain of what seemed at first to his bewildered senses, celestial music; returning consciousness, however, soon convinced him that it was *not* celestial, as the Angels are not wont to tune their harps to Scotch airs, and the one ringing in his ears, and thrilling his heart, and making the blood to tingle in his finger-ends, was decidedly Caledonian, if he knew anything of national music. It was a merry strain, a cheerful, stirring strain, full of life, and hope, and all the most welcome of the heart's emotions, and how Giacomo's heart did welcome it! Never had he heard such soul-stirring music; so he thought, at least, and as the delicious melody floated around, now high, now low, on the midnight air, the young man lay entranced and motionless, fearing to lose a note by any change of position. All at once the strain changed to an equally cheerful Irish air, one he had often heard Rose play,—which Giacomo recognized as "Nothing in life can sadden us." When this was played a few times over, the music ceased, Giacomo sprang from his bed and approached the window, just in time to hear a deep masculine voice saying words like these, rapidly spoken:

"Good morrow, Mr. Ackland! Good morrow Miss Ackland! Good morrow, Miss Rose!—good morrow, young gentleman! Good morrow, ladies, and gentlemen, all!"

The cold, sharply-pointed crescent of the waning moon was struggling through thick clouds at the moment, and by her misty light, the young man could just distinguish some four or five figures in great-coats, having, as he thought, an exceedingly ancient look about them, something like the "Charleys" who still kept watch and ward over the slumbers of the burghers of Drogheda; the faint rays fell, too, on certain brazen "instruments of sound," carried by these quaint-looking serenaders, the light of which completely dispelled from Giacomo's mind any lingering suspicion that the music he had heard might possibly be that of O'Neil's harp, or some other minstrelsy from the world of spirits. Standing opposite the windows at the rear of the house, in the street leading out from Lawrence's Gate, the musicians had thus agreeably broken the night's dead silence, and were now moving away. Had the cold been less intense, Giacomo might have been curious enough to have watched them on their way, but as it was, he was only too glad to take shelter again under the blankets from the keen frosty air of mid-winter. It was long, however, before sleep again visited his eye-lids, for the music he had heard was still ringing in his ears, filling his mind with sweet and gracious fancies, and he could not, if he would, break the charm it had cast over all his senses.

When he met the family at breakfast next morning, Giacomo went at once into the subject that occupied his thoughts, and asked if any one in the house had heard music during the night. Miss Ackland smiled, and Rose laughed.

"Music!" said she, "what music? Did *you* hear any?"

"Indeed I did, the sweetest music I ever heard before."

"Ha! ha!" cried Rose, "the Signor has been visited by the harper's ghost. Only think, grandpapa."

"Not exactly, Miss Rose," said Giacomo, "unless he was one of a company of old fellows, for such I could see they were, who thought proper to serenade us last night. Moreover, if your ancient harper was there, he forgot his harp, for I'll swear I saw only brass instruments with the performers."

"So you have been made sensible, Giacomo," said Miss Ackland, "of the meaning of those lines of our national poet—

> "'No, not more welcome the fairy numbers
> Of music fall on the sleeper's ear,
> When half awaking from fearful slumbers,
> He thinks the full choir of heaven is near.'"

"Truly I have, Miss Ackland; but pray, can **you** tell me what music it was I heard, or rather who they were that paid us such a compliment—I say 'us,' for I presume I was the 'young gentleman' so kindly greeted with the rest of the household?"

"Only fancy, aunt," said Rose with her merry laugh, "the Signor fancies that the compliment was all for us? as if that same compliment was not paid at fifty different houses last night."

"Indeed?"

"Yes, indeed!—did you never hear of 'the waits,' who go round every night in some of these old towns just before Christmas, playing on different instruments, and wishing everybody a good morrow?" No, Giacomo had never heard of them.

"Well! you have not only heard *of* them, now, but heard them your very self. Those were the waits whom you heard last night, and the waits are a very old institution in Drogheda. We purposely refrained from telling you of the custom, in order to give you a surprise."

"For which I thank you; but do you mean to say, Miss Rose, that those worthy individuals take all that trouble every year merely to regale the ears of the townspeople with their merry midnight music?"

"That—and something else," said Rose laughing at the young man's simple earnestness.

"The something else being —— ?"

"Certain silver coins ranging from a crown to a shilling, which they receive when they go round some days after to every house they serenaded, to ask their 'Christmas box.' If you are here the week after Christmas you may have a daylight view of 'the waits'—and queer, jolly old fellows they are, too!"

"I fear I have seen the last of them," said Giacomo, making an effort to imitate Rose's gaiety, "unless they may choose to pay us another visit during this week."

"They may and they may not," said Rose, "but are you really and truly going before Christmas?"

"Really and truly,—if I can."

"And you won't wait for the Midnight Mass, or to see the Crib and the Holy Infant in the Churches?"

"No, I hope to be at Midnight Mass in Leghorn, and there I shall see all, and more than all, I could possibly see here."

"You forget, Rosey," said Miss Ackland, "that all Giacomo loves await him in Leghorn."

"*All* I love?" repeated Giacomo, in a reproachful tone, turning his dark, eloquent eyes on Miss Ackland. "Do you think *all* I love are in Leghorn?"

The lady smiled, and, reaching her hand for his cup, said in her quiet way—"Perhaps I should have said 'those he *most* loves.' But, after all, *love* is a strong word, Giacomo!—seldom, indeed, can it be applied to those whom we and the world call our *friends*. Some we esteem, others we may like, but rarely, indeed, beyond the limits of our own family, do we find any to love—any whose presence is sunshine to our hearts, whose absence, gloom and weariness.

Well for those who have found such, but alas! for those who found and lost them!"

The last words were uttered in a sort of inward tone, as though the speaker were rather following out her own thoughts than addressing another; her eyes filled with tears, which she hastened to wipe away, and smile as usual, seeing her father watching her with that troubled look which she often saw on his face when a cloud rested on hers.

"Papa," said Miss Ackland, brightening up, "we must take our young friend to Oldbridge before he leaves, to see King William's Obelisk, and the scene of the famous Battle of the Boyne."

The old gentleman smiled assent. "But, dear me!" said Rose, "there are so many places he has not seen. He has not even walked up the Rathmullen Road, or out to the Mall; the beautiful Nanny-Water he has not seen,—nor scarce anything."

One word caught Giacomo's fancy—"The walk on the Rathmullen Road," said he, "surely there is time enough for that," and he looked at Rose with a heightened color. "No, no," said Miss Ackland, "you would not enjoy even that now. Wait till you come back next summer, and you shall see everything —Bellewstown Races included."

Giacomo smiled and shook his head, but said no more on the subject.

## CHAPTER VII.

By good or ill fortune as the case might be, a ship was found a few days after taking freight for Leghorn, and the captain, to whom his father was not unknown, willingly consented to take Giacomo as a passenger in his cabin. Now that the day was fixed for his departure, the young man began to feel the yearning that all loving hearts must feel for the loved and long unseen. But none the less his regret for leaving the new friends amongst whom he had spent some happy weeks, perhaps the most sensibly so of all his life. Under the influence of these feelings he much desired to revisit the places where they had been together, and most of all, Clogher Head, the scene of that disaster which had thrown him, a friendless stranger, on their bounty.

They went to Clogher, one gray, mild day, when there was neither frost, nor rain, nor snow—Miss Ackland and Rose, with a certain Mr. Cusack, an elderly young gentleman extremely well-to-do in the world, and very anxious to secure a footing in the small circle which counted the Acklands as its centre. Other and higher ambition Harry Cusack might have had, but of that more anon. He had long ago been set down by the town gossips as a would-be candidate for Miss Ackland's hand, but years passed on and nothing came of it, and people had at last made up their minds either that Harry Cusack had never "meant anything particular," or that Miss Ackland had determined to "die an old maid," now that she was nearing, if not actually on, the upper shelf. But still Harry was seen in as constant attendance as the ladies would permit, and no Mrs. Cusack was presented to the burghers and their wives. When an escort was required, Harry was always only too happy to do the amiable, nothing impeded by the claims of business, for Cusack was his own master, and the head of a thriving mercantile house of good standing in the borough. So Harry Cusack was of the party that drove down to Clogher that December day, moved thereto by some instinctive feeling that the young Italian had enjoyed more than his share of the Acklands' company. Moreover he drove them there on his own handsome and stylish jaunting car—that is to say, his man did.

The heavens were gray above, and the sea and the river gray and misty all, when, leaving the car in the village, our party made their way to the end of the bold promontory, over rough and jagged rocks, and enormous boulders thrown up probably from the deep by antediluvian tides when Clogher Head did not tower so high as it does to-day above the world of waters. Mr. Cusack had offered his arm to

Miss Ackland, but she took Giacomo's, as though not noticing the motion, and the disconcerted Harry was about trying his luck with Rose, when that volatile young lady skipped past him, and was seen the next moment, poised on the top of a huge stone to which she climbed by means of others smaller resting against its green, mossy side. Giacomo started, and would have gone to aid her in her descent from what seemed her perilous position, but Miss Ackland gently detained him, saying that Rose was in no danger whatever, and was well accustomed to clamber over the rocks.

"But they are damp to-day, Miss Ackland, and somewhat slippery."

"Oh! never mind, Rose is as sure-footed as a mountain-goat. I often tell her she ought to have been born in some Alpine *chalet*, she has such a fancy for climbing rocks. A perfect Linda di Chamouni."

"Perfect, indeed," said Giacomo, as he watched the lithe and active girl, moving to and fro on her elevated perch, in order to catch the view at different points. Even the heavy folds of her large cloak, and the close-fitting bonnet that covered her head, could not hide the grace and symmetry of her figure, or the lightness and agility of her movements.

"She'll break her neck, Miss Ackland, I'm sure she will," was Cusack's consolatory remark; "she's as wild as a deer—upon my honor she is."

"Suppose, Mr. Cusack! you went up to take care

of her," said Giacomo somewhat maliciously, as he glanced over the Louth man's goodly proportions.

"Is it I go up there?" said Cusack; "no, I thank you, I value my life and limbs too much for that. Perhaps you'd like to go yourself—eh?"

No sooner said than done; another moment and the light and graceful figure of the young Italian was traced with Rose's on the gray wintry sky. He was standing by her side on the lofty eminence.

"Now I call that a smart lad!" said Cusack, his vexation quite perceptibly shown; "I shouldn't wonder if he had served his time to a circus-rider."

Miss Ackland smiled at the idea, but she merely answered—"I rather think not,"—her mind was already wandering from the present to that past in which she loved to dwell. In vain did Cusack exert himself to keep up a show of conversation; she answered him, indeed, but, as it were, mechanically, and in monosyllables that sufficiently indicated her abstraction. Her eyes were fixed now on the surging waves, in whose depths a hoarse sullen murmur was heard, denoting a coming storm,—and now turned, as if unconsciously, on the youthful pair, who had descended from the top of the boulder, and approached the verge of the rocky precipice, at whose foot roared the white breakers evermore. What association was it that attracted Miss Ackland's grave, sad look to the animated face of the young man while he talked to Rose, and smiled at the girl's wayward answers, then looked thoughtfully out over the waters that lay between himself and home? Did his voice, his mien, his youthful grace, recall some image from the grave of time, or awake to momentary life some dream of by gone days? None knew save herself, and she was not given to revealing her thoughts or fancies, least of all to Mr. Harry Cusack.

And of what were the young people talking as they stood on the bold high bluff together? Their talk was of nothing in particular, whatever their thoughts might have been.

"Oh! do look at that gull!" said Rose, pointing to one that was describing circles between air and water, "see how gracefully and lightly he skims the water with his wing! Should you not like to be a sea-bird, Signor Giacomo?"

"Perhaps I might," he said, amused at the question, "provided I were not doomed to fly alone. But I would rather be a canary-bird, singing in a cage, in a place I know."

"Oh fie!" laughed Rose, "what a preference!—you do not, then,

"'—— dream of all things free?'"

"No, I dream of nothing free. My dreams are not of freedom, but of captivity—willing captivity."

"What, have you never felt the poet's longing when he sang'"—and she recited with theatrical emphasis—

"'Oh! to be free like the eagle of heaven,
   That roams over forests and mountains all day—
   Then flies to the rock which the thunder has riven,
     And nurtures her young with the fresh bleeding prey?'

You never have such yearnings after freedom, have you?"

"No, I stick to the canary."

"Truly, you are very humble in your aspirations."

"Not so humble as you seem to think." And turning he fixed his eyes on her laughing face. "My ambition, Signora, soars higher than you may suppose."

"Oh! pray, don't begin to confess to *me*," and the smile on Rose's cheeks and lips deepened into rosy dimples of mischievous glee, "you know I am not your spiritual director. Did you ever hear the Mermaid's song?" And without waiting for an answer, the wayward girl sang in her sweet clear tones—

> "Come, mariner, down to the deep with me,
> And hide ye under the wave,
> For I have a bed of coral for thee,
> And quiet and sound shall thy slumbers be
> In the cell of the Mermaid's cave."

'What would you think of a flying descent to the Mermaid's cave such a day as this?"

"Anywhere—anywhere with you!" was it a spirit near them that spoke those wild, passionate words, or was it the youth who stood so calmly at Rose's side, his lips firmly compressed, his cheeks pale, his eyes fixed on the dark rugged rocks beneath. Rose was silent a moment,—a thing unusual with her. At last Giacomo turned, and a faint smile was on his face—

"You forget, Miss Rose, that but few weeks have

passed since there below I was battling with the waves, amid storm and darkness—struggling for a life," he added drearily, "that was scarce worth the saving."

"I did forget it—for the moment'—Rose answered, a sweet seriousness stealing over her face, and a shudder creeping through her frame. "It was a fearful night. I shall never forget it. How thankful you ought to be, Giacomo,—I mean, Signor,—that you escaped when so many perished. Oh! that gun! that signal gun! how dismally it sounded through the wild storm!"

"You said I ought to be thankful for my escape," said Giacomo; "I am thankful, Miss Rose, very, very thankful to our good God who has spared me for some wise purpose of His own. But tell me, had you known me as you know me now, would you have been sorry had I, too, perished that dreary night?"

"Sorry!" Rose repeated with a slight start, then seeing the eagerness with which the young man awaited her answer, she laughed and said in a careless way—"Oh! of course I should have been sorry. I will not promise you, though, that I would 'to your memory drop a tear,' as the Scotch ballad says. But I *think* I should have been sorry, for it is not always, you know, one has somebody to tease, as I have many a good time teased *you*."

"Och! weary on you for a creel, for I can't hould you up, at all, at all!" said a rough coarse voice from below

"Who in the world is that?" said Giacomo, peering down amongst the rocks.

"Your Mermaid," answered Rose, laughing merrily; "see if it be not!"

The head of an uncouth female figure emerged just then above the rocks on the side of the promontory where a rough precipitous path led down towards the Pirate's Cave. Her stout and bony frame was attired in a costume half masculine, half feminine, a sailor's jacket being her upper garment, over a short drugget skirt and a gown of linsey-woolsey of the same length pinned up behind. On her head was a blue handkerchief tied under the chin, while the picture was completed by a large basket of the kind called a creel, which hung over her shoulders by a leathern strap across her chest. The basket was full of the dulse or sea-rack which the woman had been gathering amongst the rocks. "There she is," said Rose, in a low voice, "I told you so. A rare Amphitryon, is she not, oh! mighty Neptune?"

But Giacomo scarcely heard her; seeing the poor fishwoman bending, as she was, under her load, and exhausted by her toilsome and difficult ascent of the damp, slippery rocks, he had flown to assist her, and reaching his hand, which she caught fast hold of, enabled her to climb over the last remaining ledge of rock, and plant herself on *terra firma*. She gave her basket a hitch to raise it on her shoulders, and then turned to thank the young gentleman who had so kindly assisted her.

"I'm entirely obleeged to you, gentleman," said she, "an' sure it's aisy known it's a rale gentleman ye are, or ye wouldn't stretch your hand to help a poor cratur like me wid her heavy load. It's aisy seen where the bit o' dacency is. But isn't that young Miss Ackland I see wid you? Augh! sure now I know who you are, barrin' your name,—an' the Lord be praised that you didn't go to the fishes down, that night when the ship was wracked! Well! God bless you both, sure if anything comes of it, it's the purty couple you'll make. You have Catty Nugent's blessin' anyway!"

And so saying, she trudged away, dropping a curtsey to Miss Ackland as she passed her by, and glancing with broad satirical meaning at Mr. Cusack, where he stood facing the lady in a favorite attitude of his, with his overcoat thrown back, and his thumbs in the arm-holes of his handsome vest of dark-colored velvet. Whatever might be the reason, it was plain the wealthy merchant held no very high place in the fishwoman's estimation, and she belonged to a fraternity who are never chary of their opinion. The Clogher and Baltray fishwomen enjoy the enviable reputation of being able to scold down all before them, and of them it is, indeed, often said that "their tongues are no scandal!"

The broad hint so characteristically given by Catty Nugent was not lost on Giacomo and he turned to see what effect it had on his fair companion. A true Irish girl was Rose Ackland; gay and volatile as she was by nature, her modesty was of that sensitive kind that shrinks from any, even the slightest allusion to such possibilities, and though her cheeks were dyed crimson red, she strove to appear as though she had not understood the fishwoman's broad "if anything comes of it." She stooped to pick up a variegated pebble that lay at her feet, and handing it to Giacomo said, with a smile that was evidently forced—.

"Suppose you take that home to Leghorn as a *souvenir* of the rocks of Clogher."

"And of these few 'happy moments'"—he said with emphasis, "moments all too brief, and never to be forgotten. If never to be enjoyed again, these moments during which I have stood with you on the wild shore of Louth, looking out on the waste of waters, will come back to me in after times, Rose Ackland, as one bright speck on a life that may be dark—

"'And in the flight of years we trace,
  The dearest of them all.'

This little stone may one day have a value you little dream of now!" And he put it carefully away.

Before Rose spoke again she coughed once or twice, then gathered her cloak around her, drew down her veil, and finally burst into one of her merriest laughs.

"Mercy on us, Signor, how you do talk!—you are positively becoming quite serious, and such being the case, I must try the efficacy of Harry Cusack's amusing dulness, by way of specific."

"Harry Cusack is much obliged to you, Miss Rose!" said the gentleman named, who, having at length perceived that Miss Ackland paid little attention to his common-places, could no longer resist the temptation of breaking in on a *tete-a-tete* which, brief as it was, rather piqued his self-importance. He had just come up in time to hear his own name mentioned. "I wasn't aware that I was the subject of your conversation. I am quite flattered, I declare!"

"You need not be, then," said Rose, sharply; "if you heard what I said you would not."

"Oh! of course I heard, of course I did—something about my dulness, I think you said. But no matter,—no matter, Miss Rose, better some people's dulness, as you may find out, than other people's over smartness. I never was a great hand at jumping, or turning summersets, or the like," and he looked pointedly at Giacomo, "but still I'm not so dull as you may suppose, and there's one thing I can say for myself that everybody knows who I am, which is more than some people can say for themselves."

Giacomo colored, and was evidently about to make a sharp retort, when a comical look and gesture from Rose made him change his mind and turn away laughing.

"Now, you dear old Harry Cusack, you can't deny but you *are* a little dull at times," said Rose, laying her hand playfully on his shoulder. "And as for jumping and turning summersets, as you say, you know you are to be my uncle one of these days, and such performances would ill become the gravity and dignity of your position. Good gracious! only think of Harry Cusack practising gymnastics!" And away she ran to join her aunt, leaving the two gentlemen looking at each other in a sort of comical bewilderment.

"Uncle, indeed!" muttered Cusack as he turned on his heel and walked away, "what an uncle I'd make you, to be sure, Miss Rose Ackland!"

"Well! Giacomo," said Miss Ackland, when the party were once more together, and walking towards their vehicle, "have you fixed this wild scene of your perilous adventure sufficiently in your mind to describe it when you get home?"

"Yes," said Giacomo, casting his eyes over the wide expanse of water, and the rocky shore, then down on the little straggling fishing-village that nestled, as it were, under the side of the bold promontory, "yes, I think the picture is well stamped on my memory."

"Not forgetting your Mermaid," said Rose archly, "and her basket of sea-weed."

"The Mermaid shall not be forgotten." was the reply, "nor she who sang her song," he added in a lower tone that only reached Rose's ear.

"I think," said Miss Ackland, "we shall have a storm soon; I do not like those heavy clouds that are gathering on the horizon."

"Nor I," said Cusack; "it will be a rough evening, depend upon it, and I think it is the best of our play to be making the road short. There's Ned, too, making signs to us to hurry, so if you have all seen enough of Clogher, we'll start for home."

A few minutes more, and they were all comfortably seated on the car, with water-proof covers over their knees, and Ned, jumping into his seat, smacked his whip as he dashed down the village street, Catty Nugent standing at her door, dropping a curtsey, as they passed, and wishing them all safe home, and "all sorts o' good luck to the pretty young gentleman, an' the ladies, God bless them!"

Soon Clogher was left behind, and the car dashed rapidly along the somewhat lonely road back to Drogheda. The rain was falling, and the quaint old sycamores quivering in the blast, when the party reached Mr. Ackland's door. The short day was already at its close, and "the candles *were* lit in the parlor,"—and Nancy was in a state of feverish excitement because the dinner was spoiled—she was sure it was, and wondered at Miss Ackland to stay so long, knowing well enough that the chickens would be boiled to rags, and the drawn butter burned trying to keep it warm, and that nothing would be fit to put on the table. And there was Mr. Cusack, too, staying for dinner. Well! well! it *was* provoking, sure enough, and so Miss Ack'and acknowledged, soothing Nancy as no one else so well could, and praising the skill and ingenuity by which the faithful creature had endeavored to make the most of what she had to cook for dinner. Notwithstanding Nancy's lamentations the viands were declared excellent, the credit of which Nancy, well pleased, took to herself, but which Miss Ackland, in the good woman's absence, ascribed rather to the keen sea-air and the long fast, in conformity with the old adage that "hunger is good sauce." So the meal passed right pleasantly, and even Harry Cusack's brow, clouded before, grew serene as a summer sky.

The dinner was scarcely over when in came Mr. and Mrs. Brodigan, with their two daughters, the mother a fine portly matron of a certain age, making up in breadth what she wanted in height;—the daughters nothing in particular, except that Miss Brodigan was tall and rather dark-complexioned, Miss Jane small and fair, with blue eyes and light-colored hair, almost flaxen in hue; also, Miss Brodigan was very reserved, and spoke but little; Miss Jane was insipid and sentimental. Their father being wealthy, however, the young ladies had admirers—no, suitors,—by the dozen, to which circumstance might be owing the slightly supercilious air habitual to both, but especially to the elder. They had heard much of the handsome young stranger who had been so long the guest of the Acklands, yet all unseen by Drogheda belles, and were anxious to make his acquaintance before he left; so, hearing that that was to be on the morrow, they had proposed to their father and mother to go and spend the evening at Mr. Ackland's, "it was so long since they had been there."

To all except Giacomo the arrival of the Brodigans

appeared to give pleasure; he would much rather have had, for the last of his stay, one more of those delightful evenings, so quiet, yet so far from dull, of which he had spent so many under that roof. But the Brodigans were there, and Cusack was there; there was no help for it, and everybody seemed so pleased,—especially Mr. Brodigan, who asked if it wasn't quite a lucky coincidence that Mr. Cusack should happen to be there, too, and that Mrs. Brodigan's throat got well just in time.

Cusack exerted himself to shine that evening; and shine he did in his own way, with that leaden brightness peculiar to him. He and Mr. Brodigan were on extremely good terms; they had business relations not unfrequently that were of mutual advantage, and otherwise, there was sufficient in common between them to make their intercourse of the friendliest kind. The young ladies, not having the honor of Mr. Cusack's particular attention, were the more disposed to value it, and could ill brook his well-known partiality for the society of the Ackland ladies, for the wealthy and good-looking Cusack was deemed quite an authority in Drogheda circles. "Mamma" herself had a lingering hope that Mr. Cusack might one day "come round" to pay more attention to either of her daughters, who, if they were not quite so handsome as some of their neighbors, had that (in expectation) which according to Mrs. Brodigan and many others—"covers all defects." They had money (to get), and Mr. Cusack and all Drogheda knew that

—they were young enough, too,—and so their prudent mamma could afford to wait, and "let things take their course," the more so as "the girls had as good as Cusack looking after them, and were always sure of being well settled."

So on these terms the party spent a very pleasant evening together; quadrilles were danced by all in their turn, except Mr. Ackland, who was laughingly allowed the special privilege of keeping his seat near the fire; Rose Ackland and the Misses Brodigan danced the Highland Fling in character, that is to say, with tartan scarfs tied gracefully under one arm, and the whole party, with the exception of Miss Ackland who played, danced "The Triumph," and some other country-dances, for country-dances as yet maintained their ground in Irish society. Some of these dances were new to Giacomo, and his efforts to follow the figures, under the guidance of his partner for the time, created much amusement. But he turned the tables on them by proposing to teach them some of his own national dances, and nothing could be more amusing than to see good Mr. Brodigan, and even Cusack, though younger and of somewhat lighter proportions, attempting the light fantastic movements of the gay Italian dances. There was singing, too, including French *chansons* from the Miss Brodigans, and a beautiful Italian *romanza* from Giacomo, being the first time the latter had sung in that house. He had overlooked sundry hints from the fair Miss Jane that she was *so* fond of Italian music, and so forth, and even a patronizing request from her more stately sister, and it was only a little before the party separated that on Miss Ackland's whispered invitation, enforced by a "Pray do, Signor!" from Rose, he sang the little *canzonetta* which charmed all the company, though Harry Cusack shrugged his shoulders a very little, behind backs, and the sisters were not quite so loud in their applause as if the *canzonetta* had been sung at their request, expressed or understood. It was evident, indeed, that if the young stranger chose to make himself agreeable to either he might easily have succeeded, and Miss Jane's languid graces were as clearly put forth for him, but alas! put forth in vain; he was blind and deaf in her regard, as she saw with no small degree of mortification. As for Anne Brodigan, she soon perceived that the handsome and graceful young stranger was not likely to bend at the shrine of either, and though she would probably, in his case, have stooped to conquer, she shrewdly guessed that the victory was not for her, so she did *not* stoop, but kept her dignity, and was barely civil, nothing more.

It was late, for that quiet household, at least, when Cusack and the Brodigans left together, wishing the Signor a safe and pleasant voyage, though politely regretting his departure. Nancy was then summoned, and the night-prayers said, when, late as it was— eleven o'clock or so—the little circle drew their chairs around the fire to enjoy the pleasure of a last friendly chat before they retired for the night. They talked long, but not cheerfully, for though all tried to conceal the feeling of approaching separation, it would come uppermost, and was plainly visible on every face, and in the saddened tone of every voice; even Rose was not merry as her wont, although she showed the least depression of all. Mr. Ackland would have Giacomo promise that he would, if possible, visit them again in the summer, and the young man said in an under tone—"God grant I may be able to come as soon as I would wish to come, and that I may find you all as I leave you now!" So saying he left the room.

On the morrow he sailed for Leghorn, as sad for leaving his Drogheda friends as hopeful of meeting those he loved at home. Mr. Ackland, Mr. Brodigan, and Harry Cusack, with several other gentlemen of the town, had accompanied the young man to the ship, which lay alongside the quay, near the bridge. They had just left him, and he was standing on the deck, looking wistfully up at St. Catherine's Mount, then glancing over the strangely-varied features of the scene immediately around him, when he perceived a tall, slouching figure standing motionless on the quay, scanning through half-closed eyes the crowd of faces on board the Lady of the Lake. It was Jemmy Nulty, and Giacomo, suspecting the object of his visiting the quay at that particular time, crossed the gangway to where he stood, and tapped him on the shoulder. He turned slowly, without any manifestation of surprise.

"Were you looking for me, Jemmy?"

"I was, dear;—God bless you! I hard you were for lavin' us this mornin', so I thought I'd bring you an *Agnus Dei*. I got it a' purpose from the dear ladies up at the Fair street Convent. I meant to bring it to you yesterday, an' I would, too, only for a touch o' the rheumatics I got. You'll be sure an' wear it, an' I'll go bail you'll never be shipwracked again."

Giacomo promised; he did not choose to tell the kind simple old man that he had one already, the gift of Miss Ackland, which lay very close to his heart. He warmly thanked Jemmy, and asked him to remember him sometimes in his prayers.

"Oh! it's little good my poor prayers 'ill do any one," Jemmy replied in the perfect good faith of genuine humility; "there is no one needs prayers more than I do myself, God help me! But, sure, they say even sinners are hard when they pray for others, so I'll not forget you, dear young gentleman!"

Giacomo would have placed some money in the old man's hand, but he gently put it away, saying in his soft, whispering tones, "No, dear, no!—I don't want it!—I've enough for the little time I'll be here. But if you ever come back to Drogheda, an' miss poor Jemmy, I'll lay it on you to get a Mass said for me. There's my hand now, an' farewell! an' God be with you!" Somehow the tears started to the young man's eyes as he watched the large uncouth figure of the pilgrim slowly moving away.

# CHAPTER VIII.

It was Christmas Eve in Leghorn, that old-new town of Western Italy, in fair Tuscany, yet scarcely of it,—with its mixed population, comprising people from most of the maritime countries of Europe, its modern fortifications, its Turkish mosque, its Greek and Protestant churches, rising as proudly there, under that blue cold sky, as though they were not on Italian soil, and in almost the only city of Italy where all religions stood on equal ground. The Angelus-bell had long since tolled from the Duomo and the Church of the Madonna, and the streets were already thinning fast of the busy, bustling crowds who had all day long been hurrying to and fro in pursuit of their various objects. The night was cold for that southern climate, and the stars were twinkling in the dark blue depths of a moonless sky with that intense brightness peculiar to the frosty nights of midwinter.

All Leghorn is within the walls built around it by one of the magnificent Medici princes some two hundred years ago. So, within the walls, in one of the handsome streets appropriated to the dwellings of the rich merchants and the professional men of the place, we are going to enter a house, plainer than most of those around it, yet still indicating the affluent condition of its owners—in the taste displayed everywhere around it, and the more than Italian attention to comfort and convenience. In a small but handsomely-furnished parlor on the first floor, with a clear smokeless fire burning on a brasier in the centre, sat two persons, a father and daughter, it was plain to see, from the close resemblance they bore to one another. The girl might have been some eighteen years of age, although her height would have made one suppose her older, for she was rather over than under the middle size, yet slight and graceful withal; her face was not what could strictly be called handsome, but it was more than handsome, with clear blue eyes of a pensive, almost melancholy expression, and a rich profusion of fair hair smoothly braided in those Grecian bands which sculptors love to represent, as giving to the female head that classical character so full of womanly modesty and womanly grace.

The father was a remakably fine-looking man of some forty years and upwards, with a look of decision, and what might be called stern determination, for the prevailing character of his pale, and strongly-marked features. The eyes were blue, and deep-set under the finely arched brows; the forehead high and broad, shaded by hair only a little darker than his daughter's and as yet untouched by the frosts of years. The nose and mouth were singularly fine, expressing at once the decision of the gentleman's character, and a certain refinement that was scarce compatible with the sternness of the general aspect. There was, moreover, a certain air of command about the head and face that well became the tall, muscular figure; but there were lines of care and anxious thought in the still handsome face that evidently came in advance of time. He was pacing the room to and fro, with knitted brow, and folded arms, while his daughter sat near the brasier, making a Christmas wreath of evergreen branches, which she intertwined with dexterous fingers. Ever and anon, she paused in her work, to steal a look at her father, and her sweet face grew sadder and sadder as she saw the cloud darkening on his. It was not her custom, however, to break in on his meditations, and so she worked on in silence till he suddenly stopped in front of her, and said in Italian:

"Maddalena, I fear we shall have a lonely Christmas, after all. If Giacomo were coming he would be here before now."

Tears came into the girl's eyes, but she only said—
"He may come to-night yet, father."

"No, no, he will not come—he forgets us—he is like the young Telemachus, shipwrecked on Calypso's Island,—but without a Mentor," he added bitterly.

"My dear father," said the girl in her sweet soothing way, "do not be hard on Giacomo." She did not understand the classical allusion. "I am sure he will be here. I have prayed the Madonna so often to bring him home for Christmas that I know she cannot choose but hear me."

"Pray her to keep your heart pure and innocent as now, my child!" said the father, regarding her with a softened look which, seldom seen in his stern eyes, was very beautiful and very touching—so Maddalena thought, and her gentle heart glowed with pleasurable emotions. "Pray the Madonna, Maddalena, that your woman's heart may never harden in the world's icy grasp, or its freshness depart with the spring-time of your years!—pray, my child, that you be like your mother in all womanly virtues!"

He resumed his walk, nor spoke again till a loud knock came to the outer door, and before either father or daughter could reach the hall, the room-door was thrown open, and Giacomo, our Giacomo and theirs, rushed in, flushed with excitement, and radiant with joy. Oh! the ineffable delight with which Maddalena embraced him, and kissed him over and over, murmuring "Thank God! thank God! you are safe home again!" but when the youth would have thrown himself into his father's arms, he glanced in his face, and drawing back, extended his hand, while the light of joy faded from his eyes.

"Giacomo," said the father in a calm but rather severe tone, "I am glad you have come home for Christmas. But why did you stay so long? It is some weeks since you have been quite recovered.

Why should you intrude so long on ——, on strangers—not to speak of the indifference your protracted absence showed for us at home?"

"Father," Giacomo began, in a hesitating voice, "it was really impossible to get away sooner without giving offence to the kind friends to whom I am so indebted."

"Ay," said the father, with his bitter smile, "I was just saying to your sister that *our* Telemachus had been thrown on Calypso's Island without his Mentor."

"Well! even if it were so, father," the young man returned smiling, "you know Ulysses had been there before Telemachus, and all his wisdom could not shield him from the potent charms of the goddess. But for me, I found no Calypso after *my* shipwreck —no spells were woven for me."

The father turned quickly and fixed a piercing look on his son, but there was nothing in the frank, ingenuous face that sought to elude detection, and the elder gentleman smiled with evident relief as he told Maddalena to leave off gazing at her brother, and go see if supper were ready.

"And I will go down at the same time to see Paolo and Nannetta," said Giacomo, "before I go up stairs. How are they?"

"As well as can be—just as you left them."

"I saw Giulia, of course, at the door, when she let me in, and I heard her running at full speed to tell the news below."

These were the servants, a husband and wife and

their only child, whom her mother was training as a maid-of-all-work, making her very helpful to herself in discharging the easy duties of that small and quiet household.

So Giacomo *was* home for Christmas, and had had a good sleep by the time the churches were illuminated for twelve o'clock; then went with his father and sister to Midnight Mass in the Church of the Madonna near by, where, kneeling before the high altar amid the blaze of lights and the perfume of fresh green branches, he sang with the rest the soul-inspiring *Adeste Fideles*,—wishing the while that some of his Drogheda friends were there to hear an Italian congregation singing with one voice and in perfect unison the joyous strains that usher in the auspicious day of Our Lord's Nativity. Even there came up before his mind, amid all the holy associations of the place and the time, the group that greeted his eyes when last he looked on the old house by the Boyne—Miss Ackland and Rose standing side by side on the esplanade, watching him as he descended the steps, the latter waving a smiling farewell, while near them, but a little behind, stood old Nancy, raising ever and anon her apron to her eyes to wipe away the tears which she did not care to hide. "They are all at Midnight Mass, too" thought he, 'in their favorite High Lane Chapel, and dear Mr. Ackland is there, and, perhaps, Jemmy Nulty. And it may be that some of them are praying for me, as I pray for them, at this happy hour."

It was natural that Giacomo should talk much of the Acklands, and it was natural that Maddalena should listen with such interest as she had never listened before to even the most minute details of her brother's sojourn under their roof. Soon she learned to know each and all of the family, their old house by the bright Irish river, their old servant, whom she usually associated with her own good Nannetta, and even Tab, the cat. Maddalena grew familiar with them all, and it became one of the favorite amusements of her solitary hours to gather them all around her in fancy. She had her favorites amongst them, too, and her chief one was Miss Ackland, whom she somehow singled out from all the rest as more than all interesting. Sweet Maddalena had a heart full of tender, gentle affection,—a creature of feeling, still more than of thought, she clung to any one who once gained her love like ivy to the castle wall.

But it was almost always in the absence of their father that the young people talked of Drogheda and the Acklands; once or twice when some casual allusion was made to the subject in his presence, he chilled the warm hearts of his children by some cynical remark, expressive of that cold skepticism in regard to human nature, which was, unhappily, one of his prevailing traits of character. Thus, the generous care and kindness of the Acklands to his son, he collly and curtly attributed to " circumstances— nothing more," and would scarcely admit any extraordinary merit in the case. It seemed to his children as though he felt annoyed at being under such obligations to strangers, without any proper means of discharging a debt, which his pride could ill bear. But, however little he talked on the subject, he managed to possess himself of the principal circumstances connected with the Acklands, and now and then startled the young people by some abrupt question concerning them, when they were talking together in a low tone, and believed him absorbed in his book or his writing—for it was his practice to write letters sometimes of an evening, at home in their quiet parlor. Then came dimly back to Giacomo's mind the unaccountable dislike his mother had for Drogheda, which yet she had never seen, and he began to remember, what he had of late, oddly enough, forgotten, that his father had known that old town well in his younger days, and he much desired to ask him whether he had been acquainted with any of the Ackland family; but thinking, very naturally, that if such were the case, he would have mentioned it before then, the young man forbore putting the question; it was seldom, indeed, that he did take such a liberty with his father.

And yet the Signor Malvili was not a harsh man; cold he seemed always, and stern at times, but never harsh or rough; on the contrary, there was a certain degree of gentleness even in his harshest mood, something that attracted you towards him, you knew not why, and made you almost love, even while you feared him. His manner was that of a well-bred man a gentleman, easy and natural, except in so far as it was cold and reserved. There was, too, a dash of the seafaring man about him, not very perceptible, as a general thing, but most so when his manner was the least repellant. It seemed as though it were his pleasure to efface from his memory and that of others that he ever had, if, indeed, he had, gone " down to the sea in ships," or followed the roving life of a " dweller on the deep."

He had applied himself for all the years that his son remembered to the pursuit of commerce, part of the time in connection with his father-in-law, at whose death he had succeeded to the entire business of their large mercantile " concern,"—as we are wont to phrase it now-a-days. Shrinking with nervous dread from society, and from contact with a world of which he took no pains to conceal his contempt, he lived himself, and kept his family, in almost unbroken seclusion, surrounded, indeed by many of the domestic appurtenances of wealth, especially in matters of taste,—and doing more good to the poor of the city and its various public charities than many who made a greater show, and professed a greater interest in them. His children knew and well appreciated his fine qualities, yet their love of him was, as we have seen, strangely mingled with fear, and its manifestation timid and constrained.

Walking out one evening together a few weeks after Giacomo's return, while the lengthening eve of the last days of January was fading from the cold clear sky, the sister and brother talked long of the days when their young mother was with them, beautiful and gentle, and loving.

"And I *think* my father loved her," said Giacomo musingly, as though half unconscious he had a listener.

"Loved her, Giacomo?" said his sister in surprise, "of course he did, brother,—how could he help loving her whom every one loved?"

"I know, I know," said the brother absently, "but you know, Maddalena, our mother was not what our father is in many ways—she was a child always and to the last—a child in worldly wisdom, and in book knowledge, whilst he was a *man*, and a man of superior intelligence, with a heart tried in the world's furnace. Maddalena, I tell you there was little in common between our parents—they were never made for each other."

"But, Giacomo, they lived happily together. You forget that. You talk so strangely!"

"If I say now, my sister, what I never said before. it is because you are older now and can better understand these my thoughts, and they are not new ones, I assure you."

Maddalena was silent, and they walked on a little way without either saying a word; at last the sister spoke, and her tone was graver than its wont,— "Brother, it may have been as you say, but I see no use in talking of things, now past and gone. Besides, our father was never unkind to our dear mo ther, and I am sure *she* loved *him* with her whole heart."

"She did," said Giacomo, " but now I can remember that there was ever a shadow over her love, a doubt it now seems to me, though she never betrayed it to my father. But to me, even as a child, she has often expressed such a feeling, and said it was her constant prayer to overcome it. I know not if she ever did. But, after all," he added, seeing that his words impressed his young sister more deeply than he thought they would, "after all, Maddalena, these may be only fancies of mine, for, though you have never given me credit for imagination, I *have* my fancies, too, sometimes."

"Not always so gloomy as these, I hope!"

"Nay, my sweet sister, you must not take the matter so seriously. Our parents lived as happily together, I think, as most married people do, and they never gave us their children any but good example. Our dear mother is in heaven with the Madonna whom she loved so tenderly, and our father is good enough to go there, too, when death calls him hence. He loves us, I am sure, and it is idle to raise the veil from his earlier life which we cannot, if we would, penetrate."

They were almost at home, and the lingering shadows were entirely dispelled from the hearts of both by a fine manly voice from the deck of a ship that was passing out to sea, singing to an old plaintive air—

"Peggy Bawn, you are my darling,
  And my heart lies within your breast,
And although we're at a distance,
  I still love you the best.
Although the raging seas, my dear,
  Between you and I may roar,
Oh! Peggy Bawn be true to me,
  And I'll love you for evermore."

"Ha!" said Giacomo, "that should be an Irish sailor—I have heard Miss Ackland's old Nancy sing that song many a time. That poor fellow is thinking of his sweetheart, and who knows but she is in Drogheda? Can *you* see that flag that is at her mast-head, Maddalena?"

No, the night had now closed in, and Maddalena either could not see the flag, but she laughingly said: "I should like to know whether some one else has not left a sweetheart in that Irish town. What of your beautiful Rose Ackland?"

"Nothing in particular, sister mine, except what I have told you. But I know *you* would love her if you on'y knew her."

"No, brother," and Maddalena shook her head, slowly; "no, I might *like* the Signorina Rose, but I should *love* Miss Ackland. I know I should, and I pray the Madonna every day that I may one day see her, if it were only long enough to tell her how I love her, and how often I have prayed for her."

They had reached the door as Maddalena thus spoke, and her last words were overheard by her father, who had just rung the bell, and was waiting for admission.

"Of whom do you speak in such enthusiastic terms, Maddalena?" he inquired, as they all entered the vestibule together.

"Of that dear good Irish lady, father, who was so kind to our Giacomo."

"Oh! you mean Miss Ackland, I suppose. Happy child! through what a golden medium you see all the world, and all the people in it! An English, or rather a Scotch poet has said—

"'Tis distance lends enchantment to the view,'

but I think youth is, at least, as illusive as distance."

The cold philosophy with which their father treated a subject so dear to both the young people, and enlisting their warmest sympathies, was deeply painful to their sense of gratitude, and Giacomo could not help saying—

"I only wish, father, that you knew Miss Ackland as *I* know her!"

A look of some strange emotion—a sudden and sharp pain, as it were,—came into the deep thoughtful eyes of the father,—then a smile of doubtful meaning, and he said, coldly and calmly,—in a sort of mocking tone—

"And suppose I did, Giacomo! what then? I am too old a bird now to be caught with chaff. I have little faith in woman, or woman's ways." He then added, with a softening look and tone—"Yet there was one woman, at least, true,—ay! true as the needle to the pole! Your mother, children, your poor mother, was all truth, truth and innocence! So is my Maddalena!" and he laid his hand on the girl's shoulder, and looked at her with more fondness than she had seen in his eyes since she sat on his knees in her happy childhood. In a tumult of delightful emotion she escaped from the room to muse in solitude a little while over the many peculiarities which marked her father's character, and the gushing tenderness that forced its way at times through the icy coldness of his usual demeanor. Many a time she had complained to her father confessor, who had also been her mother's, of the little affection her father ever manifested for his children, and as often had the good *padre* told her that she must not judge by appearances, or trouble herself about her father's manner, but go on loving him, obeying him, and doing all she could to make him happy.

One day, a week or so after the conversation just referred to, Signor Malvili suddenly raised his head from a book he had been reading, and asked his son if Miss Ackland were as interesting as he described her how it happened that she had never been married, "for I understood you to say," said he, "that she is no longer young."

"That I cannot account for, father," said the young man, thoughtfully; "the same thought often puzzled me, as I sat and watched her when wholly unconscious of observation; she seemed to give the veins to memory, and a sweet pensiveness settled down on her fine, though faded features."

"Did she never allude to her past life in your hearing?"

"Never; and I could not help wondering, as you say, why she never won a heart to which her own might cling with woman's devotion."

"Why, Giacomo," said his father, with a melancholy smile, "were not Miss Ackland so many years your senior, I should fear that she had won *your* heart."

"Won my heart, father!" exclaimed the son, surprised to hear his father indulge in such *badinage;* "oh! there was little danger of that." He spoke with an energy that startled himself and drew his father's eyes to his face with a look of keen inquiry. The son colored to the very temples; the father shook his head and sighed. He rose from his seat, took a few turns up and down the room, then paused in front of Giacomo, and said to him with his usual calm impassibility—

"Giacomo, this quiet monotonous life of ours is not suited to your years; you must go and spend some time with your uncles and aunts in Florence and also in Pisa. You can spend the remainder of the winter between the two cities, and that will give you an opportunity of seeing something of the gay world. Nay, no objections; you shall start the day after tomorrow. I will write to your uncle Ludovico this evening. Go tell Maddalena to make the necessary preparations."

"But, father, I came home so lately, and I have no desire for seeing the gay world. Suffer me to remain with you and my dear sister!"

"Giacomo, I have said that you are to go; no entreaties can alter my determination."

There was nothing for it now but to obey this unwelcome mandate with the best grace possible, for Giacomo was not the son to dispute his father's will, and his was not the father to permit him, if he did. Maddalena was both grieved and surprised by this new and sudden idea of sending her beloved brother away from home so soon again, and for several weeks, but she knew by experience that no effort of hers could change her father's stern will, and she quietly went to work to prepare all that was necessary for Giacomo to take with him, the tears streaming from her eyes, and her heart heavy with sorrow.

That evening, the last but one that Giacomo was to be at home, for what seemed a very long time, his sister asked him to sing; she had not heard him sing since his return from Ireland. They were alone together.

"I cannot refuse you, my sweet sister," said the young man kindly and tenderly, "though I never was in less humor of singing. What shall I sing?"

"Anything you like." And she handed him her guitar.

"I will sing you a song, then, that I learned in Drogheda." And he sang a pretty ballad, old even then, but still popular in the British Islands—"Poor Bessy was a Sailor's Bride."

Maddalena was delighted with the little English ballad and its sweet sympathetic air, but she was not yet satisfied, and petitioned for another song.

"English or Italian?"

"Oh! English, to be sure, it is not often I hear English songs."

This time Giacomo sang one of the most popular of Haynes Bayley's drawing-room lyrics—"Isle of Beauty!" and his voice was full of pathos and quivering with strong emotion as he sang the last stanza, particularly—

"Whilst the waves are round me breaking,
　As I pace the deck alone,
And mine eyes in vain are seeking
　Some green leaf to rest upon,
What would I not give to wander
　Where my old companions dwell,
Absence makes the heart grow fonder,
　Isle of Beauty, fare thee well!"

He had just ended the song and was playing the symphony when his father suddenly opened the door from a small study-room where he spent many of his in-door hours, although neither the brother nor sister knew of his being there then. He was pale, paler even than usual, but his voice was calm and his tone passionless, as he said:

"I see you have been learning some songs during your absence, Giacomo! pray, of whom did you learn those you have been just singing?"

"I learned them of Miss Ackland, father, they are two of her particular favorites, and I have heard her sing them over and over so many times that I had no trouble in learning them. I heard her say that they were endeared to her by the sweetest and saddest recollections of her life."

"Indeed!—Did Miss Ackland say that? How very strange!" said the elder Malvili, with a ghastly smile; "perhaps the lady *may* have had heart-ties once,—old maid as you say she is now!"

"Nay, father, I did not call Miss Ackland an old maid," began Giacomo, but his father had left the room.

## CHAPTER IX.

Spring was abroad, and the earth was glad, and the waters bounded on their way rejoicing in the merry sunshine; the Boyne, brightest of rivers, ran cheerily on between the lovely scenes that margin its course; the fields and meadows were green, and the trees were already putting forth their earliest blossoms. The linnet and the thrush made groves and gardens vocal, and all nature was gay. The old town of Drogheda sat looking down on the placid stream that flowed in her midst, with the calm contentment of reverend age, a time-mellowed picture that bright spring day. Around the home of the Acklands on St. Catherine's Mount, the sunshine fell all goldenly; there was joy abroad in the air and on the earth, and on the glancing waters, but within the old house there was no joy, but gloom, even the gloom of death,—and were it not a Christian household there would have been dark despondency as well, for old George Ackland had been gathered to his fathers, and with him died out the slender means which had stood between the family and utter poverty. In the last days of win'er the old man passed away, tranquil

and resigned, on his own account, but troubled with
anxiety for those he left behind, now thrown entirely
on their own exertions for a maintenance, they who
might once have expected not only competence, but
wealth. These gloomy thoughts were not suffered,
however, to weigh heavily on his mind; his daughter reminded him that she and Rose were both well
able to earn a living for themselves by the exercise
of those talents which he, in the days of his prosperity, had spared no expense to cultivate; it would be
easy supporting two, Miss Ackland said, especially
when they were in a position to assist each other.
And Rose, though her heart was breaking, hid her
grief, and schooled her face and her voice into something like cheerfulness, and told her dear grandpapa
not to trouble himself about her or her aunt, for that
they would be sure to get along well; that losing him
was *their* only trouble, and they did not want to see
him fretting about anything that merely concerned
them; and besides she ridiculed the idea that "grandpapa" was going to die, and at times half persuaded
himself that the Great Summoner had not yet issued
his warrant. Never had Rose appeared to so much
advantage as during those days and nights of anxious
watching, and many a time her aunt thought, as her
eyes followed her with affectionate admiration, how
little we know people by the ordinary seeming of
their daily life.

But the suspense, the uncertainty was over; death
had claimed his own, and the venerable parent, around

whom the hearts of his daughter and granddaughter had intertwined as the missletoe round the forest oak, lay low in the earth, never to bless their eyes again till their own turn came to cross the dread bourne that separates time from eternity.

They had many friends, the Acklands, and many invitations for "long visits" had been given them in all kindness and sincerity, with a view to take them from a place so full of sad and bitter associations as their old home was then. But they could not be prevailed on to leave it, for, lonely as it was, it was still their home, dear and sacred because of its thousand memories, so sweetly soothing to their hearts, and in its still seclusion they could weep unseen and alone. As yet they had received no visits, except from a very few of their oldest friends, and most of their time was spent arranging everything, with Nancy's assistance, for the final breaking-up of their little household, to which they all three looked forward with heavy hearts. Poor Nancy was inconsolable; although a month had passed since Mr. Ackland's death, she still could not speak of him without tears, and it was her frequent remark that she "cried the old master then as fresh as the day he died, the glory of Heaven to his soul!"—"An' sure good right I have," she would add, "for it's me that lost the good friend when the breath left his body!"

So the old house was lonely, lonelier than ever, yet all its remaining inmates desired was that they might be able to stay in it. Of this there seemed at first little probability, notwithstanding the earnest injunction of Mr. Ackland during his last illness not to break up the old home, or let the old house pass into the hands of strangers unless it became actually necessary to do so. But Miss Ackland saw no way, at first, of paying off some trifling debts, and providing the means of present existence, except for Rose to take a situation as governess or companion, and herself to sell the house and most of the furniture, then remove with Nancy to lodgings, and commence giving music and drawing lessons, or, perhaps, go out as visiting governess.

But things were not destined to be quite so bad as that; Miss Ackland soon found that she had friends who were like William of Deloraine, "good at need," and were quite indignant at the thought of her giving up the old place that was so much endeared to them all.

The aunt and niece were busy in-doors that bright spring morning; they had happily left off the sad preparations before mentioned, and were now arranging the large front-parlor on the right-hand side of the hall as a school-room, for on the following Monday Miss Ackland was to open a school, and quite a number of pupils were already promised to her. The two ladies were in deep mourning, and Nancy, when she came in to help, looked every inch the respectable old follower of a good family in her black gown and clean check apron and cap as white as snow. All there were grave, but the first shock of grief having passed away, they could speak now more hopefully of the future, and of their opening prospects. On that head there was no reserve with Nancy, for Nancy was, indeed, one of the family, entirely devoted to their interests, and losing therein all thought of her own,—so long as the ladies could live together in the old house and she with them, Nancy's wishes were amply satisfied.

"Wasn't it just like Mr. Brodigan, Aunt Lydia," said Rose, as she mounted a chair to hang a map of the world on the wall—"wasn't it just like him to go and pay our little debts himself, without even saying a word about it?"

"Yes, my dear Rose, that *was* the act of a generous friend. He had asked me to put what we owed to each person on paper, just, as he said, for his own private information, and to get them to wait a little till we should be able to pay them off by degrees."

"And Harry Cusack, too, offering his services so kindly, although you didn't see fit to trouble him in any way."

"Of course not, Rose, it would not have been prudent, you know, to place ourselves under any obligation to *him*, though I am, and shall ever be deeply grateful for his genuine kindness."

"Poor fellow!" said Rose, "I declare I shall never laugh at him again—no, never!"

"You should never have laughed at him," said her aunt gravely, "his little foibles are all on the surface, and he is at bottom a very worthy man. I wish, my dear child, you would never amuse yourself at the expense of the little peculiarities of your friends and acquaintances. It is a dangerous habit."

"Oh dear, Aunt Lydia, there is no need to lecture me now on that point! I am in little humor of laughing at any one since poor dear grandpapa is gone! I don't think I shall ever, ever laugh again!" And fairly bursting into tears, the affectionate girl ran out of the room to indulge her grief unseen.

"Poor child!" said Nancy wiping her own eyes, "it'll do her good to have her cry out. It'll do her good. Ochone! she may well cry him that's gone, an' so may we all, so may we all!"

"Very true, Nancy," said Miss Ackland, with difficulty repressing her own tears, "but we must all try to bear our loss patiently, and go through the business of life as though *he* were still amongst us."

Nancy was silent, but she thought to herself—"Oh! that's her all over. She never lets any trouble in on her the same as others. An' sure it's well for her she does not, for if she did she'd be dead herself, or out of her wits, long ago, the crature!"

When the day's occupations were over and the two ladies sat by the fire which the chill evening rendered still welcome, in the dear old back-parlor so hallowed in their recollections, they remained long silent, each oppressed by the thick-coming memories that started like shadows from the gloom of their hearts.

But at length Miss Ackland made an effort to rouse both herself and Rose from their sad reflections.

"I wrote to Giacomo to-day, Rose!" she said abruptly.

"Ah! *he* will be sorry to hear of poor grandpa's death; I know he liked him very much."

"He little thought when he wrote that kind letter we had from him a few days ago that the little circle he remembered so lovingly was already broken by cruel death."

"I wonder will he ever come back again, Aunt Lydia?"

"It is not very likely, my dear, at least for a long long time."

"Poor Signor!" said Rose, "it makes me sad to think how merry we all were when he was here, and that such a very little while ago."

"Well! my dear child, that is life, as you will learn long before you are my age. To the calm succeeds the storm, to the storm, calm; to sunshine, shade, and to shade, sunshine. It is the natural course of things, and they are wisest and happiest who can bear with equanimity life's changes as they come."

"But, aunt," said Rose, drawing closer to Miss Ackland, and lowering her voice perhaps unconsciously, "do you remember how old Mabel sent you word one evening by me that she had heard the banshee often of late,—wasn't that a strange coincidence to say the least of it?"

'Not at all, my dear," said her aunt with a sad

smile, "your grandpapa would have died all the same whether Mabel heard the banshee or not—that is, what she supposed was the banshee."

"Then you don't believe in the banshee, aunt?"

"Believe in the banshee—of course I do not. That superstition, like many others, has grown out of the ardent imagination of the simple and unlettered of our people in the ages past away."

"But, aunt, every one says that the banshee follows all the old families, and when so many people hear her, there must be such a being, you know."

"Why, my dear little Rose," said Miss Ackland, with an attempt at cheerfulness, "I fear you are growing superstitious since we have been left all alone."

"No, no, aunt, indeed I am not superstitious, but I want to know how Mabel, or any one else, could hear the banshee if there were no banshee to be heard. What do you suppose Mabel heard?"

"Very possibly the winds, my dear child! If you remember we had stormy weather about that time."

"Yes, I know it was one of those very nights that the San Pietro was lost," and Rose lapsed again into thoughtfulness.

"Talking of the banshee," said Miss Ackland, with a view to change the current of her thoughts, "you remember that song of Moore's, beginning thus—

"'How oft has the banshee cried.'

How naturally and how beautifully he has embodied many of the national customs and the national superstitions in his immortal melodies! You know how gracefully he introduces one of our old fairy legends in the last stanza of 'The time I've lost in wooing?'"

"Yes, I know the lines you mean, aunt," said Rose, brightening up, and she repeated with something like her former vivacity—

> "Like him, the sprite,
>  Whom maids a night
>    Oft meet in glen that's haunted.
>  Like him, too, beauty won me,
>  But while her eyes were on me,
>  For when her gaze was turn'd away,
>    Oh! winds could not outrun me."

"You see," said her aunt, "there is just the old story of the *leprachaun*,—the fairies' shoemaker,—which Nancy has often told you."

"So it is, I declare! Well! I never thought of that, often as I sang the song."

Thus insensibly led away from her melancholy thoughts, Rose began to turn to the future, and was the first to speak of their plans, of the school arrangements, and other matters appertaining to their changing prospects.

"I wonder," said Rose, "how the Vernons and Brodigans—I mean the girls—will treat me, now that we have come down to teaching school."

"My dear Rose, why do you call it coming down? There is nothing disgraceful, surely, in turning to account whatever talents and attainments God has bestowed upon us?"

"Oh! no, aunt, I didn't mean that there was, or that I am the least ashamed of it, but then, you know, others may think differently, and girls, especially, may look down on us."

"Rose," said Miss Ackland very seriously, "the opinion of any one who could look down on us, as you say, for maintaining ourselves by our own exertions, is not worth considering, and if I am not much mistaken, we shall be more respected in our school-room than we ever were in our days of comparative idleness."

Rose shook her head and sighed; she could not see the matter in the same light that her aunt did, but she would not say so, and both lapsed into silent thought.

\* \* \* \* \* \*

The school opened on the following Monday, and the attendance of pupils was sufficiently encouraging to cheer even Rose, who, to do her justice, went into the harness with right good will, determined to do her full share of the drudgery of teaching, and save her dear aunt as much as possible. "If our school does not succeed," said Rose to herself, and also to Nancy, her trusty *confidante*, "it shall not be *my* fault, for I am going to do my very best." Poor Rose! her best was not much, for many a long day and week, but she strove hard and finally became a good teacher in those branches of instruction which devolved on her.

Her industry and perseverance were rewarded.

Contrary to her expectations, and to her very agreeable surprise she was not "looked down upon" by her young acquaintances. Invitations poured in on her after the first period of mourning had elapsed. And though she accepted none for large parties her aunt insisted on her going out evenings more than she had ever done before, forcing her own inclinations so far as to accompany her. This she did in order to keep up Rose's spirits, and counteract the depressing effect of the monotonous and fatiguing occupations of her daily life. Miss Ackland, in her watchful care of her beloved niece, acted on the homely old axiom that "all work and no play make Jack a dull boy," and she would not that the freshness of life's joyous springtime should be blighted in its fair promise by the unvarying tedium of hard work and unbroken seclusion.

And Rose made conquests during those times, conquests that much amazed some of her wealthier and better dressed acquaintances. Not to speak of Harry Cusack, who had become quite particular in his attentions, there were some of the first young men of the trading community about Drogheda who would gladly have won the hand of the portionless grandchild of George Ackland, the heiress of his good name, and the brightest and fairest of Drogheda maidens. But Rose, though gay and affable with all, appeared to make no distinction, and received the attentions of her various admirers more as a matter of course than as anything meant to be seriously taken.

Provoked and mortified by her studied indifference her would-be suitors came one after another to the same conclusion that Giacomo had reached months before, that Rose Ackland had no heart. Nevertheless, they were only the more determined to persevere to the end, whatever it might be, for Rose's careless ease was provokingly piquant, and her admirers found to their cost that she, by no means,

"——charm d them l ast wh n *she* most r p ll'd.'

Every Sunday the elder and the younger Miss Ackland were expected to spend at Mr. Brodigan's, and around the hospitable board were generally assembled some of the old familiar faces oftenest seen at Mr. Ackland's—in his more prosperous days. They were very pleasant those Sunday dinners at Mr. Brodigan's,—and we might add at many another Drogheda merchant's,—when old friends came together, as it were *en famille*, week after week, to enjoy the bounteous, yet unostentatious hospitality of the large hearted host, and his comely spouse, both the very personification of good nature; when almost every subject of interest was common to all, and the whole circle was in that happy condition prospectively described by the poet—

"Wh n fast as a fe ling bu' touches one link,
Its magic shall send it direct thro' the chain."

One peculiarity of these genial *reunions* was the remarkable absence of slander and that ill-natured criticism on the real or supposed defects, mental, moral or physical, of others, which too often makes the staple of conversation. The imperturbable good nature of the host and hostess diffused all around them such an atmosphere of kindly feeling that the poisonous weed of slander might not grow within the sphere of their influence. There was much harmless mirth, and much development of character, in the unrestrained freedom of that friendly intercoarse, and one always felt that the best feelings of their nature were somehow called into play, and that they left Mr. Brodigan's better and happier for being there, and more disposed to look kindly and lovingly on their fellow-creatures. Then there were, as might be expected, little by-plays going on amongst the well-assorted guests and the family of the house, little scenes being enacted that just served to ripple the otherwise too placid stream. There every one being perfectly at home, so every one appeared in their own proper character, and the distinctive peculiarities of all gave zest and variety to the whole. And all were perpetually furnishing "coincidences" for worthy Mr. Brodigan, sentimental reflections to his daughter Jane, and arch drollery for Rose Ackland. And rosy Mrs. Brodigan sat smiling on all in her goodly rotundity of figure, fat, fair, and well preserved, her brown hair brown as ever, and her brown eyes as soft and calm. It was hard to say whether she or her husband most enjoyed the society of their friends, or loved the most to see them gather around their table. That was Drogheda twenty years ago, and all who knew it then may well hope that it is so still!

The Sunday dinner at Mr. Brodigan's was generally preceded, in the fine season, by an excursion to some of the many beautiful places in the vicinity,— to Oldbridge and King William's Glen, to Townley Hall, or Bewly,—sometimes to the lovely pastoral banks of the Nanny-Water, and the ancient Castle of Jigginstown, or Ballygarth, or farther on to Gormanstown Castle, the baronial mansion of the Lords of that name, and the noble family of Preston. Or down to the coast the party might take their way, for a pleasant drive along the smooth white sand, past Baltray and Mornington and Bettys'own, where the people they met all knew them, and exchanged a kind, or a humorous greeting with each as they passed in their several vehicles, jaunting-car or gig, or " inside car," as the case might be. Pleasant they were, too, those rural excursions around the old borough, to places interesting of themselves, because of the lavish hand wherewith mother nature had adorned them, each in their kind, and still more interesting from their various associations with historical or legendary lore.

It was one of Miss Ackland's chief enjoyments to walk out with Rose in the early evening, when the labors and cares of the day were over, and stroll leisurely along some of the fine promenades in the immediate vicinity of the town. Above all she loved, and Rose, too, the picturesque heights of Rathmullen, and the shady walk beneath the over-arching trees, between fields and orchards and gardens in their bloom, whence ever and anon were glimpses caught of the stream far below, threading its seaward way, and through the long vistas of the sylvan alleys might be seen at no great distance up the river, the Obelisk commemorating the defeat of the too faithful Irish who fought and died for an ungrateful foreign prince.

There was a certain green meadow, or paddock it might be called, just on the verge of the precipitous heights overlooking the river; a sweet shady nook it was, surrounded by fine old trees, with a path running diagonally across it from the road to the brow of the steep; there the two ladies often sat to rest in the still evening hour when earth and air were hushed and the thin mists were hovering like shadows over the landscape far and near. They loved to hear the milkmaid singing in some adjoining field some old-time ditty of faithful love or pitiful murder; or the laborer going from work, whistling as he went. Sometimes they heard from a boat on the river, or a cart driving slowly homeward along the neighboring highway, snatches of some local song, it might be this—

"July the First at Oldbridge town,
There was a grievous battle,
Where many a man lay on the ground,
And the cannons loud did rattle."

And there was little of sympathy or compassion in the voices thereabouts that sang how

"Brave Duke Schomberg lost his life,
In crossing the Boyne Water."

But what visions of "the pomp and circumstance of glorious war" did the rustic lay conjure up as, with "Oldbridge town" full in sight, the thoughtful mind reverted to that disastrous day nigh two hundred years before, when three kingdoms were lost and bloodily won on that memorable spot, and amid those scenes, now so calm, so redolent of peace.

Anon some full manly voice would come softened to the ear over the still waters trolling—

"When first to this country a stranger I came,
 I placed my affections on a comely young dame,
 She's straight, tall, and handsome in every degree,
 She's the flower of this country and the Rose of Ardee."

Then Miss Ackland would tell her young niece of the straggling and neglected village of Ardee away in the northern part of the county, adjining Monaghan, where one of the old border-castles of the Pale still frowns, even in decay, over the quiet street beneath and the tame stretch of level country spreading around, and where, in a nameless grave somewhere amongst those sandy knolls, sleeps the outlaw Redmond O'Hanlon, treacherously murdered in the vicinity by an English captain, to whose plighted faith he had trusted his life for the purpose of holding a parley. Then Miss Ackland told Rose all the wonderful tales that her youth had heard of that strangely-misrepresented chieftain, who, instead of being the low robber he has been made to appear in latter times, was in reality an accomplished gentleman, of great personal attractions and of ancient lineage, who had served in the Austrian wars, like so many other Irish exiles of his time, and actually bore the rank of a Count of the Empire. From a chivalrous desire to aid his oppressed country and co-religionists at home, Redmond O'Hanlon returned to his native land, to whose service he bravely but ineffectually devoted himself as a leader of the outlawed Rapparees or "Tories."

Rose was inexpressibly charmed by this romantic story of the past, especially as her aunt assured her that it was as well authenticated in all its principal parts as many recorded on the historic page. The girl's ardent fancy had ample room to exercise itself on the hair-breadth 'scapes, the gallant deeds, the manifold privations of this Irish *preux chevalier*, in his roving life of incessant danger with the wild and lawless band who called him master.

Lost in this new region of old romance, Rose was almost sorry when her aunt reminded her that night was fast closing in, and that they had rather a lonely walk home.

They had just crossed the stile to the high-road when an incident occurred which alarmed Rose, and even her aunt, more than a little, and convinced them that it was not prudent to linger so late in that secluded spot, however great might be the temptation.

## CHAPTER X.

A party of officers, three in number, and evidently fresh from the mess-room, were passing at the moment; they laughed and talked in that loud excited way which indicates a certain degree of intoxication, and seeing the two ladies they probably thought it a good opportunity for having " a lark." The youngest of the three, accordingly, came up to Rose, and with a mock politeness offered his arm, asking permission to " see her home." Another did the same to Miss Ackland, whilst a third, a tall, soldierly man, stood as if enjoying the joke. Miss Ackland drew her niece's arm within her own, and merely saying—" I perceive, gentlemen, you are under a mistake," walked on with as much composure as she could assume. But the others were not to be so got rid of; declaring with ironical gravity that they could not think of allowing ladies to remain unprotected at that late hour, and exchanging glances amongst themselves, they walked on beside the aunt and niece, peering under their bonnets, and otherwise annoying them by ridiculous questions which, of course, they did not deign to notice. The two first mentioned kept their places on either side of the ladies, whilst the elder amused himself with the gambols of a magnificent grayhound, a creature of rare grace and beauty.

"Now, by Jove, I call this the rarest piece of good fortune," said suddenly the gentleman who had succeeded in getting a glimpse of Rose's face, "why, Singleton! this is the very young lady whom I saw the other day with Miss Ball."

"You don't say so, Cornell?"

"But I do!—pray, Miss—ah! excuse me—I forget your name!" speaking in that exaggerated English accent wherein young Cockney *militaires* are wont to exhibit their brainless coxcombry, "may I have the honor?" and bowing with more real politeness than before, he again offered his arm. Rose only answered by shrinking closer to her aunt, while both quickened their steps in more trepidation than they wished to have seen. But the gentlemen saw it and were much amused, asking did the ladiess uppose they were going to run away with them.

"So you will not favor me with your name, ah?" lisped the young Englishman, addressing Rose.

"Sir," said Miss Ackland stopping short in her walk, and drawing herself up with that dignity which no one better could assume, and she looked the impudent coxcomb full in the face, "Sir, *I* will tell you this young lady's name which is also mine—it is Ackland—a name old and not unhonored here in Drogheda." The young man, as if by an involuntary impulse, drew back a pace or two, and raised his military cap with the respect of a gentleman for a ady  His companion fol.owed his example.

At this moment the elder officer, with an authoritative "Down, Cato!" to his dog, eagerly approached Miss Ackland, and stopping in front of her said—in a deep and as it seemed an agitated voice—

"Ackland! Did you say, madam, that your name is Ackland?"

"Sir, I did," the lady replied, wondering much at the stranger's question and the emotion he betrayed.

"Any relation, may I ask, of George Ackland?"

"His daughter, sir, his only daughter, and this young lady is his granddaughter, and my niece."

The gentleman turned aside for a moment, pressed his hand to his forehead as though to still the throbbing brain, then turning to Miss Ackland with freezing politeness, he said—

"I have heard the name before, although I am a stranger in Drogheda, having joined my regiment he.e at Millmount but a few days since. Pass on, madam!—*Miss* Ackland, did you say?——"

"Miss Ackland."

"Strange!" he muttered, again raising his hand to his brow, then recollecting himself he bowed still coldly, but yet courteously—"Pass on, ladies! you shall receive no further annoyance!—young gentlemen! let us continue our walk!"

"As you please, Major Melville!" one of them replied

"Melville!" repeated Miss Ackland in her turn, agitated by some powerful emotion.

"Ay, Melville!" the officer replied, and, lowering his voice so as only to be heard by the person addressed, he said in a whisper—"the brother of Ralph Melville, whom *you* may have forgotten,—but *I* have not!" he sternly, almost fiercely added, then, taking the arm of one of his companions, he turned away, and the ladies were left to pursue their way in peace. Nor did they have any more boisterous laughter or loud talk from the party of officers, sobered, it would seem, by the late *rencontre*, the two younger probably ashamed of their conduct, now that they found the ladies they had so annoyed were really entitled to their respect. Of the little episode between their newly-arrived major and the elder lady they were, of course, unaware, so could form no surmises on the subject.

It was with no ordinary pleasure that the ladies found themselves back again in the secure shelter of their own quiet home; outside the door they were met by Nancy, who had grown uneasy when the night began to fall, and they not yet returned. Fervent, indeed, was her act of thanksgiving as she saw them through the dim twilight ascending the steps, and with all the alacrity of youth she hastened to meet them.

"Oh! the Lord be praised, Miss Ackland dear! sure it's beginnin' to be afeard I was that something had happened!"

Rose was just beginning to tell, in a half jesting way, that something *had* happened, but her aunt stopped her by asking Nancy if tea were ready. The old woman vanished directly.

"Now, my dear Rose," said Miss Ackland, laying her hand on her niece's arm, and Rose shrank from its touch, for it was icy cold—"now, my dear Rose, what have you to tell Nancy that is worth telling? Let us go in; I feel weak and tired."

When they reached the parlor, where two candles were burning on either end of the high, old-fashioned mantel-piece, Miss Ackland sank heavily into a chair; it was her father's "old arm-chair." The light from the mantel-piece shed a ghastly glare on her features, and Rose was shocked to see them pale as death. She would have run to fetch Nancy, but her aunt gently detained her, saying that it was only a little fatigued she was, and a cup of tea was all she required.

"I knew you were more alarmed than you allowed them to see, aunt," said Rose, as she took off Miss Ackland's bonnet and mantilla; "we really must not put ourselves again in the way of such an adventure."

"We shall have to go out earlier," said Miss Ackland in a languid tone, "and enjoy the twilight at home," she added with a wan smile.

"But did you observe, my dear aunt, what a fine-looking man that Major Melville is? I really could not help admiring him as he stood for a moment near you."

"Melville!" cried Nancy, who was just coming in with the tea-pot in one hand, and a small plate of crumpets in the other. "Who's that you're talkin' about, Miss Rosey?"

"Of a gentleman we met since we went out,' said Miss Ackland, raising herself in her chair and endeavoring to regain her usual composure.

"A gentleman? What gentleman?" persisted Nancy, laying down her light burden and fixing her eyes on her mistress.

"An officer," said Miss Ackland, smiling at the simple earnestness of her old domestic, then she added with a strange smile—"Not a dead Melville, Nancy, but a living one—no ghost, I assure you!"

The old woman appeared to understand the allusion, she muttered something to herself, unintelligible to others, and placing the two lonely-looking chairs at the table, she said, "Tea's on the table, Miss Ackland!" then withdrew to her own premises, to ponder on the circumstance—to her simple mind extraordinary—of the ladies having " come across" a gentleman of the once-familiar name of Melville, so long unnamed under that roof.

"Why, aunt," said Rose innocently, "the name of Melville seems to be familiar to Nancy. Did you, then, ever know any one of the name?"

"Yes, Rose," said Miss Ackland, laying down the cup of tea which her trembling hand refused to hold, "I once had a friend of that name—many, many years ago." Her soft eyes filled with tears, and there was a depth of sadness in her low, tremulous voice that told of such sorrow as Rose had never known. This the girl felt, and she was silent, revolving in her mind whether the *friend* so tenderly remembered might not be the gentleman of whom Nancy had once spoken to her.

"Rose," said Miss Ackland, "please to ring for Nancy. I see you have finished your tea."

The tea-things were removed, and Miss Ackland, instead of taking up a book or her knitting, as usual, threw back the curtains from the window, and stood looking out on the moonlit sky and the lovely panorama of land and water that stretched far and away beneath that gorgeous canopy. There was a chair in the deep recess of the window, and Miss Ackland seating herself there at last, beckoned Rose to her.

"Bring that ottoman, Rose, and sit down here beside me." Rose joyfully obeyed, never so happy as when near her aunt. Then both were silent for a long, long while, looking dreamily out on the fair night, whose blue depths and whose silvery light were so very like the heaven we dream of in our better moments.

"Yes, Rose," said Miss Ackland, as if resuming the theme of that brief conversation which, broken off all too soon, had so deeply interested Rose, "yes, my child, the name of Melville is one that shall live in my heart while its pulses beat—yet though sweet as music to my ears, it is the most painful of sounds, awaking the very bitterest of thoughts, and the saddest of recollections."

"My dear aunt!" whispered Rose soothingly—she had never heard her speak so before.

"Rose, you are all I have now left to comfort me," resumed Miss Ackland—"we two are alone in the world—why, then, should I not make you acquainted with the one secret of my life, that 'silent sorrow' which has preyed upon my heart so long? Whilst my dear father lived I had one who knew and understood the cause of my life-long sadness, but since he is gone, I feel the load heavier than ever, and I see no reason now why I should not admit you, the last of all my kin, into the solitude of my heart."

Rose answered only by a fond caress, and her aunt went on after a moment's recollection: "I was about your age, my dear Rose, when I first became acquainted with Ralph Melville, then some three years older; his family belonged to the county Kildare, but he had embraced a seafaring life some years before, when a mere boy, at the request and under the care of a maternal uncle, who was captain and part owner of a large merchant vessel trading chiefly between the Mediterranean ports and those of the British Islands. The captain and my father had had much connection in business—indeed, he was one of the two partners of Capt. Dillon in the ownership of the vessel. They were old and fast friends, and when Ralph began to go to sea with his uncle,—after spending some years at school in Leghorn,—he was of course, received with the same cordial welcome at our house, when their vessel came to Drogheda, first on account of his uncle, but very soon on his own. Years passed on, and the handsome youth became a man, and such a man!—oh! Rose, I shall not attempt to describe him to you,—suffice it to say that it was not in his features or his form the charm lay that won all hearts. It was in the frank and generous nature, the delicacy of feeling, and the natural grace and refinement that manifested themselves in every word and action, with a gay, dashing, *dégagé* air that was infinitely pleasing, and as far removed as could be from the self-occupation of vanity."

"It seems as though I could see him now," said Rose in a low tone, as if fearing to interrupt the narrative even by a sound; "Nancy has told me what he looked like."

"Oh! she has, has she?—poor old Nancy! she loved him, too, and so did Mabel—how could they help it, for he was kind and generous to all? And there was one who loved Ralph Melville better than all, but I think—I fear he never knew it." Rose did not ask who that one was, she knew it all too well. Miss Ackland paused, as if to collect her thoughts for the remaining portion of the narrative, but in reality to control her feelings, so as to speak with the composure that became her sober years. Having partially succeeded, she continued her recital:

"I was young then, my dear Rose, for you will remember that it was 'twenty golden years ago'—

young I was, and, as some people thought, well-favored"—she smiled—"amongst these was Ralph Melville, who, unhappily for himself, learned to love me as man, or woman either, can love but once. And how proud I was of his love I will not attempt to conceal from you. So he used to come the welcomest of guests, to this old house of ours, whenever his ship came to Drogheda; he came, to one at least,

'Like birds that bring Summer and fly when 'tis o'er.'

His first visits were with his uncle, a hale, hearty old gentleman, and a 'jolly tar' to boot, manifesting in his own proper person the very best characteristics of the profession. I believe Captain Dillon cherished the hope of making a match, as he would call it, between his favorite nephew and the only daughter of his old friend, but I soon discovered that my father had higher views for me, and began to look coldly on Ralph Melville, perceiving in what light he regarded me. But one dull Autumn day, Ralph came alone, with crape on his hat, and sorrow in his eyes and in his heart; his good old uncle, his more than father, had died suddenly whilst on a short visit at their house,—which was really his home, for he had no other. This was sad news for us all, for we loved the blunt, warm-hearted sailor, and we grieved to think that we should see his honest face no more. Alas! for 'the old familiar faces'—how they vanish one by one from our life's darkening path ever as we journey onward! The old man had fortunately left a will, and his share of the Frances Anne (the ship was named after Mrs. Melville, Ralph's mother) was left to Ralph, with a recommendation to the other partners to give him the command; the few thousand pounds the captain had had in the Bank of Ireland was the only provision now remaining for his widowed sister and two younger children, a youth of nineteen and a girl of sixteen.

"Some three months had passed before Ra'ph Melville came again to Drogheda; he appeared in somewhat better spirits, and when I made the remark to him, he said it was so, and asked me to guess why. I told him I was not good at guessing, my cheek burning all the while with the consciousness of what was coming. 'I have obtained my mother's consent,' said he, 'to woo and win a wife—that is if I can.' 'Indeed?' I replied—with an air which he mistook for cold indifference, but which was really meant to hide the joy that filled my soul. 'Indeed!' repeated Ralph, looking in my face with so keen a scrutiny that I shrank from his glance as though I had, indeed, something to conceal. Poor Ralph! I can see it yet, the shadow that fell on the brightness of his face, and till the day I die I can never forget the altered tone in which he spoke again. 'Excuse me, Miss Ackland!' he said, (it was the first time in two years he had called me so,) 'I had flattered myself that *you* were a party interested. I see I was mistaken, and have only to crave your pardon for the unwarrantable liberty I took in supposing that the heiress of Mr. Ackland's fortune could be interested in the affairs of one so humble as myself.' I know not what evil spirit it was that prompted me to leave him in the strange blindness that had come upon him, but I did so to my life-long regret. I replied with real coldness, piqued that he should not have seen and known my real feelings: 'Really, Captain Melville, you talk in riddles, and I am so dull in comprehension that I do not understand you.'—'Then you never shall understand me now,' he said in a quick, decided tone. '*I*, at least, understand it all. I refused to believe what I had heard when last in Drogheda, that your father had negociations on foot for your marriage with a certain gentleman, the owner of an estate somewhere in the county Meath—now I believe it when too late to recall my own folly!' How I longed to tell him that such a union had been proposed to me with my father's fullest approbation, but that I had refused and for his sake as much as my own! But I would not so far humble my foolish pride, and merely saying—'You are, of course, at liberty to believe what you please, Captain Melville!' I left him."

"You left him!" cried Rose; "oh! aunt, how could you act so?"

"You may well ask that, my dearest Rose!—it is the question that echoes in my heart all these long and weary years since then."

"But what did Captain Melville do then, Aunt Lydia?—Did he go away for good?"

"For good!" Miss Ackland repeated with sorrowful emphasis, and she raised her tearful eyes to heaven. After a moment's pause she continued: "In a sort of dogged resolution, I suppose, to know exactly how the matter stood, and, perhaps, with a view to justify to himself the final farewell he meant to take of us, it seems Ralph went straight to my father and asked whether he had any objection to him as a suitor for his daughter. My father told him in a hesitating sort of way that he thought his circumstances were not such as to make the match an eligible one for me with my expectations. 'Precisely so, sir,' was Ralph Melville's answer, 'I am sorry I troubled you on the subject; however, it is well to know exactly where one stands. Will you say good-bye for me to Miss Ackland in case I should not see her again before leaving Drogheda?' And he shook my father by the hand, and wishing him 'good morning,' went away before he could make up his mind what further to say. Rose, we never again saw Ralph Melville."

"Why, how was that, Aunt Lydia?"

"He sailed for Civita Vecchia that same afternoon, two days earlier than he had intended, but he never reached the Italian coast; the equinoctial gales set in that very night with unusual violence, and in the fierce storm that raged during the hours of darkness, his ship perished, with all on board. Oh, that I should live to tell it!"

"Perished!" cried Rose in horror; "oh aunt! aunt!"

Miss Ackland covered her face with her hands, and

wept long in silence, unbroken by Rose, whose tender heart was too deeply touched for verbal expression.

"I can weep now," said Miss Ackland at length, as she wiped away her tears, "I can weep now, but I could not weep then; no, not for weeks and weeks, although my heart was breaking with the double weight of sorrow and of self-reproach; by night and by day I grieved for the words that I might have said, and did not say—the words of explanation that would have made Ralph happy, and kept him near me, instead of sending him to his death by my foolish pride and petulance! Oh! how severe has been my punishment."

"My dear aunt!" said Rose very gently, "you surely accuse yourself too harshly; as you never saw Captain Melville after that, how could you be certain that you were the cause of his leaving on that day?"

"Ah! Rose, he took care to make me certain; Nancy had been into town that day on business for me, and coming back, by the lower road, she found Captain Melville walking hastily to and fro outside the gate,—seeing her, he gave her a note for me, and to her great astonishment, bade her good-bye, saying as he shook hands with her—'I am going now, Nancy, never to come back again—not with my own will, be assured, for my heart is here.' He was gone before Nancy could get over her bewilderment sufficiently to ask what he meant. The note contained but these words—*'Lydia, farewell!—It is hard to forgive you, but I do—be happy, if you can, and forget*

Ralph Melville.' My father read that fatal note, for when he came home it lay open on the table, beside which I sat in a sort of stupor; he read it and read my heart, and ever after understood the bitterness of self-reproach that mingled with my grief, and Nancy, too, rightly interpreting Captain Melville's parting words, but supposing from them that I had refused him, was long before she forgave me, indeed, I know not if she has yet, or ever will. She thought I was more in fault than I actually was, and she blamed me all the more because I did not choose to let her see the deep wound festering in my heart."

"My poor dear aunt!" whispered Rose, "who could have dreamed of all this?"

"It was known only to my poor father," said Miss Ackland, in a voice of strong emotion; "that is, the real state of the case, and since he died I have borne my load of vain regret alone—all alone—as far as my fellow-mortals are concerned. This evening something occurred that has torn open again the wounds half-healed by time."

Rose started. "How? is it anything connected with those officers?"

"Yes, my dear Rose, you will not wonder at my agitation when I tell you that in the eldest of the three I discovered Guy Melville, the only brother of my lost Ralph!"

"You did?"

"Yes, I did, and he contrived to make me sensible that he, too, blames me as the indirect cause of his brother's untimely death!—strange that he should know what occurred on that last sad day, but he evidently does, all too well. Oh Rose! Rose! I am miserably punished for a fault that of itself was only trivial, and certainly unintentional! To think how *I* loved Ralph Melville—the long years I have mourned him, and the gloom that settled down on my path of life when I lost him, and to know that his nearest and dearest do me such cruel injustice! This is hard—hard—and it is only from above I ask and obtain strength to bear it. Rose, my dear child, it is selfish of me to make you acquainted with my life's great sorrow. But the heart will pine for human sympathy, and it lightens the burden of grief to know that we possess it."

The fond embrace with which Rose answered, and the tears that filled her eyes, gave assurance to her aunt that there was still one heart she could call her own, and whose sympathies were all bound up with hers. There was comfort in the thought, and she marvelled much during the wakeful hours of that night how much feeling lay concealed under the youthful buoyancy of her niece's outward bearing.

The truth was that the revelations of that night wrought a change in Rose's interior that was very perceptible to herself, if not to others. She felt as though years had passed over her head, and left their seared impress on her heart during that one still moonlight hour when she listened to her aunt's simple tale of sorrow, and learned, for the first time the strange power that one heart may exercise over another, and the deeper depths that may lie hidden from mortal eye beneath the outward seeming of ordinary life. A veil seemed suddenly to have been lifted from before her eyes, and the world appeared to her under a new aspect. Or rather, her aunt's story was to Rose Ackland's perceptions, like the ointment in the fairy tale which, rubbed on mortal eyes, opens them to the sights and seeings of another sphere of existence. Thoughts and feelings unknown before all at once started into life, seeming now as old companions, and Rose felt all the happier for the change that had taken place within her, and the new range of vision opened before her. Yet outwardly she was still the same, perhaps a shade more thoughtful and subdued, but still habitually the gay, laughing girl who made sunshine all around her in her little sphere of life. But it was very touching to see the new relation in which the aunt and niece stood to each other; a tie, far stronger than that of blood, had suddenly bound their hearts together, and in the gentle sympathy of Rose, so sweetly and tenderly manifested, her aunt found a solace for her woes, such as she had never dreamed of obtaining. Her past being now all known to her niece, she could talk to her at times of her loved and early lost, and it seemed as though her heart were lightened of its heaviest burden by the privilege of weaving over with Rose the web of her life, the joys and griefs, the pleasures and the pains of those by-gone years of whose flight no record now remained save in her own heart.

It was long a source of trouble and apprehension to Miss Ackland that the brother of Ralph Melville should be in Drogheda and might at any moment cross her path again, with his stern look, and settled dislike, and his voice so like one never-to-be-forgotten, yet so full of anger and contempt. But weeks past away, and no Major Melville was seen, and her fears gradually subsided. The stream of her life flowed on as before in its calm monotony,—for how long, who could tell?

## CHAPTER XI.

Two weeks had passed after the conversation of that memorable evening, without any further interruption to the placid tranquillity which marked the daily life of the aunt and niece. At the end of that time, they walked down to Baltray one lovely afternoon, immediately after school was dismissed, to see old Mabel, who was now too feeble to leave the cottage, and spent the time she was not in bed, sitting at the door in the sunshine, talking drearily to herself, or watching her grandchildren, as they rolled and tumbled in the sand hard by.

"I thought you'd come the day, Miss Liddy," was her reply to Miss Ackland's kindly greeting; "somethin' was tellin' me ever since mornin' that I'd see you before night. An' Miss Rose, too—sure, but it does me good to see you both, an' it's thankful I am that I *can* see you, for the sight is goin' fast from me."

"Mabel!" said Miss Ackland, sitting down beside her on the rough wooden bench, "who do you think I met since I saw you last?"

"Who?" asked the old woman curtly but anxiously, turning towards the lady whom she still regarded as her mistress.

" Why, Mr. Guy Melville," and she lowered her voice.

"Guy Melville!' repeated the old woman with suddenly awakened interest. ' Why, that should be *his* brother—it was Gay he used to call him. An' where did you meet him, Miss Liddy, asthore?'

"On the Rathmullen road when Miss Rose and I were taking our evening walk, about two weeks ago. It appears Mr. Melville is an officer in the army, and belongs to the 88th, now stationed at Millmount."

"Well! an' what did he say? Did he know you, Miss Liddy, dear?"

"Yes—but not till I had told him who I was. There did not much pass between us then, and I have not seen him since."

"But *I* have seen him, aunt," said Rose, who had been standing an apparently unconcerned listener, watching the fleecy white clouds that were sailing slowly over the face of the western sky, their upper edges tipped with the gold of the still gorgeous sunshine. "I forgot to tell you that I had seen Major Melville once or twice,—but not to speak to him. It was only yesterday that I met him and one of those officers who were with him that evening, as I came along Palace street from Georgina Neville's."

It did not escape Miss Ackland's watchful eyes that Rose said this with a somewhat heightened color, but that was not the place or the time to make any sort of comment, so she merely said, "Oh indeed?" and turned again to old Mabel.

"You see I speak now of—of Capt. Melville"—she added, getting rapidly over the name—" even before Miss Rose. I have told her all, Mabel."

"An' I'm glad you did," said the crone, with an oracular nod, "it's what you should have done many's the day ago. It 'll do you good, asthore, to open your mind to somebody, an' now that the ould master is gone—the heavens be his bed!—I b'lieve there was nobody livin'—hereabouts, anyway,—that knew anything about what's come an' gone, in regard to the Captain that was, barrin' myself an' Nancy. An' sure, in the coorse of nature, neither of us 'ill be long in it. Then you'd have no one at all to spake a word to about what's ever more in your mind."

"Very true, Mabel, and that is just the reason why I told my niece the sad story."

"Ah! Miss Liddy dear!" said the old woman after a long pause, "I think I could die happy if I could once see *you* in the way of bein' happy. But, och one! sure there's little chance o' that, in this world, anyhow!"

"Little chance, indeed," said Miss Ackland, rising, "unless either the dead could come back to life, or somebody convince me that the past was all a dream. But still, Mabel, we must work our passage through in the best way we can, and take things as they come. Happiness is not for this world, you know! We shall all meet, I hope, where happiness is, and is eternal. Good-bye, Mabel! be sure and send me word if you want anything."

"I will, asthore! I will, for I know it 'id fret you to think that poor Mabel *did* want for anything. Well! all I can do is to pray for you an' Miss Rose, an' that I do from my heart out, night an' mornin', on my bended knees; an' when the world's sleepin', an' only the dead to the fore, I pray for you, too, an' sometimes I think the dead answers me, an' there comes like a whisper in my ear that there's bright days before you still! Go now, an' God be with you!"

Going out from the cottage, the ladies stopped a moment to speak to the children, when as they turned to regain the high road through the village, they were startled to see on the smooth white sand the name *Giacomo* plainly written in large fair characters.

"What *can* it mean?" said Miss Ackland to her niece who stood gazing on the name with a wild, startled look, her color changing like the April sky.

"It is hard to say," Rose replied, "he cannot have been here, yet who could have written his name in such a place?"

A thought struck Miss Ackland; she once more approached the children and asked them who wrote that, pointing to the name on the sand.

"That!" replied the eldest, "oh! the gentleman made that there a while ago when you were in with granny."

"What gentleman? Did you know him?"

No, none of the children knew him, so the ladies were forced to return home in the anxious suspense arising from this singular incident. They half expected on reaching home to find the young Leghorner there before them, but in answer to their eager inquiry, whether any one had been there since they left, Nancy replied in her matter-of-fact way—"Oh the sorra one, then, barrin' Catty Nugent that called to see if we wanted any fish for the morrow. She says she has the best of haddock, an' some rale good pike, if we'd be for havin' any. An' she'll have sole an' fresh herrin's the morrow mornin', she expects, for her man is out all day."

"Oh! dear me, Nancy," cried Rose with an impatient gesture, "do let us alone about Catty Nugent's fish. We don't care if she never had any."

"Why, then, Miss Rose," said Nancy with an air of offended dignity, "it's newens for you *not* to care about your Friday's dinner. There's nobody in the house so hard to plase, I'm sure, any day in the week, in regard to what's put before you. But all's one to me. It's little fish sarves *my* turn, or mate, aither, for the matter of that." And she betook herself to her own quarter of the house, closing the kitchen door after her with no gentle motion.

"You must go, by and by, and pacify poor Nancy," said Miss Ackland, ever alive to the feelings of others.

"Oh! that is easily done, Aunt Lydia!—but you see Giacomo has not come. How very strange!"

"He may have arrived," said her aunt thoughtfully "although he has not been here yet. We may probably see him before long. Yet even if he had come,

I wonder what could have taken him to Baltray, or why he should go write his name in the sand near Mabel's door!"

"That is just what puzzles me, aunt!"

"Well! in any case, it is useless to waste time in idle speculations on the subject. I declare it is almost tea-time. I will go myself to the kitchen, and I shall tell Nancy at the same time what we saw at Baltray, in order to excuse your impatience."

A day or two after, who should drop in for an afternoon call but the two Miss Brodigans. After some desultory conversation, Miss Jane said in her languid way—

"So your Italian friend is come back. Of course you have seen him?"

"Why no," Miss Ackland replied, "we have not seen him."

"Have *you* seen him?" asked Rose in a careless tone.

"Well! no, but a friend of ours did!"

"And where, pray!" said Rose in the same tone.

"In Lawrence street, not so far from here," said Miss Brodigan; "it is strange he did not call on you immediately. It was the evening before last, I think, that Tiernan saw him."

"Or thought he saw him," said Rose with a smile of incredulity. Yet she and her aunt exchanged meaning glances, for that was the evening of the day on which they had been to Baltray.

"I see you are incredulous, Rose," said Anne Brodi

gan, a little annoyed by her tone and manner; "of course, you think, and you ought to know best, that the young gentleman could not possibly be an hour, much less a day, in Drogheda without your seeing him."

"Without *my* seeing him?" said Rose haughtily; "you are much mistaken, Miss Brodigan, if you suppose I have any special claims on Signor Giacomo's attention. My aunt *may* have, for she was very kind to him during his illness, but as for me, he owes me nothing, and I expect nothing from him."

"Oh! of course not, now," lisped languid Miss Jane.

"No, nor *then*," replied Rose with increasing vehemence; she was really annoyed at their meddling insinuations.

"Not since the military came into favor, at all events," said Miss Brodigan, with a meaning smile as she and her sister rose to take their departure.

"What do you mean by that, Anne Brodigan?" said Rose, with a sudden change of voice and manner, and her aunt was pained to see that her face was all in a glow.

"Oh! nothing at all," was the reply, "only you know, Rose, the *scarlet fever* is prevalent here just now, and I really did not know whether you had escaped it or not. Good-bye, Miss Ackland! Good-bye, Rosey! I forgot to say that mamma sends her kind love to you both, fair ladies of the hill! Good-bye!" Miss Jane nodded and smiled, hands were mutually shaken, and the visitors retired. There was a short silence after they left, then Miss Ackland said somewhat abstractedly—

"I begin to think that Giacomo may be here, or has been here. But if so, it is passing strange that we have not seen him."

"So strange, indeed," said Rose, "that I cannot believe it."

"The evening is fine," said Miss Ackland, an hour or two later, when the sun was sinking in the west, "let us walk a while in the garden," and she drew her niece's arm within her own. After taking a few turns round the garden, which was not very large, and for the most part exhibiting the useful rather than the ornamental in its botanic arrangement, they stopped to catch the last faint glow of sunset flushing the distant sea with crimson, and Miss Ackland said—

"Rose, I have a question to ask you."

"Indeed, Aunt Lydia?—and pray what is it?" said Rose in a hesitating sort of way.

"What did Anne Brodigan mean about the military, and the *scarlet fever*. She spoke with a pointedness which you seemed to understand."

Rose laughed, but her laugh was not the same free, joyous one that her aunt was accustomed to hear. "Why, my dear Aunt Lydia, what importance can you possibly attach to Anne's silly *badinage?* You ought to know her by this time?"

There was a slight rustling amongst the bushes near by, that made both ladies start and turn quickly in the direction of the sound. No living thing was to be seen, however, except a linnet that sat on the topmost bough of an apple-tree warbling its vesper song.

"Yet, Rose, I fancied there was a consciousness in your look and manner, while she spoke, that somehow reminded me of what you said yourself in Mabel's cottage the other day."

"What was that, Aunt Lydia?"

"That you had met Major Melville more than once, and with him some of his brother officers. Why did you not tell me that before?"

"Well! I told you *then*, my dear aunt, and I'll tell about it now, although it is scarcely worth the telling." Was it the linnet that shook the branches, and crushed the dry leaves on the ground as though human foot were there?

"The truth is, aunt," resumed Rose with a cheerfulness that re-assured Miss Ackland, "I have been a little annoyed by some of those same military gentlemen, especially that Lieutenant Cornell, since we were so unlucky as to meet them that evening. They *will* salute me when we meet, on the street, and that is oftener than I could wish, and as for Cornell he has once or twice addressed me with the familiarity of an old acquaintance."

"But you have not answered him, have you? or recognized any of the others?"

"Certainly not, Aunt Lydia! I should do little credit to your teaching were I capable of exchanging salutes with gentlemen who have never been introduced to me, and whom I only know as imprudent and intrusive."

"There spoke my own Rose," said the aunt with proud affection; "shall I confess that you have taken a load off my heart?"

"Why, surely, you did not suspect me of encouraging any advances from these gentlemen, or noticing them in any way?"

"No matter what I suspected, Rose, I find you are a true Ackland, and know how to keep such people at a proper distance. But tell me, Rose, did Major Melville act in the same way as the others?"

"Not he, indeed, aunt!—he never pretended to recognize me, although I could not help seeing that he knew me again at the first glance."

"That is just what I would expect," said Miss Ackland in a low, tremulous tone; "to be a Melville he must be the soul of honor, and a gentleman in the truest sense. Let us go in, my dear, the night-dews are beginning to fall."

They were turning to go into the house by the front door, when a figure presented itself to their view at the corner of the esplanade from behind the drooping branches of a laburnum-tree. Rose clung closer to her aunt's arm, with difficulty suppressing a scream, and Miss Ackland herself was somewhat alarmed. But alarm soon gave place to joy when a well-known voice said—

"You do not know me, then?—have you already forgotten Giacomo?"

"Giacomo! Can it be possible?"

It was, indeed, Giacomo, his very self; there was no mistaking the friendly grasp of his hand, the heart-warm tones of his voice, unheard for long,—and truly he had no reason to complain of his reception. Miss Ackland was rejoiced to see him, and frankly said so, and even Rose manifested more pleasure than could have been expected from her former demeanor towards him. At first no questions were asked, and they all three entered the house. Nancy was rather surprised on seeing what she took for a strange gentleman with the ladies, but, on recognizing her young favorite, the good old soul could scarcely find words to express her joy.

Tea was long over, and Giacomo had had his, he said, but it was hard to persuade Nancy from going to work to get tea for him, "An' sure a cup of tay would do him good, an' he must take something, after bein' so long away from them."

At last the faithful creature was got rid of, the candles were lit, and Giacomo ran his eye over the well-remembered room, as if to see that all was the same there as when he left it; but all was not the same, and the young man's eyes filled with tears as they rested on the old arm-chair still in its olden place, but vacant now. The ladies saw his emotion, and well understood its cause, but they were silent.

"How much you must miss him!" said Giacomo after a long pause.

"Yes, we miss him, indeed!" Rose replied,—her

aunt could not trust her voice to speak, "every day, and every hour we miss him, and shall, I think, for years to come."

After another pause, Miss Ackland said—"By-the-bye, Giacomo, when did you arrive?"

There was a slight confusion visible in the young man's manner as he replied—"Three days ago."

"Three days!" said Miss Ackland reproachfully, "three days in Drogheda without coming to see us?"

"I came on business, and have been much occupied."

"Yet," cried Rose with the arch smile of other days, "you found time to go to Baltray!"

"Oh! that is true," said Miss Ackland; "we saw your name in the sand near Mabel's cottage, and have been ever since puzzling our wits imagining how it came there."

"You flatter me, Miss Ackland," he replied laughing, "I could not have hoped that the sight of my name should have attracted so much of your attention."

"Not of mine," said Rose, saucy as ever, "not of mine, I assure you. I for one take little heed of words *written in the sand*. But my aunt thought it strange to get the first token of your arrival on the beach at Baltray. A new way of leaving one's card, that!"

"But who told you I was there at all?"

"Why, Mabel's grandchildren told us—that is they told Aunt Lydia that 'a gentleman' wrote that, and it was very natural to conclude that no gentleman was so likely to write your name as yourself. Then Miss Brodigan told us you were in town, for that a friend of theirs had seen you."

"And did you believe her on her friend's word?"

"No, that she did not," said Miss Ackland, answering for her niece; "she gave Miss Brodigan no small offence by refusing to believe it."

"And why would you not believe it, Miss Rose?" said Giacomo, evidently much pleased.

"I'll answer that question," Rose quickly replied, "when you tell me, Signor, why you were three days in Drogheda without coming to see my aunt."

"A fair proposal, Giacomo," said Miss Ackland smiling, "come, give an account of yourself."

"Some other time I will – not now," said Giacomo, "but I was forgetting my sister's letter, Miss Ackland!" and he handed her the letter, which she glanced over with evident pleasure, then handed it to Rose.

"What a sweet girl your sister Maddalena must be," observed Miss Ackland; "somehow I feel a longing desire to make her acquaintance—that is in person—for I fancy I know her now in heart and mind as well as I ever could know her. It seems to me that I should love her dearly."

"Why, that is just what Maddalena says of you," said Giacomo laughing; "Miss Rose she thinks she could *like*, Miss Ackland she would *love*, nay, loves even now."

"What a remarkable coincidence!" said Rose in a tone so like that of worthy Mr. Brodigan that even her grave aunt could not refuse a smile.

"I was much amused yesterday evening," said Giacomo, after a short and rather awkward silence, "by a scene I witnessed at the Tholsel—I believe you call it—that gloomy town-hall of yours. I was passing by there about eight o'clock, when I saw the building lighted up, and some people going in, but what most attracted my attention was that funny old bellman of yours, walking in that lazy way that is peculiar to him, up and down in front of the building, neither faster nor slower.—slower he couldn't well go—ringing his big bell and repeating these words—'Walk in, gentlemen! walk in! Hell open, gentlemen!—Hell open!'\* Hearing such a singular invitation given to the public, I thought *I* would 'step in' and see what was going on, noticing, as I did so, that those who went in were few, compared with those who laughed and passed on."

"Well! and what was it?" said Miss Ackland, exchanging a glance of intelligence with Rose; she knew well enough, but she wished to hear Giacomo's account of it.

"Why, it was a meeting of 'The Irish Church Missionary Society,' as I afterwards saw by the placards on the walls, but the whole business of the meeting seemed to be to abuse and vilify the Catholic religion. Such stories as I heard **told** there by grave

---

\* This really occurred in Drogheda.

looking men, well-dressed, and, you would think, sensible enough, concerning what they called 'Romish superstition,' I never heard in all my life before. They were so childish, so ridiculous, and all about people without a name, and with no particular place of residence, that I could scarce keep from laughing to see how attentively they were listened to. Some of them were located in my country, at the village of A or B, and so forth, and always to some C or D, or some other letter of the alphabet. I only wish you could have heard them, Miss Ackland! for I know it would have given you much amusement. For my part, I might have been annoyed, only I wondered so much at the gravity with which the speakers spoke, and the audience listened, to such nonsensical rigmaroles that I forgot it was of my own religion such absurd stories were being told."

"Oh! that is nothing new to us here," said Miss Ackland, "but we only laugh at those knaves or fanatics, whichever they may be. You see how the bellman was employed to turn them into ridicule. That is just how we treat them here in Drogheda. We have 'soupers' here, as they are called (from their attempts to bribe the poor through their appetites), but they never succeed in making one pervert, unless it be some miserable wretch who is willing to barter his or her soul, like Esau, for a mess of pottage. The townspeople only laugh at the efforts of these Missionaries' to make Protestants. I rather think they find our old borough too hot to hold them, at times, for the very boys on the streets plague them with questions about religion which they cannot answer. Have you none of these Protestant missionaries in Italy?"

"Yes, we have them in shoals; they every year come to us in greater numbers; they call themselves there 'evangelists' and other such names."

"Well! and how do they succeed there in making perverts?"

"They make no perverts, so to say, from the Church; those whom they induce to join them outwardly, are already deprived of faith,—on account of their bad morals, I suppose,—and, therefore, have none to lose. But even they are only few in numbers, as I have always understood."

The conversation then turned on matters of more immediate interest, and the evening passed so pleasantly, that all were surprised when the clock struck ten, soon after which Giacomo took his leave.

## CHAPTER XII.

**Whatever** Giacomo's business might have been in Drogheda, he seemed to have an abundance of time for all purposes of amusement and of social enjoyment. He said that his father had given him permission to remain some weeks after his business arrangements were completed, in order to see some more of the country around Drogheda. It annoyed him more than a little when he found that Miss Ackland and Rose were necessarily confined to the schoolroom during the greater part of the day, so that he could not have their company in all his excursions. But Saturday was at their disposal, and he contrived to visit the most interesting scenes and localities on that day, when most of all he enjoyed their beauties, and learned the most of their historical and legendary lore. Jemmy Nulty was one of the first for whom he inquired, but Jemmy, he learned, had " shuffled off his mortal coil," and gone to rest till Doomsday in the little monastic graveyard by the side of the brother he loved so well, his brother in faith, hope, and charity, no less than in blood. " Happy pair!" said Giacomo, when Miss Ackland, with tearful eyes, spoke of the truly Christian brothers now reunited in the calm sleep of death. "Happy pair! who would not envy such a death? Poor Jemmy seemed to have a presentiment that we should meet no more on earth, for he asked me, if I 'missed him' on returning to Drogheda, to remember him in my prayers  Kind old man! indeed I shall not forget him! he reminded me of nothing so much as the simple anchorets of other days, who lived in the desert with God and their own souls."

A shade of deeper thought passed over his face as he thus spoke, and when he raised his eyes again, he found Rose watching him with an earnestness of which she herself was hardly conscious, yet she blushed slightly, and turned away with some degree of embarrassment, laughing the while at Giacomo's unwonted seriousness.

"Let Jemmy rest in peace," said she, taking up her tapestry frame, "which I have no doubt he does, the good old soul. You intend, of course, to go to Beliewstown races, Signor?—They come off next week."

"I should certainly like to go," was the reply, "and I have invitations from the Brodigans, Tiernans and others, to go with them, but——" he stopped short and looked at Miss Ackland, "I do not know whether I shall go or not."

"But you shall go, my dear Giacomo," said Miss Ackland with a smile, rightly interpreting his hesitation; "if respect for the unforgotten dead will not permit all your Drogheda friends to be there, that is no reason why you should miss seeing what will be new to you, and is really in itself worth seeing, especially for a stranger. You must go to Bellewstown."

"With whom would you wish me to go, if go I must?" said Giacomo in a listless way.

"Oh! the Brodigans, of course; they would naturally feel hurt, being *our* most intimate friends, if you did not go with them. Harry Cusack, I suppose, will join their party."

"I do not think so, Aunt Lydia," said Rose, "he told me he had promised to go with the people out Duleek Gate. It seems they have friends coming down from Dublin for the Races, and expect to have quite a large party there."

It was settled then and there, however, that Giacomo was to go with the Brodigans, and accordingly the young ladies of that family had the triumph of parading the handsome stranger as one of their attendant cavaliers the first day of the Races. And truly it was a novel sight to our young Italian, and one that was characteristic of Drogheda, to whose genial, free-hearted burghers those annual Races at Bellewstown were (and we suppose are) a sort of carnival, during which all, or nearly all, business was suspended in the town, and all of its population who could manage to go, were, day after day, "off to Bellewstown," the rich riding or driving, the poor trudging on foot,—the distance is only a few miles—and all in the best possible humor for being happy themselves and making others happy. At Bellewstown the generous hospitality of that proverbially hospitable town seemed to reach its height. The Drogheda people made it a point to have as many of their friends from other places for that great occasion as they possibly could, and it was a stirring scene of harmless mirth and jollity when hundreds of different parties were bivouacking *a la pic-nic* on the smooth green sward at some particular hour of the day when "the horses were not running." It was a scene to be remembered. What with the merry music of pipes and fiddles from the tents, the countless multitude of happy, joyous faces, all intent on sport, the numerous groups scattered over the spacious green surrounding the Course, enjoying their creature comforts with laugh and jest, in which the passers-by often shared; the rows of carriages of all kinds drawn up without the ropes which marked the limits of the Course, from the handsome and elegant barouche of the nobleman with its heraldric devices and liveried servants, to the plain gig and jaunting-car of the respectable shopkeeper, or the wealthy farmer, "the ladies" being generally stationed in the latter class to see the Races, whilst the very highest ascended the stand in the centre, where might be found almost any year, about the time we write of, the Lord Lieutenant of the day, all the eighteen miles of way from Dublin, and the heads of the Louth, Meath, and Dublin aristocracy, the stand-house itself being a gay sight to look upon, with its national and other flags and streamers dancing in the summer-breeze that swept across that high table-land from the Irish Sea on one side, and on the other the Bay of Dundalk, whose blue waters were visible in the distance, with the shapely forms of the Mourne Mountains rising vague and misty beyond it. It *was* a scene of life, and beauty, and animation, and our young Leghorner thought, as he cast his eyes over the rich plains of three level counties lying in beauty and freshness below on every side, then looked through the vistas opening between hills and mountains to the bolder outlines of the northern scenery, far away in the counties of Cavan and Monaghan, that even his own sunny Italy presented few scenes by nature fairer than that to which worthy Mr. Brodigan took care to call his attention. But it was only to Mr. Brodigan or his plain but intelligent wife that Giacomo listened with any degree of pleasure; in vain did Miss Jane quote sentimental poetry, and compose fine sentences descriptive of the surrounding scenery; in vain did Miss Brodigan unbend from her usual *hauteur*, and condescend to hang on his arm, when they all took a turn round the green during the intervals of the races; his thoughts were in the old house by the Boyne, and the schoolroom where two bright kindred spirits were shut up at their wearisome, monotonous task—

"Pent in the weary schoolroom during summer."

There he would rather be, he sadly thought, than where he was on the breezy plain with the beauty of earth, and sea, and sky before him, and a world of life and gay festivity around him.

"If they were only here," he thought, " or I with

them—oh! that we might live together always—always—then life would be life indeed!" He thought of Maddalena, then of his father, and the glow faded from his cheek.

It was after sundown when Giacomo and his party reached the city, and politely declining Mrs. Brodigan's pressing invitation to go home with them and spend the evening, he hastened at once to the old house on the hill, where he found the aunt and niece seated on the esplanade enjoying the rare beauty of the evening. They seemed surprised to see him, and Rose said, as her aunt made place for him on the rustic bench beside her—

"Why, Signor, I had no idea that we should see you this evening. I thought you would have gone home with the Brodigans."

"No, I was kindly invited to do so, but after the bustle and excitement of the day, I longed for quiet, so I came where I was sure to find it."

Miss Ackland smiled gratefully, she knew that he came to them because he feared that being all alone, they must feel lonely at such a time. Rose exclaimed with her usual animation,—but a trifle more eagerly than usual—

"So, then, you didn't like Bellewstown—you didn't enjoy the Races, or anything, as we hoped you would?"

Giacomo fixed a meaning glance on her as he replied—"On the contrary, Miss Rose, I did like Bellewstown, very, very much, and I did enjoy the Races and all the rest, but shall I confess that the excite ment and general bustle was too much for me, and that I was really glad to return into town?"

"But you will, of course, go back to-morrow?"

"No, I have had quite enough of it, Miss Ackland! I saw to-day all I desire to see of Bellewstown and the Races. Only let me accompany you and Miss Rose in your walk to-morrow evening, and I shall enjoy it more in one little hour than an hundred such days as this."

"My dear Giacomo, you are very kind to say so; if that be the case, come and take tea with us to-morrow, an early tea, at six o'clock, and we shall take you to our favorite walk up the Rathmullen Road."

"The Rathmullen Road! oh! I remember Miss Rose speaking of it once before—that is to say last winter when I was here. I shall be much pleased to see it."

"We have not been there for some time," said Rose, addressing her aunt, "I shall be glad to see the dear old place myself; especially as we can stay longer and later, having an escort with us," she added smiling.

"Are escorts then necessary here?" said Giacomo, observing that she laid a certain emphasis on the word. "I should think in a quiet old town like this, ladies might walk abroad at all hours of the day, or even of the early night."

"So it would be," replied Miss Ackland, "were we left to our own population, but you forget, Giacomo, that this is a garrison town," she said pointedly.

"Oh! then it is the military who make it unsafe?" said Giacomo, and he looked at Rose who was bending in silence over a volume of engravings, her color higher than usual, it appeared to him. "Your gentlemen of the army, then, are not the *preux chevaliers* they ought to be?"

"Yes," said Rose, perhaps, in the spirit of contradiction, "there are some of them here—one especially—who looks as though he might be a veritable Bayard or Du Guesclin, and whom I have never seen act indecorously!"

Giacomo looked surprised, and so did Miss Ackland; the latter, however, tried to pass it off as a jest, and said with her sweet, sad smile—

"Oh! you mean Major Melville, Rose!—I see you praise *him*, by force of contrast. And I believe you are right; compared with those younger brother-officers of his, he does appear very much of a gentleman."

Giacomo looked from one to the other, wondering what it all meant; at last he said—

"Miss Rose appears to have seen a good deal of these military gentlemen of late."

"There you are mistaken, Signor," said Rose quickly; "I have never been introduced to one of them, and have only met them on the road or the street."

"It is not so said here in Drogheda," Giacomo replied in a tone of forced composure. "I was told the very day after my arrival that some of them were your particular admirers."

He looked so grave that Rose could not help laughing. "And do you suppose, Signor, that any young lady hereabouts would consider that a misfortune?"

"Not if the admirer were such as you describe your Major Melville," he replied still more seriously.

"*My* Major Melville," cried Rose with her merriest laugh; "he certainly is not my Major Melville, and it is more than probable that he is somebody else's Major Melville long before now. Do pray, Aunt Lydia! tell this puzzled Signor how we came to meet the gentleman in question!"

Miss Ackland, pleased to see the turn Rose had given the conversation, willingly complied, and related the adventure with the officers on the Rathmullen Road, with the exception of the episode between Major Melville and herself. When she had finished Giacomo drew a long breath, like one who felt relieved:

"So this was the beginning of the affair; and the sequel was—those annoyances to which Miss Rose has been subjected by these *gentlemen*," with a bitter emphasis on the last word.

"Annoyances!" Rose repeated with some surprise; "what annoyances do you mean?"

"Those of which I heard you complain to your aunt the first evening I saw you after my return."

"So you heard her?" said Miss Ackland.

"Yes, I did; I was just crossing the esplanade to the front door, when, hearing your voices in the garden, I thought I would take you by surprise, and having ascertained what part of the garden you were in, I went round by the shady walk at the further end, and met you as you know."

Miss Ackland and Rose both thought of the rustling amongst the branches, but they merely exchanged looks, and Giacomo went on: "You will not, I hope, think the worse of me, ladies, when I tell you that I purposely waited to hear the conclusion of Miss Rose's explanation."

"And I hope you found it satisfactory, Signor?" said Rose with ironical gravity.

"Perfectly so," he said with a look that brought the eloquent blood to her cheek. Yet she laughed lightly and carelessly.

"How satisfactory! Well! really, Signor, you do talk strangely at times!—do you know, Aunt Lydia, I sometimes think that that bump his head got against the rocks at Clogher may have seriously affected his brain. Are you subject to headaches, Signor?"

"No," said Giacomo laughing, and as Miss Ackland turned away with a gentle "For shame, Rose! what a silly girl you are!" he added in a low whisper, "but I am to heart-aches—can you account for *them*?"

"You give me credit for more skill than I possess, Signor!—what should I know of heart-aches or their cause?" Was it the red cloud which the sun had left at his setting "to preside o'er the scene" that crimsoned her cheek just then?

"Did you ever see a lovelier evening?" said Miss Ackland, returning from the western end of the esplanade, where she had stood a moment regarding with that ardent love of the beautiful, which was one of her strongest characteristics, the sunset glow that lit up the lovely scene around. "How one's heart expands at such a moment, and one's spirit casts off its weary load in the last fair hour of day!" Then she murmured low, as she threw herself wearily on the bench beside Giacomo—

'The twilight hour! the twilight hour! which poets vie to praise,
And it is now a weariness so loved in other days."

He who watched her read her heart, for he loved her as a dear elder sister; he took her hand, and said with a tenderness of sympathy that brought tears to her eyes—

"You have known many sorrows, my friend, my benefactress! would that I could do anything to efface their remembrance!"

Miss Ackland turned and laid her hand on his shoulder, and her voice was tremulous with emotion as she replied—"Giacomo, my dear young friend! I would not forget my sorrows if I could, but believe me, your sympathy consoles me. It reminds me of one whose voice I shall never hear again on earth."

"Then there was one whom you regarded with favor?"

"Yes, Giacomo, I will not conceal it from you towards whom I feel as a mother to a very dear child —yes

'There was one who once with me so woo'd this quiet hour,
As young hearts tired of revelry woo slumber's gentle power'—
one who loved me, and whom I loved—oh how well —how truly."

"I knew it," he said with a strange earnestness, "I knew you had loved and been beloved. How could it be otherwise?"

There was dead silence for a while; the spell of the hour and the scene had fallen on all; the moon was rising slowly above the horizon, and her light still veiled and subdued shed a solemn glory over the picture of sea and land and town and river that lay spread like a map below; the sounds of busy life had died, it would seem, with the departing day, and only the watch-dog's bark broke on the ear, or at long intervals the shrill whistle of some passer-by on the road beneath, or the creaking voice of the corn-crake in the meadows behind the town. Silence was on the land and the water, and as the shadows of twilight gradually gave place to the beams of the rising orb of night the scene was beautiful beyond expression.

"Does your Tuscan Val d'Arno much exceed that?" said Rose at length, as if anxious to break a silence which she, at least, felt oppressive; could you by any stretch of imagination suppose our Boyne to be the Arno?"

"As regards the river itself I might easily get up the illusion, for your Boyne is as bright, its banks, in many places, at least, to the full as picturesque, and I believe it is to your history and tradition very much what the Arno is to us Tuscans, but——"

"Oh! of course, there's a *but*—what is it, Signor?"

"Why," said Giacomo, laughing, "it would require a greater stretch of imagination than I could boast, to transform yonder old town into Florence, the fair queen of the Arno. Truly she is Fiorenza il bella—Florence the Beautiful!"

"I should like to see Florence, and Rome, and Venice," said Rose half abstractedly, as she watched the broad yellow disk of the lady-moon rising over the shining sea.

"Why not Leghorn?" said Giacomo; "it is a fair city, too, looking out from orange groves and myrtle bowers on the broad bosom of the Mediterranean."

"Oh! Leghorn! who cares about Leghorn?" said Rose, falling back on her old ways.

"I do, for one," said the young man reproachfully. "If it be not equal to other Italian cities in beauty, in splendor, or in old and high renown, it is my city, and I love it best of all."

"Forgive me, Signor!" said Rose very gently; "I did not mean to speak disrespectfully of your native city—I only meant to say that it has not the same hold on the imagination as any of the other cities I mentioned. You yourself must admit that."

"Some day," he replied in a low tone, "I will hope to convince you that the city of Pietro di Medici is not altogether unworthy of its founder. But here comes Nancy," he said, seeing the old woman protruding her head from the doorway.

"Do you want me, Nancy?" said Miss Ackland standing up.

"It's one from Baltray that's within, Miss Ackland, an' wants to see you very bad."

With a slight apology to Giacomo, Miss Ackland entered the house, but Nancy seemed inclined to linger, and on a kind invitation from Rose to come out and talk to Signor Giacomo, squatted herself on the ground beside the bench where he sat.

"You are keeping your health well, Nancy!" said the young gentleman with that easy condescension that marks the really well-bred in their intercourse with their inferiors.

"Well then, I am, sir, thank God, an' you for the askin'; but you don't know how lonesome I am for the ould master, God rest his soul!"

"I can well believe that, Nancy!—but now I think of it, I forgot to ask after your old friend Tab: I have not seen her since I came."

"Ah! poor thing, she's dead, too," said the old woman with a melancholy shake of the head, her chin resting on her hand, her elbow on her knee.

"Dead, is she?"

"Aye, indeed, and do you know, Mr. Jacomy! (so she always called him), I miss her more than I ever thought I'd miss one of her kind."

"What! and she an enchanted Dane?"

"Ooh! the sorra Dane or Dane she was, the poor

harmless crature, an' many's the time I was sorry since she died for the grudge I had again her."

"There's a touch of human nature," said Rose in an under tone, "death, you see, like charity, covers a multitude of sins, and sometimes sheds a halo round those who in life we did not value as we ought."

"So that if even *I* were dead, who knows but some one might encircle my memory with the halo you speak of——"

Here Nancy started to her feet and hastened into the house, having, as she said, heard Miss Ackland call her.

"Do you think any one would miss me if I were gone?" persisted Giacomo, bending forward to look in the face of his companion.

"Why, how can I tell?" said Rose in her laughing way; "I suppose, though, you would have no worse chance than our old Tab. You see *she* is not forgotten."

"You are really quite complimentary, Miss Rose!— Well! *I* know one who *would* be remembered and would never be forgotten while one heart throbbed with life."

Rose Ackland smiled, and a softened expression stole over the brightness of her face; but it passed way in an instant, and she said in a sort of musing way—"And *I* know one, or at least, I knew *of* one who though many, many years dead, is still as fondly beloved, as well remembered as though he died but yesterday."

Giacomo was silent for a moment; then he asked somewhat abruptly, Rose thought—"But is he dead, then, of whom you speak?"

"Why, of whom do you think I am speaking? I did not tell you, did I?"

"No, but somehow it seemed to me as though I knew."

Rose turned and fixed her eyes on him with a startled look; he smiled and went on—"That is, I thought I might have known, but since you say the person so long and tenderly remembered is *dead*, that changes the whole affair. I find I was mistaken—that is to say, that my imagination was running away with my reason. But it is half-past nine o'clock," looking at his watch, "and I must away to my solitary room in West street."

"But tell me before you go, Signor, why it was that you did not come into Mabel's cottage that day, but left, instead, your name on the strand? Were you there, or were you not?"

"I was there; I had gone down to see Mabel, for I really feel interested in that old woman, but when I got there I changed my mind——"

"You heard we were there—was that the reason?"

"It was."

"You are very candid, Signor Giacomo,—more candid than polite, I think."

"You asked me a plain question; truth obliged me to give a plain answer."

"But why write your name on the sand?"

"To let you know I had been there, and was gone."

"Well, really, you grow worse and worse."

"Sincerity is a virtue, you know, Signora!"

"Tell me, then, in your sincerity, why you wished to avoid us."

"Your aunt I never wished to avoid, it was you, Miss Rose, and for the same reason that would have prevented me from visiting your house—at least from seeing *you*—had I not chanced to overhear what passed between your aunt and you that evening in the garden. I had heard of you immediately on my arrival what grieved and mortified me beyond expression."

Rose stood up, her cheek burning, and an angry light in her dark eyes:

"And did you suppose, Signor, that your absenting yourself from our house would punish me for my supposed folly and indiscretion?—If you did, you have more vanity than I would have suspected.'

"Miss Rose Ackland," said Giacomo, also rising, the warm southern blood rushing from his heart to his face, "I am *not* so vain as to imagine anything idea, be assured there is little danger of my now lapsing so preposterous, but if I ever had entertained such an into such folly. Were I disposed to enter into explanations, you might see my conduct in a different light; but I am not, and so let the matter rest. I will merely say 'good night' to your aunt, then rid you of my company—for the present. May I have the honor?' and he offered her his arm with cool politeness. Rose did not choose to notice the motion, and they walked in together. They found Miss Ackland preparing to go down to Baltray, having learned that Mabel was unusually ill, and wished to see her. Giacomo at once offered to accompany her, and his offer being gladly accepted, they immediately set out for Baltray. It was a pleasant walk they had by the Boyne side in the clear moonlight, Giacomo talking the while of his father and Maddalena, till Miss Ackland imagined she could see both one and the other of those who, for his sake, she already loved, she said.

"My sister cherishes the same feelings towards you, my kind dear friend," said the warm-hearted young Italian; "she desires, more than almost anything else, to see you, and thank you in person for your more than kindness to her only brother."

"And your father?" questioned Miss Ackland, half unconscious that she was betraying the surprise she felt at hearing so little of *his* gratitude.

"Oh! my father," replied the youth, with some degree of embarrassment—"my father is never demonstrative; he seldom talks of his feelings. But I am sure he appreciates your goodness to me, stranger as I then was to you."

"My dear Giacomo," said Miss Ackland, "you overrate the trifling service I had in my power to render to you, so, I believe, does your sweet sister, but it cannot be expected that your father should feel as fervently as you do. Why, here we are at Baltray; truly, we have

'With talk of various kinds beguiled the way,'—

it is long since I found the road so short."

They entered the cottage; Mabel was not so ill as her son's affectionate fears had represented, for it was he who had gone to let Miss Ackland know the change that had taken place. She was already recovering from the death-like swoon that had so alarmed her relatives, and Miss Ackland had the satisfaction of seeing her restored to consciousness, and likely to improve before she left the cottage.

"I'll not die yit awhile, Miss Lyddy!" were the old woman's parting words; "I'll live, plaze God, to see something turn up for you, *asthore!*"

With a kind but incredulous smile Miss Ackland left her faithful follower.

## CHAPTER XIII.

CONTRARY to Rose's expectation, Giacomo came next evening punctual to his appointment, with no perceptible difference in his manner, yet she could see that he addressed more of his conversation than usual to her aunt. and less to herself, and was, moreover, a little more ceremonious than usual when he did speak to her. Nancy's best skill had been put forth " to have something nice for tea," on that particular evening, and the meal was a pleasant one, in that cheerful little room with the slanting sunbeams from the window resting on the table and its equipage, the quaint old *garde-vin* that stood in the farther corner, and the high mantel-piece with its old-fashioned china ornaments, surmounted by a fine engraving in a heavy gilt frame of Leonardo di Vinci's famous Last Supper. *Apropos* to the engraving, Giacomo told the story of the discovery, by mere accident, of that noble painting originally frescoed on the walls of the refectory in an Italian convent where it had been for ages concealed by a coat of cement laid over it by the good monks to protect it from some expected foreign invasion; its very existence was forgotten,—at least its whereabouts, for the painting of such a work by so great a master as Di

Vinci was, of course, on record, in the traditional history of art.

"I was so fortunate since my return to Italy," said he, "as to be able to visit the native place of the divine Raffaelo, away amongst the purple hills of Umbria, just the place to inspire a poet-painter; I visited Rome at the same time, and by the way, Miss Ackland, what discovery do you think I made while there?"

"I am sure I cannot tell; I know so little of the Eternal City, except from the descriptions of ordinary travellers,\* and they, I know, are not always, indeed, scarcely ever, reliable."

"Well! apart from things of greater interest and importance, I have traced the origin of your old Christmas *waits* to Rome."

"Is it possible?"

"Yes, I then heard for the first time of a band of peasants who descend from their mountains every year about the Feast of the Immaculate Conception, to usher in the joyous Christmas time, and to delight the Romans with their sweet and simple lays, chiefly in honor of the Blessed Virgin. I have heard it said many times during my short stay in Rome that their music is of the sweetest, and gives greater pleasure

---

\* It will be remembered that all our best Catholic works on modern Rome, both in French and English, and even in Italian, have appeared since the date of this story. Amongst the English we may reckon Maguire's "Rome and its Ruler," and Nelligan's "Rome and its Institutions."

to those who hear it than the most artistic performances. Their instruments are few and simple, such as shepherds' pipes, and the like, but it is the very simplicity of the music that constitutes its greatest charm; that and the devotion to the Madonna which, animating the hearts of those pious mountaineers, gives touching expression to their rustic lays."

"But our *waits* do not sing hymns to the Blessed Virgin," said Rose; "they don't sing anything, you know,—but the airs they play, even, are not of a religious character."

"I know that from my own experience, Miss Rose, but, nevertheless, it is easy to see that the custom was at first a religious one, and I assure you I was agreeably surprised to find something so very much like it existing in Rome."

"I wonder could you find in Rome," said Rose with her characteristic archness, "anything like our Shrovetide mummers?"

"What do they do?"

"Why, they dress up in the most ridiculous and fantastic costumes, for the most part representing municipal dignitaries, with the Lord Mayor at the head of the procession, mounted on an ass, a string of potatoes hanging from his neck by way of gold chain, and in his hand a long pole with a bladder on the top, which his lordship amuses himself by dabbling in the mud from time to time, and shaking it over the heads of the passers-by, to the great delight of the noisy ragamuffins who form his guard of honor wo be to the showily or pretentiously dressed female who is unlucky enough to meet the mummers, her fine dress is sure to be none the better for it, for his worship, the chief mummer, is sure to direct his attentions towards her. Then his lordship rides into shops, hotel-halls, and such like, to collect his tribute, and ill they fare who refuse to pay it."

"Why, that is plainly from us, too," said Giacomo; "those are precisely the sports of our Italian Carnival. The difference is that we have innumerable others, whereas you here seem to retain but that one of our Shrovetide sports."

"You can find no religious origin for that, can you?" more archly than before.

"Well! of course not, but still it is an old *Catholic* custom, indicating the approach of the penitential season, when all public amusements are suspended."

"That is so true," said Miss Ackland, "that I believe it is only in one or two other towns or cities of Ireland that the custom is still observed; these, of course, are the most thoroughly Catholic—in all the other localities the Shrovetide mummeries have long since fallen into disuse, and been forgotten. But I see you have finished your tea, Giacomo, had we not better set out at once, the sun will soon go down?"

"The very thing I was wishing for, Miss Ackland! we shall lose the finest of the evening, if we delay much longer."

Some twenty minutes' walk brought them to the romantic heights of Rathmullen, with the road crossing the top of the bold bluff, winding away around the hill-side, disappearing ever from the view under the dense shade of overarching beeches, elms, and sycamores; the sun streamed down all goldenly through the tangled branches, forming a net-work of yellow light on the well-paved road beneath, with its grass-fringed sidewalks, and its hawthorn hedges, all blooming then in their summer garb of white, and filling the air with their delicious fragrance. The sun was setting in the crimson west far over the sea, and the waters far and near, the sea and the river, were tinged with the same roseate hue.

> Never did Ariel's plume,
> At golden sunset hover,
> O'er scenes of richer bloom

than those which lay beneath that evening sky from the storied heights of Oldbridge, and its graceful commemorative Obelisk, to the Boyne's mouth at Bettystown, with the ancient and picturesque town between, girt round, as it were, with mouldering relics of the past.

"And this," said Giacomo, "is the Rathmullen Road," as he turned to take a parting glance at the near surroundings and the far prospects. "What a lovely spot it is, this green quiet nook, so high above the river, and commanding such a view! Truly existence might glide smoothly away amid such scenes as these. How my father would appreciate this!—But," he added musingly, "it is more than probable that he has seen it."

"Has your father, then, been in Drogheda?" asked Miss Ackland, stooping to pick up something from the grass at her feet.

"What have you got there, aunt?" said Rose in her girlish way.

"A four-leaved shamrock, my dear!"

"Oh! give it to me, give it to me," cried Rose clapping her hands.

"Nay," said Miss Ackland, in a jesting way, "I cannot afford to give away my *luck*. If I did, you know I might forfeit the favor of some benignant fairy."

Giacomo looked puzzled, whereupon Miss Ackland explained to him the popular superstition concerning the four-leaved shamrock, promising that she or Rose would sing for him, perhaps, that evening, Lover's beautiful ballad of that name, one of the songs of the superstitions of Ireland—

"I'll seek a four-leaved Shamrock.
In every fairy dell,'

hummed Rose, catching the word, and she would probably have continued the song, being bent, it would seem, on showing just then the greatest amount of careless ease, but all at once, she stopped short, and said—

"Oh aunt! do look! why, there is Major Melville!"

And so it was the Major himself and alone, walking slowly with his hands behind his back, and his eyes fixed on the ground like one whose thoughts were of engrossing interest.

He started on seeing the party, and contrary to Miss Ackland's expectation, raised his cap as they passed. His eye rested for a moment on Miss Ackland with a sort of keen scrutiny, then turned to the young man on whose arm she leaned, and the one who watched him understandingly either saw, or thought she saw a strange intensity in that momentary glance, as though he would fain have looked longer. Giacomo had caught the glance, and he said when the officer was out of hearing—.

"And that is Major Melville; I wonder why he looks so earnestly at *me*." Then he thought of Rose, and her admiration of the Major, which, from all he had heard, might well be mutual.

"Because he sees you are a foreigner," suggested Miss Ackland, giving the only probable reason she could think of. Rose smiled but she said nothing; whatever her thoughts were she kept them to herself.

Miss Ackland's reason seemed to satisfy Giacomo in a matter of so little importance, and he dismissed, or appeared to dismiss, the matter from his mind. Having accompanied the ladies home he bade them good-bye at the door, declining Miss Ackland's invitation to go in.

"I am leaving town early to-morrow," said he, "and I shall not see you for some days."

"May I ask where you are going to?" said Miss Ackland.

"Certainly; I have been often asked by Mr. Callinan to go with him the next time he visits his her-ring-fishery on the coast of Scotland, and as he goes to-morrow I think of going with him; not that I expect much from the excursion, but, as I have never seen any part of Scotland, I may as well take this opportunity of having a glimpse of it."

"And I know you will be pleased that you went," said Miss Ackland; "these fisheries are on the Lochaber coast in the wildest region of the Highlands. I know Mr. Callinan usually starts early when he goes, so I shall not insist on your remaining this evening,— expecting, however, to see you very soon after your return."

He promised with all good will, and then commenced his descent of the long flight of steps with the lightness and agility of youth; the ladies watched him in silence till he turned at the gate below and waved a smiling farewell, then disappeared behind the high wall that skirted the road.

"Aunt," said Rose, in a way half jest, half earnest, as they walked to and fro on the esplanade in the darkening twilight, while the stars came peeping through the blue in the depths above, "Aunt, did you observe what a thoughtful anxious look Major Melville had that time when we met him, and how sharply he looked at you and Giacomo?"

"If *I* didn't observe it," said Miss Ackland smiling, "I see *you* did, *ma chere petite Rose!*"

"And he saluted *you* very graciously! I could scarce believe my eyes after what you told me of his manner of speaking to you at your last meeting."

"At our only meeting; I had never seen Guy—I mean Major Melville—before that evening."

"It was all along of the four-leaved shamrock, aunt," said Rose with her arch smile. "Who knows what form your *luck* may take? Heigho! I wish *I* could find a four-leaved shamrock, or some other token of good luck!" And she sighed with such a conical look of doleful despondency that her aunt could not help laughing.

"Never mind, my dear, we shall, at worst, find 'luck' for you at Painstown with worthy Mr. Ledwich, or nearer home with our friend Harry Cusack."

"Yes, by way of *dernier ressort*—many thanks, Aunt Lydia, but I could not think of depriving *you* of either of two such constant swains who, to my knowledge, have been bowing full fifteen years before your ladyship, like young Edwin in Goldsmith's ballad, though, like him, they 'never talk of love.'"

"Fie, fie, Rose! you cannot, I am sure, longer mistake the nature or the object of Cusack's attentions. Harry has little taste for ancient maidens of such very mature years as mine. Come, let us go in,—it wears late, and the dew is falling."

A week or so had passed before Giacomo again made his appearance, and then he was so full of what he had seen and heard that for some days he could speak of nothing but the wild grandeur of the scenes amid which he had been sojourning, so different from anything he had ever seen before. He would have come all the way from Leghorn, he said, and farther still, to stand on one of those steep hill-sides, "Among the Highland heather," to inhale those mountain-breezes, and look forth over the waste of waters from the dizzy height where the eagle sheltered her young far up in the voiceless solitude. He had lodged with his friend in the cottage of one of the fishermen, and had heard with delight, by the evening fire, the wild superstitions of those Scottish Gael, there of a wilder character still, from the sea-faring habits of the people. Marvellous tales of second-sight had he heard, and ghost stories that made the blood curdle in one's veins, and of shapes that fashioned themselves from the gray mountain-mists to warn those simple children of the Gael of impending death or doom; of maidens white and fair, but with neither flesh, nor blood, nor bone, who appeared at the prow of the lonely corrie, to apprise the fisherman of danger at hand. Then there were legends of faithful love, and dark revenge, and wild adventure, and all the many forms that romance is likely to assume amongst sea-coast mountaineers.

"And then the 'bonnie Jeans' of Highland song," said Rose with her characteristic smile; "who has not heard of Lochaber in connection with a certain rustic fair one, the beloved of some 'Highland laddie' who went like that other famed in Scottish song ' to fight the French' or some other foreign foe, 'for King George upon his throne?'"

"I, for one, never heard of either," said Giacomo

"What! you have never heard either 'Farewell to Lochaber,' or 'The Blue Bells of Scotland?'"

Giacomo shook his head.

"Then you have heard little of Scottish minstrelsy, my aunt will tell you about the best of its kind in Europe. But if I had known you had never heard 'Lochaber' you should have gone there with that sweetest and most touching of airs echoing in your heart, and mingling with the breezes that sweep those heathery hills."

"Is it so very beautiful, then?"

"Yes, and even more so; you should hear my aunt sing it—then you can judge of the spirit that breathes in it. Aunt Lydia, won't you sing 'Lochaber' for Signor Giacomo?"

"Not now, Rose, not now—some other time," said her aunt hastily; then she went on with the same rapid utterance, as if to get through with the subject as soon as might be—"the air is a very sweet one, touching some of the tenderest chords of the heart, but you must not call it a Scotch air."

"No; and why not, Aunt Lydia?"

"Because, it is one of those airs the origin of which we Irish dispute with the Scotch. Moore was so certain of its being Irish that he has introduced it amongst his Irish Melodies, with one of his most beautiful songs—'*When cold in the earth lies the friend thou hast loved.*'"

"Oh! I know that well," said Giacomo, "I have

heard my father sing it many a time, at least snatches of it; I remember these words particularly—

> 'From thee and thy innocent beauty first came,
>   The reveaiings that taught him true love to adore—
> To feel thy bright presence and turn him with shame,
>   From the idols he blindly had knelt to before.'

So that air is the same as the 'Lochaber' of which Miss Rose speaks?"

"The very same. Moore says of it, in one of the notes to his Melodies, that the old Irish name of it was 'The Lamentation of Aughrim.'"

"But, Aunt Lydia, how does he account for its being so long and well known in the Highlands as an old Scottish air?"

"Simply by the fact that it was introduced into the Highlands by Lawrence O'Connellan, an Irish harper, brother of the composer. It *may*, after all, be considered an *old* Scottish air, for it has been common amongst the Scottish Gael for over two hundred years."

"So it was composed by O'Connellan?" said Rose musingly; she was but half familiar with the name.

"You seem to have forgotten, Rose," said Miss Ackland, "what quite took your fancy at the time, those fine verses we once read together on 'O'Connellan's Harp,' beginning—

> 'Harp so lov'd in days of old,
>   Unhonor'd now,
> The hand that swept thy strings is **cold**,
>   And tuneless now.'"

"Oh! yes, I remember now," said Rose, in her eager, girlish way; "how could I forget the name and the resting-place of the bard?" And she repeated one whole stanza of the poem—

> "By Lough Gur's waters, lone, and low,
>   The minstrel's laid,—
> Where mould'ring cloisters dimly throw
>   Sepulchral shade ;—
> Where clust'ring ivy darkly weeps
>   Upon his bed,
> To blot the legend where he sleeps,
>   The tuneful dead!"

"And you also remember those fine verses translated from the Irish—I think by Ferguson—apostrophizing the minstrel, and commencing thus—

> 'Enchanter who reignest
>   Supreme o'er the North,
> Who hast wiled the coy spirit
>   Of true music forth ;
> In vain Europe's minstrels
>   To honor aspire,
> When thy swift slender fingers
>   Go forth on the lyre.'

How beautiful are the last lines:

> 'Who hear thee they praise thee ;
>   They weep while they praise ;
> For, charmer, from Fairyland,
>   Fresh are thy lays!'"

"Beautiful, indeed," said Giacomo; "I should like to have heard some of those old Irish harpers—Carolan, of whom I have so often heard you speak, Miss Ackland,—or that O'Neil, of whom your poor father told us so much one evening, sitting in this very room."

"And less than a year ago!" said Miss Ackland sadly, as she cast her tearful eyes over the smiling prospect that lay spread without. Silence fell on all, the silence of tender recollection; a light wind played in the clustering vines about the open window; the breath of the jasmine and clematis was wafted fresh and balmy into the room,—beautiful and touching emblem of the odor of sweetness which the good leave on earth behind them when they have passed to the spirit-land!

Rose was the first to break the silence, evidently with the intention of diverting her aunt from her gloomy thoughts—" What were we talking of before we turned off, by way of digression, to Scotch airs and Irish harpers?—oh! the Highlands, and Lochaber, to be sure—well, really, Signor, I never thought you had so much enthusiasm as I see you have—it is quite refreshing to hear you talk of those wild scenes and wild people!—I don't know but I shall pay them a visit myself some day—that is if anybody will be so kind as to take me?" Then she sang in her real or affected exuberance of feeling,—

"Hurrah for the Highlands, the stern Scottish Highlands,
The home of the clansman, the brave and the free,
Where the clouds love to rest o'er the mountain's rough breast,
E'er they journ y afar o'er the islandless sea!"

"Well done, Miss Rose!" said a cheery, but not over sweet voice without; "I give you my word, I couldn't do it better myself!" And Harry Cusack made his appearance at the open window, raising his hat politely to the ladies, nodding stiffly to their companion.

"You!" said Rose, "why you have no more voice than a jack-daw!"

"Who said I had?" was the good-humored answer "didn't I say I couldn't do it better myself? But who's for a drive this fine evening? It's a pity to be in the house, so I thought I'd come and see if you ladies wouldn't like a moonlight drive by the river side."

"Oh! you dear Harry Cusack, the very thing we *would* like!" said Rose clapping her hands; "of course you will come, Signor?" turning to Giacomo.

"Thank you," he replied with icy coldness, "I promised to drop in this evening at Mr. Brodigan's; I should have been there before now."

"Could you not postpone your visit till to-morrow evening, and come with us?" Miss Ackland inquired; she looked at Cusack, so did Giacomo, but Cusack was looking another way, and Miss Ackland had too much tact to renew an invitation which ought to come from another. Giacomo hurried away, anxious, as he said, to keep his appointment, and Rose made no effort to detain him, wishing him, on the contrary, a very pleasant evening.

"You might have had the politeness to ask the Signor, too," said Rose somewhat pettishly, as she helped her aunt to "wrap up."

"I've got my horse to think of, Miss Rose!"

"I vow you're as gruff as a bear."

"Thank you kindly, Miss Rose! Allow me to put on your shawl!"

"Thank you kindly, I have it on! But, do you know, Mr. Harry Cusack, I have half a mind not to go, when you are so fearful of overloading your horse, you know!" And she stood swinging her bonnet by the ties, as if irresolute.

"Fie, fie, Rose!" said her aunt; "how childishly you talk! Put on your bonnet, and let us go!" Rose left the room. "I wonder, Mr. Cusack, will Rose ever learn to control her tongue?"

"That depends," said Cusack, shrugging his shoulders as naturally as though he were a born Frenchman. "Are you ready now, ladies?" As Rose tripped in, shawled and bonnetted, looking so pretty that even her aunt could not help noticing it, to herself, of course,—she was ever chary of compliments, especially to her niece.

"This is very pleasant," said Rose, as having descended the steps to the lower road, they found the car waiting, and started at a brisk trot along the white smooth road, running close by the river-side. "This is very pleasant, if none of the dead are walking abroad in the moonlight. Suppose, now, we were to meet Tom Cullen, the cooper!"

"Oh! you shocking girl, what ideas come into your head!"

"Very shocking, I know, Aunt Lydia! but very

natural, when one is out at night on the Boyne side Mr. Cusack!" turning to that gentleman who sat, *dos-a-dos*, on the opposite side of the car, " did you ever see Tom Cullen, the cooper?"

"I can't say I did, Miss Rose, and I hope I'll be longer so!—drive on faster, Ned!" to his man. The subject was not to Mr Cusack's liking, it was plain.

"I wonder is it true that so many people have seen that most unlucky of coopers," went on Rose; " the steps on which they say he stands ought to be somewhere about here. No, I believe they are farther up towards the bridge Dear me! what a thing it must be for any one going up or down to see him standing at a turn of the steps, where they can't avoid passing him, without stepping into the river. A nice dilemma, that, isn't it, Mr. Cusack?"

"Ye-es!—nice, indeed, but not over pleasant!— shall we take the Baltray road, Miss Ackland?"

"As you please, Mr Cusack!—we have no choice!" and Miss Ackland, dropping her voice to a whisper, begged Rose to let Tom Cullen rest in peace, and if she must talk, to choose some other subject.

Rose promised with a smile of doubtful meaning, and she kept silent for a while, but all at once, she said: " Mr. Cusack! did you ever see the headless woman in white that is said to walk this road by night?"

"An' sure if she didn't walk by night, Miss, it isn't by day she'd walk!" put in Ned from his perch in front, looking round with so knowing a look on his face that it seemed as though he thoroughly understood, and sufficiently enjoyed the young lady's persistent efforts to "make night hideous."

"Don't speak till you're spoken to!" said his master sharply, then answered Rose's question in the negative.

"Nor the big black dog with fiery eyes?"

Oh! the villain o' the world!" ejaculated Ned, low and slow, "sure he most put the life out o' me one night last winther!"

"Didn't I tell you not to put in your tongue, you blockhead?" said the master still more sharply than before.

"Sure I know you did, sir,' but I thought it was no harm to answer the young lady's question, as I had seen the dog, an' I thought maybe *you* hadn't, Mr. Cusack!"

"It was a harm, then; see that you don't do it again!"

"Sure I won't, sir; I'd be long sorry when you onst forbid me."

Ned was silenced, but not so Rose, for the more she saw it annoyed poor Cusack, the more she kept on talking of all the ghosts whose "local habitation" was anywhere in that vicinity, for, thanks to Nancy's story-telling propensities, and her own fondness (as a child) for ghost-stories, she knew them all. In vain did her aunt endeavor many times to change the subject of conversation; still the wayward girl returned to the same dismal themes, always addressing her discourse to Mr. Cusack, and winding up by saying with sly meaning when he handed her down at the gate on their return—

'*I hope you enjoyed the drive, Mr. Cusack?*—I did amazingly!" He muttered something, and bidding Miss Ackland " good night," stepped on his car, and told Ned to drive on, without so much as looking at Rose.

" Serve you right!" said her aunt, as they ascended the steps together.

" Serve *him* right!" and Rose laughed merrily, "he was so rude to Signor Giacomo!"

## CHAPTER XIV.

It was St. John's Eve, and the bonfires were blazing in the streets of the old borough, shedding a reddish light on the dark walls, and sharp angles, and irregular outlines of the quaint old-time fabrics, and giving to all that picturesque character which broad light and deep shadow alternating are sure to produce. Every eminence the country over sent up its cheerful glow to the blue mid-summer sky, and all along the river side were seen at short intervals, the merry groups of the young dancing around the symbol-fires, which their fathers lit of old in honor of their god Baal, and which they, of more favored times, made commemorative of the light of Christianity happily shed over the island in after-times.

The evening was beautiful, apart from the joyous celebration, and Miss Ackland proposed to Rose and Giacomo, who had taken tea with them, that they should go down and have a walk by the river side. The young people were delighted with the proposal, and they all three sallied forth, leaving Nancy sitting on the door-step under the deep porch, watching with much interest the fires that shot up here and there in quick succession, flashing out through the deepening gloom of twilight.

After a pleasant walk along the river road, pausing occasionally to watch the dancers who were footing it merrily round some of the fires to the sound of pipes or violin, our little party returned home, with the addition of Harry Cusack and Mr. Brodigan who had joined them on the way. To those who understood the reason, it was amusing to see how studiously the former gentleman avoided Rose whilst they were out of doors, and Mr. Brodigan, *not* understanding it, began to twit him with his want of gallantry.

"When I was a young man, Harry!" said he, "it isn't a pair of black eyes that would frighten me!"

"And do you mean to say, Mr. Brodigan, that eyes black or blue frighten Mr. Cusack?" said Rose with a mischievous glance at the latter.

"Well! I declare it looks like it," said honest Mr. Brodigan; "I never saw Harry so backward before in regard to the ladies. I'm afraid some of you have been trying his patience overmuch."

"Not a bit of it, Mr. Brodigan!" responded Rose quickly; "you know my aunt never tries anybody's patience, so there would be nobody here to do such a naughty thing only me, and Mr. Cusack knows himself what pains *I* took to keep him in good spirits and in good humor the last time we saw him. Didn't I, Harry?"

A grim and somewhat woe-begone smile was Harry's answer; he coughed slightly, and then, with a sudden flush, glanced at Giacomo, as though suspecting that he might have heard of Rose's experiments in the way of keeping up his spirits; but Giacomo was talking to Miss Ackland, and as Harry did not chance to perceive the peculiar smile that curved his lip at the moment, he felt relieved, and soon glided back into his old manner. But Rose was not going to let him off so easily.

"Wasn't it quite a coincidence," said she, "Mr. Brodigan, that, of all things or people, who should come into my head the other night, when Mr. Cusack was good enough to take Aunt Lydia and myself out for a drive, but Tom Cullen, the cooper, whose troubled spirit, you know, haunts the spot where he was murdered? We were passing somewhere near there at the time, and nothing would serve the cooper but he must pop into my head just when I least wished to see him? *Wasn't* it a coincidence?"

"A disagreeable one, I should say," returned Mr. Brodigan, sufficiently acquainted with his friend's nocturnal weakness regarding the inhabitants of the other world to catch the point of the allusion. "I'd rather think of something else were I in your place just then. Why didn't you think of Harry Cusack, eh?—or the Signor, here, or some other fine young fellow?"

"One of the red-coats," put in Cusack, determined to give Rose tit for tat, as he said to himself; "most of the young ladies hereabouts would be thinking of some gallant son of Mars these times, who is alive and hearty, instead of a dead cooper. Eh, Miss Rose?—don't you think so?"

"Decidedly I do, Mr. Cusack! I, for one, love the red-coats dearly, and my heart begins to beat—oh! ever so fast, when I hear the drum."

"I guessed as much!"

"You did, eh?—well! I'm glad to find you can guess so well—now you know how to keep up *my* spirits, any time you may see them down low, and feel charitably disposed to raise them. After all," she added, as if with kindling enthusiasm, "there *is* no sight like a military show,—oh! I do so love it!" Then throwing herself into an attitude, she sang in her gayest way—

> "No music for me like the row-dow-dow,
> And no you h like the Captain with smart cockade."

"Yes, that's what comes of it!" said Cusack looking very grave; "if young ladies *will* be allowed to pick up with such snobs of fellows, and run after their fife and drum, they'll never be worth a pin to themselves or any one else, for they get their heads full of all sorts of wild, ridiculous notions, and can't settle their minds to anything!"

"Very true, Mr. Cusack!" said Miss Ackland, surprised herself at what seemed the strange levity of Rose's manner, although understanding, or fancying she understood, her motive, but I must beg that you will not judge Rose by her words; you do not suspect *her*," and she smiled, of "*picking up*, or *me* of allowing her to pick up, with strangers, whether in red or black coats, do you?"

"Oh! well, as for that, Miss Ackland! I wouldn't suspect *you* of anything except what was prudent and proper, but then the wisest in the world can't always have their wits about them—they're subject to make mistakes as well as others"—and he looked full at Giacomo, who sat a rather puzzled listener, not knowing exactly what to make of the conversation.

Miss Ackland smiled, but she colored, too, and was evidently a little annoyed; but too polite to seem to take a hint that she well knew was meant for her, she said—

"I think, Mr. Cusack, we had better change the subject of conversation."

"And *I* think it's about time we were going. Miss Lydia," said Mr. Brodigan rising; "what with the ghost and the red-coats, we have had quite a little stir of it. Very pleasant, and very exciting—ha! ha! I see Miss Rose is able to hold her own with you, Harry, my boy?"

"I should think she was," replied Cusack dryly, " her tongue has quite a military rattle of late."

"Thank you, Mr. Cusack!" said Rose with a smile and a very low curtsey, "I am practising *a la militaire*, you see, and it is encouraging to have your opinion that I succeed so well. Thank you, very much! Should I make up my mind to try my luck in the *Fille du Regiment*, I shall know where to apply for a reference as to capability."

More than ever bewildered by this sally, poor Cusack made no answer, though he tried to echo Brodigan's good-humored laugh as they shook hands with the ladies.

"Are we friends now, Mr. Cusack?" said Rose running after him to the parlor-door. "I am afraid you are the least bit angry with me."

"Oh! dear me! not at all, Miss Rose! why should *I* be angry?—I never was in better humor in my life."

"I'm exceedingly glad to hear it—good night then, and once again 'good night.' Happy be your dreams—*and not of Tom Cullen*," she called after him down the steps.

"You are cruel, are you not?" whispered Giacomo, as he lingered a moment after saying "good night."

"Not at all—why do you ask?"

"You remind me of a cat playing with the unfortunate mouse it has caught, and is ready to devour!"

Rose's laugh rang out clear and musical, as she almost pushed the young man down the steps—"Get you gone, Signor! you are losing all the politeness you ever had!—I a cat, seeking to devour Harry Cusack!—Mercy on us! what an idea!"

"A very natural idea!—don't you think so, Miss Ackland?"

"Not exactly as you take it, Giacomo!—playing with the mouse she may be, this naughty kitten of ours, but for any further design on its mouse-ship, I think I can acquit her of *that* piece of cruelty."

"Oh! pray don't excuse me, Aunt Lydia! pray don't—let him think as he likes of me, I shall take the same liberty with him, and think something very, very bad of him?"

"Very, very bad—will you?—how candid!—But I must hurry after the others—I should like to have the benefit of their company into town—as Miss Rose will have us all afraid of ghosts!" he added laughing, as he ran down the steps to overtake the other gentlemen. A word reached his ear as he left the side of Rose Ackland that half induced him to turn back, but he would not do what he would have found it hard to account for, so he went on his way as before.

It was old Nancy that had spoken the word, having been evidently waiting for the opportunity. "Miss Ackland dear!" said she, "if I hadn't a fright since!—there was an officer here while you were gone!" That was all Giacomo heard.

"An officer!" cried both the ladies. "What officer?"

"Och! sure myself can't tell you that, but he was a fine, tall, portly gentleman, that 'id put you in mind, Miss Lyddy, if you seen him, of—him, you know."

"Major Melville, I'm sure!" said Rose to her aunt, as the latter sank trembling on the bench in the porch.

"Major Melville!" repeated Nancy, "the gentleman you met by chance one evenin' in the spring, an' that took such a start out of you? Ah! then, I wasn't far wrong—I'm sure he's some near relation of the poor dear Captain, the darlin' o' the world he was!"

"He is his brother," said Miss Ackland, "his only brother—I may as well tell you, at once!—but what brought him here?—what did he want?—what did he say to you, Nancy?"

"Well! as for what brought him, Miss Lyddy, I can't take upon me to say,—I suppose if you had been in, he'd have tould you his business, but he didn't tell me, and for what would he?"

"But did he not speak to you?" asked Rose, on a motion from her aunt.

"Did he spake to me, is it? Well! he did, an', indeed, a fine, well-spoken gentleman he is, too!—he asked me if the old place wasn't for sale, an' when I said no, it wasn't, he said there was some house about here that he was tould *was* for sale, but he supposed he had mistaken the place."

"So, then, he *had* business, after all!" cried Rose; "I thought you said he had none."

"Did I?—Well whether or not, that's what he said; but, anyhow, we had a *shanachus*, him an' me."

"You had?" said Miss Ackland, raising herself from her half-recumbent posture, "and what about?"

"He asked me if any of the family were in, an', of course, I said no, but that there wasn't many of them now to be in or out, for the Acklands were most all gone, barrin' two ladies of them that live here all alone. 'Are they sisters,' says he.—'Why no!' says I, 'it's the aunt an' the niece; my mistress, Miss Ackland, is the daughter of the ould master, George Ackland, esquare, an' the young lady, Miss Rose, is her brother's daughter, Mr. Alexander Ackland, that was,—rest them all in pace!' So, my dears! with that he sits down there on the bench, jist about where you are now, Miss Lyddy dear, an' he claps his eyes on me mighty sharp like, an' says he—'You're old Nancy, I suppose.'—'That's my name, your honor,' says I, makin' a curchey down to the ground, to let him see that I hadn't lived so long in a gentleman's family without knowin' what manners is.—'You're a long time in this family,' says he to me.—'Your honor may say that,' says I; 'it's thirty good years, an' three or four to the back of it, since I came to mind Miss Lyddy, the darlin', that was then a little weeny one toddlin' about.' 'Do you remember a Captain Melville that used to visit here?'"

"My God!" murmured Miss Ackland, "to think of *him* putting such questions to you! But go on—go on, Nancy!"

"I will, asthore, I will!—where was I?"

"At where the Major asked you if you remembered Captain Melville," said Rose.

"Ay! that was it—to be sure, I said I did well.— 'Was it true?' said he, 'that the Captain and Miss Ackland came near being married; I have heard that there was something of that kind on foot.'—'Well!' says I, 'I don't know that it ever went so far as that; I know the Captain, the heavens be his bed! used to be a great deal here when he'd come into port, and there was ever and always a warm welcome for him when he came—but beyant that I can't say, your honor!'—Then he looked at me very hard, and says he—'Don't you think Captain Melville wanted to marry Miss Ackland?' Well! I didn't know what I had best say, then, so I paused a while, but at last I began to think that there's nothing like the truth, so I says to him—'I b'lieve he did, sir!' 'An' Miss Ackland,' he says, after musin' a while, lookin' down on the ground, I could see, though it was most dark, 'Did she—do you think she cared for—for him.'"

"Oh! Nancy, what *did* you say, then?" cried Miss Ackland, clasping her hands, and looking the pitiable anxiety she felt.

"Well! now, Miss Lyddy! whether you like it or not, I'll jist tell you what I said, bekase truth is truth, an', as I said before, there's nothing like it, after all. Says I to him, 'I b'lieve if Captain Melville had a notion of Miss Lyddy—Miss Ackland, I mane, there was no love lost between them.'—'Do you tell me so?' says he; 'why I thought she didn't care anything about him—didn't she refuse him, just when he thought he was almost sure of a favorable answer?'—'She didn't mane it, your honor,' says I back aga'n; 'it was all along of a word she said that the Cap'ain took a wrong meanin' out of, and when she seen he was so ready to take her up wrong, she got vexed that he didn't see an' know the wish she had for him, an' so she spoke to him a little short, an' he got angry, an' went away, an' she wouldn't say a word to keep him though she felt as bad as he did, an' worse, too, maybe, —but she thought he'd be back in a day or two, an' that then all 'id be made right—but ochone! that was the last she seen of him, he went away in anger, an was lost in a great storm that came on that very night.'—'And was Miss Ackland very sorry?' says he

Sorry!' says I, 'sorry!—it most broke her heart, an' I think she never got over it since.' "

"Oh Nancy!" cried Rose, "why did you tell him that?"

' Well! God help me, I didn't know what I had best say, Miss Rose, so I thought I'd tell the honest truth."

' And I am thankful that you did," said Miss Ackland, "oh! very, very thankful!—You said what you ought to say, just what I would have you say were I within hearing."

" Well! God bless you, Miss Lyddy, that's a comfort to me, anyhow!—I'd never forgive myself, never, never, if I had said anything that 'id grieve you to hear."

' I know that, Nancy! I know it well; but was that all that passed?"

" There's very little more, Miss Lyddy! When I tould the gentleman what I'm after tellin' you, he gave a heavy sigh, an' says he, as if talkin' to himself, 'Oh! that Ralph had known this in time!—'Yis, your honor,' says I, ' he might be a livin' man this day, an' himself an' my poor dear mistress as happy as the day is long together: but I suppose it wasn't their luck!'—' I suppose so,' says he, an' with that up he gets an' goes away, jist a little while before you got in. Wasn't it mighty quare, Miss Lyddy, for him to happen here in a mistake, an' get talkin' to me, an' me to see sich a likeness between him an' his brother, that's so many years dead an' gone, though not knowin' the gentleman from Adam? An' to happen on sayin' to him the very words that you'd wish me to say to Captain Melville's brother, poor simple, ignorant body that I am! Well, sure enough, strange things does happen in this world, an' that's one o' them!"

"It is, indeed, Nancy!" said Miss Ackland, now quite composed, and even cheerful,—"let us go in now and say our night-prayers. It is after nine o'clock."

Next day, early in the forenoon, Giacomo called, to say good-bye; he was going to Dublin where he had not yet been, and as his stay in Ireland was drawing to a close, he must, of course, see the metropolis before leaving.

"And when you return from Dublin," said Miss Ackland, "if you have still a few days to spare, we must take you to see Tara Hill, where the Kings of Ireland dwelt of old, and Slane, another place of historic interest, with some few more which combine both legendary and historical associations.

"And since you are so kind, my dear Miss Ackland, I should like to visit once again the place where that great battle was fought, up the river."

"Oh! you mean Oldbridge. Well! we shall go

there, too!—I will ask Mr. Brodigan to drive us there some day; I know he will be happy to do so, for he is fond of doing the honors of our old town and the classic scenes around it."

Giacomo longed to ask who the officer was that had called the day previous. He lingered in hopes that some allusion might possibly be made to the subject, but he hoped in vain; not a word was said that could tend to gratify his curiosity, and he was compelled to leave in the same state of suspense, rendered still more painful by the evident improvement in Miss Ackland's spirits;—had the officer's visit any connection with her unwonted cheerfulness? Who was the officer? could it have been Major Melville? These were the questions that troubled Giacomo's mind, and kept it in a tumult all unknown before, during the two hours' ride to the metropolis, on the top of a stage-coach—the Dublin and Drogheda Railway was then in the womb of the future, perhaps undreamed of by mortal man.

Whether he found as much to interest him in Dublin as he had hoped and expected, our friend had been only three or four days absent when he again presented himself in the parlor of the old house by the Boyne, to Miss Ackland's no small surprise, and to Rose's no small amusement.

"Well! I declare!" said Rose, "if here is not the Signor—unless it be his ghost." And she held up her hands in well-feigned amazement. "Let me look at you!—why, positively, it is himself, Aunt Lydia!"

"So I am glad to perceive, my dear! very glad indeed!"

"Well! but, where *did* you come from, Signor?"

"From the coach-office in West street," said Giacomo, a very little annoyed by her show of astonishment. "Where else did you suppose I came from, Signorina?"

"Oh! goodness knows! from Leghorn, perhaps,— or the Peak of Teneriffe, or some such outlandish place. But, seriously, what brought you back so soon? I suppose you didn't see much in Dublin to admire?"

"Well! not a great deal; and then, being all alone, I found it rather dull work driving and walking around. I got tired to death of seeing that muddiest of rivers, the Liffey, everywhere I went, and the really fine buildings on some of the quays lost half their charms for me when I saw them reflected in those turbid waters."

"Ha' ha!" laughed Rose, and she shook her head saucily; "the Liffey is very different from the Boyne. Here you see 'the purest of crystal,' as well as 'the brightest of green.'"

"But Dublin is a handsome city," observed Miss Ackland; "did you not think so, Giacomo? The squares, for instance, are very fine, and one of them, Stephen's Green, very spacious. Then the public buildings are beautiful, at least many of them. But I fear you did not wait to see much of the city, or yet of its environs."

"I confess I did not; I begin to feel as though I ought to be at home, and as I promised to spend a few days in Drogheda before leaving, I thought I would make no delay in Dublin. When can we go to Oldbridge, Miss Ackland?"

"To-morrow, if you like; as it will be Saturday—our *demi-congé*—we shall have the afternoon to ourselves, Rose and I, and we shall go this evening and see if Mr. Brodigan can come. Stay and have tea with us, and we can all go together; they will be glad to see you."

Giacomo staid, nothing loth, and as school was not yet dismissed, he went down to the river side for a quiet stroll.

When he returned it was almost tea-time; the ladies were in the garden, and thither he went to find them. There was a cloud on his usually calm brow which rather surprised the ladies, and Rose was tempted to ask what had happened, but on second thoughts she did not, and went on making up her nosegay, singing—"Love was once a hunter boy." Giacomo threw himself moodily on a rustic bench hard by.

"Miss Ackland," said he, "who do you think I met down below?"

"I am sure I cannot tell, Giacomo!—Who was it?"

"Why that Major Melville; he was riding along with another officer, and he stared at me as though I had two heads on me, or some other monstrosity.

I wonder why he honors me with so keen a scrutiny."

"Oh! my dear Giacomo, you only imagine it," said Miss Ackland in perfect good faith; "why should he look at you more than any one else?"

"That's just what I intend to ask him at our next meeting; as for my only imagining that he watches me closely, I assure you, it is no such thing, Miss Ackland. But I'm determined to know why he takes the liberty of staring at me."

"And if you do," said Rose, "he will probably tell you that *a cat may look at a king*. I advise you to let Major Melville alone."

"You do? Well! I shall not take your advice, Miss Rose, on this occasion. I shall take my own."

"Very well! do as you please!"

"You appear to know more of this gentleman, Miss Rose, than you choose to tell."

"Not I, indeed!—I never exchanged half a dozen words with him;" then she gaily carolled forth—

> "Oh if I had a beau
> For a soldier who'd go,
> Do you think I'd say no?
> No, not I."

"I wish I were a soldier," thought Giacomo, as he watched the blithe and graceful creature bounding along the old garden walks in search of her favorite flowers—"who knows what my chances might be, then!"

Nancy's voice was now heard, and her picture-like

face seen at the backdoor of the hall, announcing that tea was ready.

The meal being over, our trio proceeded, as pre-arranged, to Mr. Brodigan's, where their unexpected arrival was hailed, as usual, with sincere cordiality. Cusack was there too, and so was a certain Mr. Bellew, a new pretender to the hand of Miss Brodigan, senior; on hearing of the intended visit to O'dbridge and Donore, they both proposed to be of the party.

"Yes," said Mrs. Brodigan, never more at home than in getting up excursions, and pic-nics, and all such rural entertainments, "yes, and we'll bring our dinner with us; I'll have all ready by the time Miss Ackland gets rid of her scholars—weary on them for scholars! but it's hard to be tied down to them, especially the like of Miss Ackland and Miss Rose!"

"I appreciate your kind sympathy, my dear Mrs. Brodigan," said Miss Ackland with her grave, sweet smile, "but you must not say anything against my pupils—I assure you I was very glad to get them, and I should find it hard to get along without them. Every one cannot be rich, or the same person always in good circumstances: *we* had our turn of prosperity, and I solemnly declare I am just as happy now, and so, I am sure, is Rose. It is not fortune that either of us regrets in our past." There was a deep pathos in her voice that sufficiently conveyed her meaning, and more than one of her auditors, even those all unused to the melting mood, turned away to hide the tear that would come, to the cherished memory of him who had been as a patriarch in their genial circle.

Next day the sun shone out in the gorgeous splendor of the long mid-summer day; early in the afternoon, our party set out on their pleasant drive up the river side to the picturesque and storied heights of Oldbridge, where, for an hour or two, they wandered through those romantic scenes so suggestive of serious thought, so rich in their associations. Giacomo was delighted with all he saw; the gloomy grandeur of King William's Glen, through whose wooded depths William of Orange led himself his hardy veterans from the Rhine against the brave but ungeneralled Irish army on the opposite bank. He was shown the identical spot where Caillemote, the leader of the French Huguenots, fell descending the heights, and Duke Schomberg in mid-stream leading his command across the ford; and George Walker, famous for his defence of Derry.

"Irish gunners aimed well," said Mr. Brodigan, "and they would have taken higher aim still, only for the rascally chicken-heart that was in that James Stuart—faugh! I don't wonder at the name that Irish tongues put on him after—the poor, pitiful poltroon! You must know, Signor Giacomo, that in the thick of the battle, an Irish gunner came to tell him that he had King William under cover, and could shoot him dead in a minute, if he only gave the word. 'Oh!' says the old hen-wife of a man, 'would you leave my daughter a widow?' So the gunner did not shoot, but he fired no more, he was so disgusted."

Giacomo could not view the king's conduct in the same light as Mr. Brodigan; he thought him more entitled to respect than to censure for his tenderness of heart, but, seeing the good man so full of indignation against the unfortunate monarch, he kept his mind to himself, and turned to admire the stately Obelisk, the ornament of the Glen, hewn out of a massive rock, to commemorate the success of William's arms, and the defeat of the too chivalrous and devoted Irish who fought the battle for James, and lost it by his miserable incapacity. Giacomo sighed as he read the inscription on the Obelisk—

SACRED TO THE GLORIOUS MEMORY OF KING WILLIAM THE THIRD, &c.*

He thought of the heroic devotion of the "Popish army" mentioned in it, to a prince who, by all ac-

* Many of our readers, who have not seen, and never may see, the Boyne Obelisk, may desire to see the whole of the inscription, which is as follows:

"Sacred to the memory of King William the Third, who, on the 1st of July, 1690, crossed the Boyne near this place, to attack James the Second at the head of a Popish army, advantageously posted on the south side of it, and did on that day, by a successful battle, secure to us and our posterity our liberty, laws, and religion. In consequence of this action James the Second left this kingdom, and fled to France. This memorial of our deliverance was erected in the ninth year of the reign of George the Second, the first stone being laid by Lionel Sack-

counts, was so little worthy of the sacrifices they made for him—a prince who was not of their own blood, but belonged, on the contrary, to a race who had never given Ireland aught but promises, broken as soon as made—a prince who had nothing in common with those so faithful followers but the religion he and they professed. Yet they sacrificed all for him, those true-hearted sons of Catholic Ireland, who erred only in trusting an English *Stuart!*

It was on the hill of Donore, overlooking the Glen, on the southern or Meath side, that our party dined, just without the boundaries—walled no longer—of the ancient graveyard, from whose church, even then in ruins, King James is said by tradition to have watched the progress of the battle, and witnessed the extinction of his last hope in the final defeat of the Irish army. The scene was grand and solemn as the associations connected with it; the deep, dark glen, with its shelving sides thickly wooded, the bright river running in its midst far below, and the graceful Obelisk standing boldly out from the green woods at the lower opening of the Glen; the hill of Donore, from which our party looked down on the river and the valley, and close beside them the deserted grave-

ville, Duke of Dorset, Lord Lieutenant of the Kingdom of Ireland,

MDCCXXXVI.

This monument was erected by the grateful contributions of several Protestants of Great Britain and Ireland."—D<small>ALTON</small>'<small>S</small> *History of Drogheda.*

yard with its sunken tombs, and long-tangled grass, and the little that remains of the ancient church, pointing back to a period long anterior to the Reformation. On a tombstone near the ruins, James was said to have sat watching the terrible struggle going on below—how appropriate a seat for the fallen monarch whom even his nearest of kin had deserted!—Oh! the place was drear, and sad, and lonely; and yet it had so many attractions for Giacomo, there was such an indefinable blending of old romance and ever-youthful beauty, such a cloud of historical and legendary interest hung over the place, that he thought he could have staid there forever, provided the same company, or part of it, was there to enjoy it with him—and he, perhaps others, too, of the party, left it with regret.

# CHAPTER XV.

Those few pleasant days passed all too quickly; Giacomo came one afternoon to say that he was ordered home immediately, and he added with a smile, "Delays are never excusable with my father, so, go I must, without fail."

Miss Ackland, summoned from the school-room to receive his visit, expressed herself much disappointed; "I had planned so much," said she, "and have accomplished so little in the way of entertaining you, and now it is all over!"

"My dear, kind friend," the young man replied with unwonted emotion, "it was the best of all entertainments to me to come and go here at pleasure, to enjoy, when I would, the calm delight of a quiet evening in your society, and that of—of Miss Rose."

"And yet," said Miss Ackland smiling, "I am afraid Rose gave you some annoyance of late by her girlish waywardness."

"None but what I could easily overlook—in her."

"You are very kind and very indulgent," said Miss Ackland; "oh! how much I shall miss you!"—and her eyes filled with tears—"somehow, it seemed to me as though you were a sort of link between me and some long-lost phase of my existence that was pleasant while it lasted,—what it was that attracted me to you I never could satisfactorily explain to myself,—but there was something from the very first,—something, I fancy, like what mothers feel for very dear children—only not quite so strong, I suppose!" and she smiled through her tears.

"It is very strange," said Giacomo, after a short pause, "that I have been attracted to you, my kindest, dearest friend, in just the same way, and, like you, I have many a time tried to explain it to myself, but never could succeed. Would that your country was mine, or mine yours!"

"Wishes are vain, my dear young friend,—we must only resign ourselves to the hard necessity that places broad seas between us! We cannot have things as we would wish in this probationary world! Should you not like to see Rose?"

"Certainly I should—just for a moment, to say good-bye;—if Miss Rose can be spared so long from the school-room." A scarcely perceptible smile accompanied these last words, but Miss Ackland was gone, and, of course, did not perceive it.

A minute or two after Rose made her appearance;—she looked just as usual, only better, Giacomo thought, in the plain mourning-calico dress which she wore in the school-room, with the prettiest and tiniest of black silk aprons. She was perfectly calm, even subdued in her demeanor—her school-room manner, Giacomo said to himself.

"So you are really going home, Signor?" she said on entering.

"Yes, my father wishes me to return as soon as possible."

"And I suppose we shall see you here no more?" still more calmly than before.

"I really cannot say as to that; if it should be so, the sorrow, fortunately, will be all my own."

"Pray do not say so, Signor Giacomo!" said Rose with unwonted earnestness; "you know, I am sure, how much my aunt likes to have you near her, and how she, at least, will miss you!"

"She has been good enough to tell me so—and, indeed, I shall miss her."

He paused a moment, walked to the window, and returned to where he had been standing, then looked full in Rose's face. "Should we never meet again, Signorina, I wish you to understand that you have my best wishes for your happiness; if you are as happy in the future as I wish you, you need desire no more."

"Dear me! what a solemn affair you make of it!" exclaimed Rose, in a tone of good-natured raillery; "I'm sure I never doubted your good wish to all our family, Signor Giacomo! and I'm sure we all wish you just as well as you do us. But where's the use of making your good-bye so tragical?—I suppose we shall meet again some day!"

"Are you ever sorry to part with any one, Miss Rose?"

"Mercy on me! what a question!" and the girl burst into one of her light-hearted fits of laughter. "I declare you grow stranger and stranger every day! Of course I do feel sorry to part with people once in a while, that is——"

"Suppose it were Major Melville who was going, instead of me?"

"Oh! that would be quite another thing," Rose quickly replied, and a smile of peculiar meaning curved her lip, and brightened her eyes; "you have no right to inquire what my feelings would be in such case made and provided. It would be something very dreadful to part with Major Melville——ahem! Dear me! it would be shocking!—But I am waiting too long—I hear my young subjects becoming noisy, they are sure to take advantage of my absence!—good-bye, Signor!" and she frankly and kindly, yet unconcernedly, held out her hand, which the young man took abstractedly as one but half conscious—"good-bye! give my love to Maddalena, and my—respect—to your father!" she could not repress a smile, for she had almost said *fear* instead of *respect*. "Good-bye! and I wish you a pleasant and safe voyage home."

Her aunt came in at the moment, and Rose was in her place in the school-room before Giacomo had recovered from his bewilderment. A hasty shake-hands with Miss Ackland; a cordially expressed hope from her that they might soon meet again—an affectionate message for his sister,—a civil one for his father, and Giacomo left the old house by the Boyne, with feelings that he could scarcely define, even to himself. He had reached the top of the steps when he heard Nancy at the hall-door calling after him, and stopped till she overtook him.

"Ah! then, Mister Jacomy," she cried all breathless with the race she had had from the kitchen when Miss Ackland told her Giacomo was gone; "ah then, is it goin' away without seein' *me* you'd be? Dear knows but that's bad *shanagh*, for it's not what *I'd* do to *you*, Mister Jacomy!"

"Do, pray, excuse me, Nancy!" said the young man, kindly shaking her by the hand; "I know I should have asked for you, but somehow I forgot it at the last moment. I should be sorry, indeed, to forget *you!* No one that knows you so well as I do would willingly forget you leaving here!"

This mollified the old woman. "Well, someway or another," said she, "all the quality that ever comes back and for'ads here does take notice of me. Didn't Major Melville, even, ask me if I wasn't 'old Nancy?' —he did, indeed!"

"Major Melville!" said Giacomo, with a sudden flash of recollection, "so he was the officer who called here on St. John's Eve?"

"To be sure—who else would it be?" said Nancy in her desire to exalt the family importance.

"Was that his first visit?"

"In coorse it was—but," and Nancy lowered her voice to a confidential tone, and looked mysterious—"but—

he had met *the ladies before*—an' though he came all as one as thinkin' the house was for sale—it wasn't that, at all, that brought him—I seen that as plain as a pike-staff." Then approaching the young man, very near, she said in an emphatic whisper—" *He jist wanted an excuse to get in!*'—that was it!—But, my goodness! don't let on that I was tellin' you, for Miss Ackland is so very partick'lar, she mightn't be pleased at me!—Well, God be with you. I must hurry in, for this is my washin' day, an' I'm very busy! I hope you'll be back soon!"

Poor old Nancy! little she knew, as she bent again over her wash-tub, the effect of her well-meaning gossip on him who heard it! Strange to say, it quickened his step, and dispelled the sadness that was weighing his heart down, and sent forth a new man, with a new heart, as he said himself, to battle with the storms of life. A new spirit had come into him, and though he went not on his way rejoicing, he walked with a firmer step, and a prouder mien, looking the future sternly in the face, and resolved to forget the warm visions of the past before entering on the cold realities of his coming life. Doubt and fear had now given place to certainty in a matter near and dear to his heart, and he haughtily, defiantly, cast away the hope that had gilt many an hour of his life during the past months!

He left Drogheda on the following day, not without hearing Mass at early morning in the High Lane Chapel, almost in the shadow of Lawrence's Gate, and there offering up his prayers with the simple piety of a true Italian for those he was leaving, perhaps forever. The Madonna, his own Madonna, looked down on him with her sweet, motherly eyes from the ancient wall of the humble temple, and he bowed his head before her as he used to do when a little child in his far Tuscan home, and asked her maternal blessing and her powerful aid in the trials and troubles that might still await him in a life that as yet had been smooth and tranquil. Then he went forth more hopeful, more resigned, and bade a cheerful farewell to the friends who went to see him off, thinking the while of poor Jemmy Nulty, whom he should see no more on earth, and breathing a prayer which he almost felt to be superfluous, for the pilgrim's soul.

Miss Ackland missed her young friend even more than she had anticipated; she often spoke of him, and always in terms of praise, regretting that they had seen so much of him only to lose his society when she, at least, had learned to value it most.

"I feel precisely towards him," she would say, "as though he were a near and dear relation. We see so few like him, now-a-days,—he is so gentle in his ways, so kind and so considerate, so refined, too, in his sentiments."

Rose shrugged her shoulders; she was not quite so great an admirer of the Signor as her aunt, so she said; the young man was pretty fair and might pass in a crowd, but she really did not see what her aunt saw in him to make her rate him so highly To

Nancy she talked in the same strain of Giacomo, when his name came up, and sometimes got a sharp rebuff for the same from the warm-hearted old woman who could never bear to hear any one she loved spoken lightly of. At such times Rose would laugh merrily, and say, "Why, you don't expect, Nancy, that every one should think as much of your 'Mister Jacomy' as you do? every one is free to have their opinion, you know!" But from a spirit of contradiction she would herself introduce the subject, enjoying of all things the annoyance her want of appreciation of Giacomo gave the old woman.

It was one gray, soft evening in the early part of August, and Miss Ackland stood on the esplanade with a gentleman who had been paying her a visit and was now leaving. He was a priest, that was plain, though his black, clerical coat was of the rustiest, and his whole appearance that of a man who had little to boast of on the score of wealth. He was rather stout built, and would have been tall were it not for a slight stoop that took somewhat from his height. His face was rather sallow, and far from handsome, but its expression was so benignant, there was such a simplicity of look, and air, and gesture about the man, and such an unmistakeable air of humility withal, that you said to yourself as you looked upon him—"There is a man who though in this world is not of it;" then you looked again and found yet other peculiarities to admire, and most of all the happy, contented smile, the ineffable smile that was the light beaming from within—the light of a good conscience, and a heart whose affections were in heaven, safe from the jarring elements of passion and all wordliness. It was Father O'Regan, the piritual director of Miss Ackland and also of Rose, as he had been of her grandfather during all the latter years of his life.

Father O'Regan was well acquainted with the family history of the Acklands; he had been the adviser and consoler of Lydia in all her worst troubles, and none knew so well as he the grief that had preyed on her heart for so many weary years, and the self-reproach that embittered her life. It had been his constant care to combat this feeling, and to persuade her that she was not so much to blame as her acute sensibility and her tender conscience led her to suppose.

They had been talking now on the same painful subject—painful to one of the two, but nothing was ever painful to Father O'Regan,—at least, if anything *did* trouble him, no one ever saw it by his outward bearing—the tranquil smile was ever on his face, meet him when you might, like one whose life was half in heaven, and scarcely half on earth. Dear old friar! humble, simple, happy, contented son of St. Francis! true lover of evangelical poverty, how far above the world's pomps and the world's vanities, which to him were less than a dream—the shadow of a shade—the echo of a voice—something seen far off as in a dream, with no hold on his heart, and having no other in terest for him than its power of affecting his fellow creatures for good or ill!

"My dear child!" said Father O'Regan, "you have borne up well;—you have, indeed!—our dear Lord has given you many graces, if it has pleased Him to give you many trials. Yet a little longer, my daughter! yet a little longer; light will break through the darkness, and you shall see the perfect day! Courage, my child, courage!"

"Ah! but, Father O'Regan, it is hard to have courage when hope is gone, and the weary heart fainting beneath its life-long load!"

The Franciscan turned full on the lady;—"And why should hope be gone?—isn't God as powerful as ever, and as good and kind?—if hope is a divine virtue, what has it to do with the poor little pitiful troubles of this world? Does it not take a higher flight, and look forward to eternity? Don't talk of losing hope, then, or I'll not be pleased with you; indeed I will not!"

"I wish, father! I could only raise my heart as far above earthly things as you do, and apparently without an effort. You do not know how much it costs me to keep my poor human heart in subjection to the promptings of divine grace.'

"I do know it, my child, but I know, too, that your merit will be all the greater—greater far than mine, for instance, because I care nothing about the world"—the smile grew brighter on his face—"nothing at all, at all! God pity them that do, and *I* pity them from my heart out!"

"You often remind me, Father O'Regan, of what an English poet lately wrote of the monks of old?"

"Indeed?" said the friar with simple curiosity—"and what was that, my child?"

> "I envy them, those monks of old,
> Their books they read, and their beads they told,
> To human softness dead and cold
> And all life's vanity."

Father O'Regan scarcely ever disturbed his equanimity so far as to laugh, but he almost laughed then, with a sort of childish glee,—"Just so, just so," he said, nodding his head in assent to the words—"only why did he say that they were 'to human softness dead and cold'—if they were, it's queer monks they'd be, an' it's queer monks we'd be, too, without 'human softness.' Where would charity be, and where would piety be without human softness, for I suppose that means feeling and tender-heartedness. No! that gentleman didn't know either the monks of old, or any other monks, or he wouldn't say that of them? Wasn't the blessed and holy St. Francis one of the tenderest-hearted men that ever lived, and didn't he leave that same love of God and men as a legacy to all his children in religion? So I object to any one saying, my dear, that monks, old or new, are dead to 'human softness,' and do you never say it again, my child! Poets write a great deal of nonsense, and that's some of it. But have you seen Major Melville of late?"

"Not since his strange colloquy with Nancy. None of us has seen him since. He must be a singular man Don't you think so, father?"

"Well, then, I do, but, after all, he may have reasons for what he does that you or I doesn't know. I have a great mind to go and see him some day. He is a Catholic, is he not?—I know his brother was."

"Oh! of course he is; it is not very likely that he has fallen away from the faith, for I have heard poor Ralph say that their mother was very pious, and I know *he* had a great devotion to the Blessed Virgin. Oh father! I used to hope that she would protect him in his perilous profession and save him from a sudden death. And as soon as I heard of his having gone to sea that last sad time, I commended him specially to her safe keeping. Was it not hard to find that, my strongest, surest hope, so cruelly disappointed?"

"Well! it was, in one sense, my child, but in another sense it was not; he might never have died in a better time, and you may be sure our Holy Mother would not have suffered him to perish, then, only, she knew he was fit to die. Don't be dwelling on these thoughts, my child, don't now, and God bless you!—What can't be cured must be endured, you know. So resign yourself perfectly to the holy will of God, and don't be tormenting yourself with things so long past. Remember my words—*No one ever trusted in our good Mother, without feeling the effects of it.*"

"I have never for a moment doubted that, father!—You know the *Memorare* is, and has been my favorite prayer."

"Very good; keep to that, my child! and peace will come down on your soul at last, and the clouds will vanish from your mind, like the shades of night before the rising sun. I'll be going now, my dear! So you'll say good-bye for me to Rose, and be sure to keep up your heart. God is good, and so is our holy Mother—good and kind, and very powerful! Good-bye!"

"Good-bye, father!"

Miss Ackland stood and watched the good friar in his descent of the long flight of steps; she thought of all the long years she had known him, the admirable simplicity of heart, the tender charity and entire detachment from the world which distinguished him even amongst his brother religious, and she said to herself—"Wonderful is the power of religion!—What but it could form such a character as that—so wise, yet so simple; so high above the world, yet so meek and humble of heart. Truly, such as he *are* 'the good odor of Christ!'—Happy, oh! how happy it is to serve God so lovingly, and so sincerely!"

Half unconsciously she seated herself on the bench near the door, and resting her head against the trellised porch, she fell into a fit of abstraction, thinking of nothing in particular, but of many things in general, with that dreamy sense of repose so dear to the world-weary heart, which the shades of evening often bring. She might have been thinking of Ralph Melville, for he was seldom absent from her mind, at least for any length of time, but whether his image was then before her mental vision or not, she suddenly beheld with the eyes of her body a figure which she instantly recognized as his, walk towards her across the esplanade as if from the top of the steps, pause a moment almost in front of her, at the distance of a few feet, fixing his eyes on her with a pleased expression, then walk slowly past her and into the house, through the hall-door which lay wide open, as it often did those sultry summer evenings.

So great was the shock of this apparition, that Miss Ackland was struck motionless and speechless; with straining eyes she watched the door, hoping that the welcome visitor might reappear, disembodied spirit though he was; but instead of him came Rose, wondering much at her aunt's delay.

"Dear me, aunt! are you all alone?" she exclaimed; "why I didn't think Father O'Regan was gone; I saw him here only a few minutes ago! But, my goodness, Aunt Lydia! what's the matter? why, you look like death!"

"Do I?" said her aunt, partially recovering from her stupor. "Well! no wonder,—Ralph Melville has been here since Father O Regan left."

"Ralph Melville! good gracious, aunt, you frighten me to death!—don't talk so, I beg of you!"

"But, I tell you, Rose, he was here—I saw him as plain as I see you now—he crossed the esplanade, and stopped a moment just there"—rising and showing the spot—"he looked at me with his old, old smile, and passed on into the house,—just a moment or two before you came out. Oh Rose, how happy I feel to have seen him—for he looked as though he were at rest—oh! that I were too!—but I shall be, in God's good time!"

"My dear aunt," said Rose soothingly, "you must have imagined it; I suppose you had been thinking of Captain Melville."

"No, I do not remember that I was, at that particular moment; but, Rose, there was no imagination in it,—I saw him distinctly, and I only wish that you had been with me, for then you might have seen him, too!"

"Heaven forbid!" said Rose with a shudder, and she cast a timid glance around through the gathering gloom. "Had we not better go in, Aunt Lydia?"

"As you please, my dear!" And they went in. "Oh! Rose," said Miss Ackland, pausing a moment in the doorway; "to think that *he* passed in here within the last five minutes!"

"I don't want to think of it," said Rose shortly; "I'd rather see the living any day than the dead. Come now, and I'll play something very lively for you, just to put this strange fancy out of your head."

"No need to do that, my dear! that strange fancy, as you call it, is more cheering to me than your livefiest music; I only wish I could often have such fancies! but why should I hope it? why should the spirit-land be opened to me more than others?"

It was not Miss Ackland's intention to tell Nancy of what she had seen that evening, but she forgot to warn Rose on the subject, and before noon next day, Nancy was in full possession of the whole affair. Her mistress was no little surprised when the old woman went out to her in the garden where she had gone to gather some flowers for her table in the school-room, and asked her in a tone of great trepidation, if it was true that she had seen the poor dear Captain the evening before.

Miss Ackland started and turned pale; she was shocked to hear *his* name mentioned in such a way, and was sorry that Nancy knew of what had occurred, but she could not prevaricate when a plain question was put to her, and she said—"I did, Nancy!"

"You did!—The Lord save us!"

"Would *you* be afraid to see him, Nancy?" said the lady in a tone of gentle reproach that brought the tears to Nancy's eyes.

"Well! now, don't blame me, Miss Lyddy, darlin'!—I had a great wish for him entirely when he was flesh and blood like myself, but the nearest an' dearest I ever had in the world, I wouldn't want to see them when they're dead!—it's hard to stand the sight of a sperit—did you look him in the face, Miss Lyddy!"

"Yes, and he looked me in the face—why do you ask!"

Nancy groaned and shook her head, before she replied—" Well! the Lord save you an' every one else from harm, they say a body never gets the better of it that meets the eyes of the dead, or hears their voice. You didn't spake to it, did you?"

" No! I wish I had!"

" Don't wish any sich a thing, then,—don't, an' God bless you!"

Miss Ackland smiled sadly, as she laid her hand on Nancy's arm;—

" I thank you for your good advice, Nancy!—but I will give you another:—be sure you say nothing of this to any one!"

" Is it me, Miss Lyddy?—is it me tell any one that the Captain, rest his sowl! is comin' back again!—do you think I'd make so little of him or you either,—an' have people sayin' that the house was haunted!—do you think I'd be so foolish as all that comes to, Miss Lyddy?"

" No, I scarcely thought you would; but it is no harm to put you on your guard, you know! You'd better go in now to your ironing."

Still Nancy lingered, and at last Miss Ackland asked her had she anything more to say to her.

" Oh! not a thing, Miss Lyddy dear!" She moved a few steps away, then turned back, and said in a hesitating sort of way—

" Wouldn't it be well to get Father O'Regan to come an' say a Mass in the house?"

" What for pray?"

'Oh well! it 'id do no harm anyhow, and maybe it 'id do good!'

"Go to your work, Nancy!" said Miss Ackland so sharply that poor Nancy's heart sank within her; the tears were in her eyes as she took her way back to the kitchen, and her voice was not heard all day in the house. Miss Ackland spoke to her no more on the subject; nor to Rose, either, though it annoyed her more than a little to see that both were more timid than usual in moving around the house after nightfall, and could scarcely be got to go out of doors alone. For herself, she had grown fond of walking at night in the garden, or on the esplanade, especially when the moon shed her mild rays over the earth, and the world lay still in the hush of night beneath the glittering stars. But Ralph Melville came not again; days and weeks passed away; August glided into September, and the beautiful harvest moon showed her pale crescent in the blue sky of evening; but in vain did Lydia Ackland keep her lone watch "beneath the stars." Ralph Melville's ghost did *not* revisit the glimpses of the moon, and Nancy felt quite convinced that their prayers had won for his troubled spirit peace eternal. "Well, now, Miss Rosy," she would say to Rose, in confidence, when the twain were stealthily exchanging their fears and hopes touching the ghost, "I'm in great hopes that he's in a fair way now of gettin' to rest; how could he miss of it, the dear gentleman! on' all the prayers *I* say for him, not to say you an'

Miss Lyddy? Please God, he'll never trouble us any more!"

"I'm sure I hope so, Nancy!" would Rose reply and there the whispered consultation would end for that time, to be renewed at the first opportunity. It was, however, a continual source of trouble and of serious apprehension to Nancy that a Mass had not been said in the house, and she was free to give her opinion (only to Rose, of course,) that "there was something comin' over Miss Lyddy, God help her! when she wouldn't so much as hear to havin' Father O'Regan say Mass in the house. If only herself was in it, a body mightn't wonder so much, but she ought to remember that there was others in it that didn't want to see a sperit in any shape or form.'

## CHAPTER XVI.

A MONTH or so after Giacomo's departure, the Brodigans, father and daughters, came one evening to Miss Ackland's, the father, as usual, with the kind intention of cheering the aunt and niece in the solitude from which he and his amiable wife could not draw them so often as they wished, the daughters with a little private object of their own which the reader will presently ascertain. There was music, as usual, and Rose sang at her aunt's request, with her guitar, a pretty ballad just then new and popular—long since passed into the realm of things forgotten, beginning thus—

> "Do you ever think of me, love,
> Do you ever think of me,
> When I'm far away from thee, love,
> With my bark upon the sea?
> My thoughts are ever turning
> To thee where'er I roam,
> And my heart is ever yearning
> For the quiet scenes of home."

"How very sweet!" lisped Jane Brodigan in her sentimental way, "and how expressively you do sing it, Rose!—Talking of being 'far away,' have you heard, Miss Ackland, that our handsome Leghorner has been taking a wife to himself?"

"Why no!—can it be possible?"

"Why should it not be possible, my dear Miss Ackland?" said Ann, with somewhat more than her wonted stiffness; "it is very natural, I presume, that Signor Giacomo Malvili would marry one time or another,—most young men do."

"Yes, but somehow I thought—I thought *he* had no idea of being married so soon—and if it were so I thought he would let *me* know of it."

"Oh! of course, you would expect that," said Miss Brodigan, in a somewhat softer tone; she and every one else *liked* Miss Ackland, even those who could not fully appreciate her; "considering your kindness to him,—but people are not always as grateful as they should be."

"Very true, my dear! but I cannot believe that Giacomo is one of those who are likely to forget friends or friendship."

"Believe what you may," said Ann, drawing herself up, "I have reason to think that the report is true."

"But how did you come to hear of it, Ann?" said her father, who had heard the news with much surprise.

"That is of no importance, father! We have it on good authority. Haven't we, Jane?"

"Oh! decidedly, the very best and most reliable. But, my dear Rose! how very silent you are. You do not seem at all surprised."

Rose had gone to the piano, and was busily engaged looking over her music for a piece she wanted. She answered without interrupting her employment— "Surprised! why should I be surprised?—As if it was any wonder to hear of a wedding! I thought I should hear of one soon! Dear me! where *can* that Overture to *Tancredi* be? Aunt! did you see it lately?"

"No, my dear! I have not been arranging the music for some days. But, my dear Miss Brodigan! do you think it is really true that Giacomo is married?"

"I really cannot say, Miss Ackland!—I can only repeat that we have the news from good authority."

"Who is that, Ann?" said her father.

"Tom Lanigan, father!—you know *he* wouldn't be likely to tell a falsehood."

"I know that, but how did *he* hear it? Who told him?'

"Well! I really didn't ask—only he had reason to think it was true, I know he wouldn't repeat it."

"It is very strange," said Miss Ackland, in a sort of soliloquizing tone; "it was one of the last things I should have expected to hear."

"Oh! here is *Tancredi*," said Rose, "and, Mr. Brodigan, here is another favorite of yours, 'Miss Forbes' Farewell to Banff,' with variations. I will play that first." And she took her seat at the piano.

"Don't you want light?" said Ann Brodigan, taking a girandole from the mantel-piece, and placing it on the piano, looking full in Rose's face as she did so.

"Thank you, Ann," said Rose very quietly, "you are always so very considerate."

"Isn't the light too strong for you, Rose? You look as though you had a head-ache."

"Oh! dear me, no! I have no head-ache. Thank you, that will do."

"Don't you want me to turn over the leaves?"

"It is quite unnecessary, I know the piece so well."

Ann Brodigan resumed her seat, glancing at her sister with an expression that seemed to say—"I really can't understand her. Can you?"

When Rose had finished, Mr. Brodigan said, rising—"Come, girls, let us be off. Your mother will be alone, for the young ones are all a-bed by this time." It was early to leave, but the young ladies made no objection, so they all bade good night and retired.

When they were gone, Miss Ackland and Rose sat together for a few moments in silence; by some impulse perhaps scarcely known to herself, Rose moved nearer to her aunt and looked inquiringly in her face. Miss Ackland laid her hand on her head and smiled in her gentle, quiet way, a little abstractedly, Rose thought.

"Aunt!" said Rose at length, "do you think Signor Giacomo is really married?"

"He may be, Rose!—But if so, it is not what I would expect. I think he would let us know if any such thing were in contemplation."

"Perhaps yes,—perhaps no," said Rose carelessly.—"how much longer do you intend to sit up, Aunt

Lydia?—I feel tired and drowsy—I think I will go to bed."

"Very well, Rose! ring for Nancy, and we will get our prayers said, then you can go."

When the prayers were over, Miss Ackland said she would read a while, before going up stairs, so Rose took her night-light and left the room. Closing the parlor door after her, she went softly to the kitchen, and asked Nancy if she was very much hurried just then.

"Well no! do you want me to do anything, Miss Rosey?"

"Only to come up and sit with me," said Rose almost in a whisper; "my aunt is not coming up just yet, and I don't like to be up there all alone. You know that's the room Captain Melville used to sleep in, any time he was here overnight."

"I know, dear! I know," and Nancy nodded and looked solemn; "I don't care to go into that room myself after nightfall. I'll go with you in a minute, when I fasten the doors and windows down here."

So the doors and windows being made fast, the two stole past the parlor door and up stairs. Nancy squatted herself on the carpet while her young lady prepared for bed, talking the while of all the pleasant days she used to have when the old house was blithe and merry, and the dead alive, and the careworn and sorrowful young and gay. But she carefully avoided mentioning *one name*, and when she had even the most distant allusion to make to him who had borne it, Rose stopped her with a terrified "Hush!" and both looked fearfully round into those corners of the large room where the light did not fully penetrate. It might have been expected that Rose would have told her faithful old confidant of the news Miss Brodigan had brought, but for once she kept something to herself, and said not a word about it, probably forgetting it altogether in the engrossing interest with which she listened to Nancy's reminiscences of old-time life in the old house.

A door was heard closing down stairs, and Rose who was now in bed, made a sign for Nancy to hurry away; Nancy was not slow in obeying, both having an instinctive fear of Miss Ackland's noticing their newly-awakened fears concerning the ghost. But Miss Ackland, coming up stairs at the time, saw Nancy stealing along the corridor, though Nancy did not see her, and guessing at once how matters stood, she could not help laughing, though her heart was heavy with the thoughts that ever weighed on her mind when alone.

Next day was Saturday, and when, at one o'clock, the school was dismissed, Miss Ackland proposed to Rose that they should walk down to see Mabel, whom they had not seen for some weeks. They sat long with the old woman, whom they found, as they often did, all alone in the cottage; she had strange news for them—Major Mellville had been to visit her, a day or two before, and had given her a bright gold sovereign, which she showed with a sort of hesitation, as though she were half afraid that, like the fairy gifts of her own stories, it might turn into some meaner substance for the showing. But the gold was " good red gold," and proof against all chances, and there was no getting over so substantial a proof that Major Melville had really found old Mabel out, though how he did so, or from what motive, even Miss Ackland's keen wits could not imagine.

Like one in a dream, she rose and left the cottage, barely bidding Mabel good-bye, and Rose followed quickly, telling the old woman that they would soon come again. When they had walked a little way, Miss Ackland said to Rose:

" What *can* this mean? I cannot understand it. How came Guy to know anything of Mabel, and why should he go to see her?"

" It is very odd, Aunt Lydia!" said Rose with a more thoughtful air than usual; " he is certainly a strange man, though he does not look so," she added as if to herself. Then both were silent.

It was one of those rich mellow evenings which the autumn only brings, when the whole earth and the boundless fields of air are a-glow with gold and crimson, and nor cloud nor cloudlet skims the surface of heaven's bright glorious sea. The Boyne rippled past with a gentle tremulous motion,

" The waters calm reflecting bright,
The golden glory of the light,"

and the fair scene around was a picture of tranquil beauty; but, each absorbed in her own thoughts, the aunt and niece little heeded the smile that nature wore, and few words passed between them till they came to their own gate, when both screamed with surprise; it was opened by Giacomo, who had evidently been awaiting their coming

"Why, Giacomo, is it, can it be possible?" cried Miss Ackland, as she warmly shook him by the hand.

"Very possible, indeed, Miss Ackland; you see I am back sooner than I expected."

"Why did you come?" said Rose abruptly and carelessly, as though little heeding what she said. She had stumbled going up the first steps, and Giacomo offered his arm, which she, however, declined with a grave bow.

Giacomo smiled at the question; it was so characteristic: "An event of some importance to myself and one other, at least, has given me an opportunity that I did not dare to expect."

"Oh! indeed?" said Rose quickly; "I guessed as much."

"You did; and pray what did you guess?"

Before Rose could answer her aunt spoke—"So it is true, then, what we heard?"

"That I cannot tell you, my dear Miss Ackland, till you have told me what it was that you heard."

They had reached the top of the steps, and the word on Miss Ackland's lips was changed into an exclamation of surprise. A strain of music came from the house, through the open windows of the front parlor—a female voice low and sweet singing to the tinkling sound of the guitar; both the ladies stopped short and looked at each other in amazement——

"She is here, then?" said Rose, turning full on Giacomo.

"Who is here?"

"Your wife."

"My wife!" he repeated, with a start of surprise; he paused a moment, then said laughing, "Oh! of course!—you wouldn't have me come without her, would you?"

The hall-door was open, and Miss Ackland was already at the parlor door which she hastily threw open, and stood looking as if spell-bound at a slight, delicate-looking, and very lovely girl who laid down the guitar and arose to meet her.

"Miss Ackland!" said a gentle voice with a strong foreign accent, and the young lady advanced like one who was sure of a cordial greeting.

But Miss Ackland spoke not; she stood with her eyes fixed on the fair girl's face, her whole frame trembling, and her pale cheek paler still. When Giacomo came near where she stood, she caught him by the arm and hoarsely whispered—"Who is she?"

"His wife!" said Rose, making her way into the room.

"My sister!" said Giacomo, with a proud, fond look at the graceful, fawn-like creature who stood waiting in her gentle beauty for the embrace of her brother's friend.

"Your sister!—Maddalena?"

"Yes, Maddalena!—my own, my only sister!"

No mother ever welcomed a long-absent child to her bosom more tenderly than Miss Ackland did that fair and gentle girl, to whom her innermost heart was at once thrown open, and for life; again and again she pressed her to her heart, and kissed her white forehead with all the warmth of affection. Rose, smiling through the tears of joy that filled her eyes, reminded her aunt that it was her turn then, and half reluctantly, as it seemed, Miss Ackland resigned Maddalena to her sisterly embrace, whilst Giacomo walked to the window to hide his emotion.

"Dear me!' said Rose, as she wiped away her tears, "who'd have thought it?—oh' you naughty, naughty Signor!" shaking her little hand at Giacomo, "how dare you play such a trick on us?"

"Trick! what trick did I play? Did I tell you I was married, or that Maddalena was my wife?'

"Well! no, I believe you did not—but then you allowed us to think so."

"I knew of old that there would be little use in trying to restrain *your* thoughts, Miss Rose!"

"Or my tongue, either, I suppose you would say! How very polite your brother is, Signora Maddalena!"

"Polite! oh yes, Giacomo is very polite," and the sister smiled fondly on her brother; she took Rose's compliment in good faith.

Miss Ackland seemed scarcely conscious of what was passing; she was watching Maddalena with an expression of eager curiosity on her calm face; at length she asked Giacomo who his sister was like.

"I believe she resembles my father," he replied, "as I do my mother. Maddalena has my father's complexion,—a very fair one, as you may perceive, and very uncommon amongst our country people."

"Then your father must be handsome?" said Rose, at which Giacomo smiled, and Maddalena eagerly replied in her sweet, simple, earnest way—

"Oh yes! my father is handsome, very, very handsome."

"So you say, *mia cara*," said Giacomo smiling, then turning to Miss Ackland he added, "you see my little sister has an extraordinary good opinion of her father and brother!—I believe she thinks nobody ever had such a father and brother as she has."

"Dear child!" said Miss Ackland, smoothing down the girl's fair tresses.

"But you don't ask me," said Giacomo, "why Maddalena came?"

"No," said Miss Ackland, "it is sufficient for us to know that she is here."

"Yes, but you ought to know why she came. My father is anxious that she should spend some time with you, as a pupil, my dear Miss Ackland!—he wishes her to prosecute her English studies, in which she is rather backward. She is to speak, or write nothing but English. Will you take her as a boarder and a pupil?"

"As a friend, as a daughter—as your sister, Giacomo!" And again Miss Ackland kissed Maddalena's fair brow, and welcomed her to Drogheda, apologizing for not having done so before.

"And now, Rose," said she, "you will take Maddalena up stairs; she can share your room for the present, as she might be lonely in a strange house, and I will resign you to her."

"The very thing," said Rose joyfully; "come along Maddalena! Oh! how happy I am to have a companion of my own age!" she added as they went up stairs arm in arm. "Do you know, Maddalena, I never had one before."

"Nor I, any more," said Maddalena in her imperfect English; "ever since my mother is dead, I have only my father and Giacomo for company."

"Oh! I was not so bad as that—my mother died, it is true, when I was very young, but I have always had my dear aunt; still I have often wished for a younger and gayer companion, for Aunt Lydia is, at times, in poor spirits, and then I find it very dull in this old house of ours."

"Oh! it is a dear old house; I like it before I see it, because my brother, he like it, oh! very much."

"Indeed?"

"Yes, indeed; better than our own at home, I think; he wanted so much to come back, but he would not ask my father; and he was glad, so glad I cannot tell you when my father he tell him to take me here."

"And were you glad?"

"Yes, I was glad, too; I wanted so much to see Miss Ackland, my brother's Miss Ackland—and you, too, Signora Rosa!"

"Don't call me Signora—call me Rose—you see I call you Maddalena."

"Very well! I will do it as you say. I wanted much, very much, to see you and Miss Ackland—and old Nancy. I wanted to see your cat, too—your cat Tabby, you know—but Giacomo told me she was dead, poor cat! And old Nancy, when I speak of her, she nearly cry, before you came in."

In such a pleasant chat the girls passed the time, sitting by a window, till Miss Ackland came up to say that tea was ready, and they all three went down together. How pleasant it was when they took their seats around the table in the early twilight of September's last days, Maddalena at Miss Ackland's right hand, opposite Rose and Giacomo for the fourth at the small square table, all around, so neat, so *cozy*, as Rose said, and the evening star shedding its faint silvery light into the apartment, through an opening in the purple clouds that were draping the western sky in regal splendor.

"What a beautiful star!" said Giacomo, pointing to the fair planet.

"Perhaps our dear father sees it now, Giacomo?" asked his sister. "I am sorry he is all alone."

"You are a good girl, Maddalena!" said Miss Ackland, who followed with increasing interest the words and ways of her interesting visitor. "I see you are not disposed to forget the absent. Don't you think, Giacomo, that your father will miss Maddalena very much?"

"Oh! I dare say he will, but only for a little while; I am not sure that he would miss any one for very long."

"Oh! Giacomo, how can you say so?" cried his sister, her delicate cheek all a-glow; " that is not right. My father will be sad, very sad for you and me. I know he will."

"So much the worse for him, then, *mia cara*," said Giacomo carelessly, as he finished his tea. "Miss Ackland, shall we not go out on the esplanade? it is a pity to be in-doors such a lovely evening."

The proposal was agreeable to all, but as the evening was chill Rose ran up stairs to fetch some muffling; Nancy came in just then to remove the tea-things, and when her eyes fell on the Italian girl whom she had only seen before with her bonnet on and her back to the light—she started, looked at Miss Ackland, and came near dropping the tray she had lifted from the table.

"What's the matter, Nancy?" inquired Giacomo, noticing her agitation.

"Oh! nothing," said Miss Ackland, endeavoring to catch her eye; "she is subject to fits of nervous excitement."

"Fits, Miss Lyddy! is it me subject to fits?" said the old woman somewhat testily; "no, nor the sorra fit ever *I* was subject to. It's the likeness I see in that young lady—Master Jacomy's sister there, that put me a little through-other.* Fits, indeed?"

"Why, who is she like?" said Giacomo.

"Nancy,' said Miss Ackland, "you are forgetting what you came in for. Remove the tea-things now, and you can talk of this again."

"I will, Miss Lyddy." but turning her eyes again on Maddalena, who was now smiling at the old woman's earnestness, "it's mighty quare, so it is,—I never seen two faces more like one another! sure it's his own smile she has—I'd know it if I seen her in America beyant!"

Rose came in with the shawls and bonnets, and Nancy went out with her tray. Miss Ackland took occasion to glide into the kitchen on her way out, and whispered to Nancy—"What put it in your head to talk so? Let us hear no more of that likeness, for you only imagine it, after all."

"And what harm is it to spake of it, Miss Lyddy?" said Nancy, still on her mettle; "I don't see what harm there's in it, that a body need talk of one havin fits,—a thing that no one belongin' to *me* ever had—no, not one of my breed, seed, or generation ever *had* a fit, that ever I hard tell of. As for the young lady, she *is* like Captain Melville, and that's all about it!"

"I know she is, but you know I do not like to have his name brought in, at all, amongst people that never knew him. So you will remember what I tell you. As for the fits, you entirely mistook my mean-

Anglicé!—"made me a little confused."

ing—I will tell you another time what I meant." She hurried away without waiting for an answer.

When Miss Ackland reached the esplanade, Rose was singing—

> " 'Tis the first star of evening,
>   So lovely and clear—
> Hasten home from the mountains,
>   My own muleteer!
>
> " At the door of thy cottage,
>   O'erhung by the grove,
> Is waiting to meet thee
>   The bride of thy love.
>
> " Yes, my fond heart expects thee,
>   It wishes thee here,
> Hasten home from the mountains,
>   My own muleteer!
>
> " 'Tis his form on the moun'ain,
>   His loved voice I h ar,
> Welcome home, fondly welcome,
>   My own muleteer!"

She was sitting near the top of the steps, with Middalena by her side, and on the next step above them sat Giacomo, listening to the song, his eyes fixed dreamily on the silvery star that now shone out from the deep blue sky of night like a diamond on the brow of some dark eastern queen. The group was a fine one, and Miss Ackland stopped at a little distance to contemplate the picture before she advanced, thinking the while of just such scenes in the long-past years when hope was fresh and life was young, and the future bright as summer skies at even. Strange to herself it was that even then her eyes rested longest on Maddalena where she sat in the bright star-light with her arm resting on Rose's shoulder, and the delicate outline of her face dimly seen in profile.

Next day, after school, Rose Ackland went to pay a visit to her friends, the Brodigans, while her aunt took Maddalena for a walk by the river side. Giacomo had business to transact during the afternoon, but had promised to come in the evening, so Rose went to ask the Brodigans to spend the evening, in order to treat them to a surprise. They had not heard of Giacomo's arrival, and Rose took good care that they should not hear it from her.

It was amusing, therefore, to see the astonishment of the sisters, in particular, when, on entering Miss Ackland's parlor, the first they saw was Giacomo.

"Why, Signor! you here?—is it possible?" cried Ann.

"Dear me! I am *so* surprised!" lisped Jane. "Who in the world would have thought to see you back so soon?"

"Upon my word, I'm delighted to see you!— Come on your wedding-tour, eh?" was Mr. Brodigan's hearty salutation.

"Not exactly," said Giacomo laughing; "ladies!" to the Misses Brodigan, "permit me to introduce my sister!" he saw that the shrinking girl was an object of great curiosity to the sisters.

"Your sister!" exclaimed Ann and Jane together, it almost seemed as though they were disappointed. "Then you are not married after all?"

"Not that I know of, although it really does appear as if some one here had been marrying me without my knowledge or consent."

"Quite a coincidence!" said Mr. Brodigan, rubbing his hands; he rather enjoyed the bewilderment of his daughters, that was plain.

"As how, Mr. Brodigan?" said Giacomo.

"Why, your sister coming back with you at this particular time, when people here would all have it that you were married."

"Not all the people here, Mr. Brodigan," said Miss Ackland smiling—"I for one did not believe it."

"Did *you* believe it?" said Giacomo in an undertone to Rose.

"Of course—why should I not?—Ann Brodigan told it as a fact."

"And you believed her?"

"I told you, yes! Why do you ask?"

"Because I gave you credit for more penetration."

"Well! don't give me credit for anything in future."

Harry Cusack just then made his appearance, whereupon the sisters brightened up, and the conversation became general.

## CHAPTER XVII.

It was night, an Italian night, and the air was heavy with the rich perfumes of southern gardens in their autumnal bloom; through the open windows of a first floor apartment in Leghorn the breath of the myrtle and the acacia was wafted in from the garden on which the room opened by a glass door in the centre, and the light branches of the overhanging creepers were traced in shadowy outlines on the tesselated floor; the waning moon was declining in the heavens, and her gentle light streamed in with mellow radiance, full, bright and yellow, for it was the Harvest Moon.

A solitary watcher was in the room, reading at a table by the flickering light of a lamp. One who has seen him before can easily recognize him again; it is Signor Malvili, the father of Giacomo and Maddalena, now alone in the solitude of his quiet dwelling. The night wore on and still he read, absorbed, it would seem, in the volume before him, old Froissart's delightful "Chronicles."

At length he closed the book, and looking at his watch, started to find that the night was already far spent; he arose, went to the door and stood awhile looking out on the trees and the flowers of his garden, and the grass-grown alleys half seen, half hid in the yellow light. He looked up to the moonlit sky and

"The spangled heavens, a shining frame"

which, to all the generations of men,

"Their Great Original proclaim."

His heart was uplifted to the Author of creation; he was well accustom'd to "look thro' Nature, up to nature's God," for he had studied that noble science in a noble school; he had "been down to the sea in ships, and had seen the wonders of the Lord on the great deep." Then he thought of times long past when he was wont to exchange his thoughts and feelings with one whom he loved, and by whom he thought himself beloved. He thought of the rude shock that had dispelled his youth's bright dreams, and left his life to the dull routine of duty. Throwing himself on a sofa, he covered his eyes with his hands and lay amid the shadows of the past, unconscious of the flight of time, till warned by the clock striking the third hour of morning, when he slowly arose, and muttering to himself—"Can it be true what they tell me? shall I not have parted with my darling child in vain? God knows! God only knows!" he lit his night-lamp which stood on a small table at the further end of the room, and after fastening the door and the windows, extinguished the lamp on the centre-table and went up stairs. There was a beautiful Madonna in his chamber, a small cabinet picture painted by some old master; it might have been the blessed Fra Angelico himself, so ineffable, so divine was the expression, or Raffaelo, in the graceful air of the head, the *pose*, as painters are wont to term it. It was before this exquisite picture of Our Lady that Signor Malvili usually said his night and morning prayers, and if that image could have spoken it could have told the story of his life for many a year past. When he knelt before it that night, or rather morning, in the dimly lighted room, it seemed to him as though the gracious countenance wore a sweeter smile even than usual, and a tenderer look of maternal love and pity beamed from the sad, soft eyes. A feeling of peace, that was almost joy, took possession of the soul of that pilgrim of life, who knelt so lovingly, so trustingly there, and from that hour, he felt no more as he had felt, the bitterness was gone, and the sweetness of hope came again, not as of old, but yet soothing and encouraging to the heart that had long ceased to look forward to aught that was of earth. His dreams that night were pleasant: Maddalena was there, and Giacomo, and one other long lost and dead to him, and all were glad and happy wandering together in some far bright land of dreams where music of celestial sweetness floated round, and light and joy and beauty seemed to reign forever.

A few more lonely days passed slowly by, made duller and sadder in the house by the sullen looks of old Nannetta, who could not forgive her master for sending her young mistress so far away from home;

bluff Paolo himself looked disconsolate, and little Giulia smiled no more; the sunshine appeared to have vanished from every heart. Maddalena's bird sat all day long motionless in his cage, tuneful now no longer, and the very cat had ceased to purr; the house was silent as the grave.

But the master of the house was neither so sad, nor gloomy as usual, and he smiled often to himself, thinking how bright and joyous all would be again when his Maddalena came home, and Giacomo,— and — who else? — he asked himself, then smiled again, and went on his way, almost rejoicing. For so lonely a man, and one outwardly so calm and cold, he enjoyed much of the sunshine of the heart at that particular time, though why it was so, was not very clear to himself.

One day Signor Malvili received a letter from Giacomo inclosing one from Maddalena; the latter drew tears from his eyes, though little given was he to the melting mood. Maddalena's letter, which was in Italian, ran as follows:

"My Dearest Father:—I cannot tell you how sorry I am to be away so very far from you; I hope you are not so sorry for your poor Maddalena's absence as she is for yours. But I am glad to be here, if you were only with me, for I do so love Giacomo's Miss Ackland, and I like Miss Rose very much, though not half so well as I do her aunt. Oh! if you only knew Miss Ackland! I am sure you would love her dearly; she is so sweet to look at, and I love to hear her speak. I never saw any one like her,—not for that she is so handsome,—but so gentle and so graceful. I fancy she is like some pictures I have seen of our sweet Madonna. Oh! I wish you knew her! Could you not come and see us while I am here? I should like you to see the old house, and the garden, and everything; it is so nice, and quiet, with such an old-fashioned look all about it. Do try and come! I cannot be happy when I think that I shall not see my dearest father for a long time.

"Ever your own
"MADDALENA."

The father, much affected, laid down the letter, and, resting his head on his hand, remained awhile in deep thought, his eyes fixed on vacancy; at length he started, and took up Giacomo's letter, which was written in English. He had not read far when he began to laugh, and laughed as he had not laughed for many a long year; this was the passage of the letter that excited his risible faculties:

"Our little Maddalena is delighted with the old house, but she would not be quite so taken with it did she know what I know about it, or rather what old Nancy knows. It appears the house is haunted by the ghost of a certain Captain Melville who used to be a visitor here a very long time ago, and who was actually seen by Miss Ackland not many weeks since so the old woman told me in confidence, and she further informed me that 'Miss Rosey' is just as much afraid as she is herself, only they *dusn't let on to Miss Lyddy!* As yet Maddalena is not in the secret, as Nancy says 'the poor thing' would be frightened out of her wits if she only knew it."

When Signor Malvili having enjoyed his laugh, had regained his usual composure, he glanced once more over the letter, and he repeated to himself— "They hide their fears from her, though it was she who saw the—the ghost; then *she* does not fear the apparition." There was a subdued tenderness in his tone, and a soft emotion in his eyes, that seemed foreign to his character, and indicated a new train of thought; he arose and made several turns to and fro across the room—stopped at the window and looked out, though little heeding, it would seem, what was passing in the street below; neither did the beauty of the bright autumnal day arrest his eye; his thoughts were far distant, and there was a strange trouble in his look and on his face that grew into a calm and settled determination; he smiled, then, and drew himself up as one who had gained a victory over some ancient enemy within himself, or had cast off a weary load that for long had crushed the heart within him. He took another letter from his pocket, one he had received some days before, and he said half aloud as his eye ran over the lines:

"How much of his boyish temperament still remains, and how many of his boyish peculiarities! And I shall see him, too! I wonder what he looks like now! How my heart swells at the thought of seeing them all once again!" Then he added, after a pause.—" Whoever told me this a year ago, how I would have scouted the idea!"

The evening of that day came on gray and gusty, such as we often see in the early autumn, when "the melancholy days" are drawing near, and the year is passing into the sear and yellow leaf. Signor Malvili loved such cloudy skies, such boisterous weather, better than the brightness of summer or the fair promise of spring, for he had been a sailor in his youth, and the sailor's instincts were yet strong within him. He loved to wander on the shore when the winds were abroad, and the billows surged and heaved, and the curlew shrieked among the rocks; such an evening was that which followed the receipt of those letters, and he strolled down to the beach an hour or so before sundown, to enjoy the wild commotion of the elements, and admire the dread Omnipotence of Him who commands both wind and wave. Walking slowly along the beach, the waves at times almost washing his feet, he pondered over the years of his life, the various phases through which that life had passed, and the causes that had produced the most important results. One scene of the past was before him, as it often was; the recollection of it had many a time raised a tumult in his soul that only the voice of religion could calm, and that only after a hard struggle. Now in silence and in solitude, with only the voice of winds and waters in his ear, and the lowering sky and the angry sea before him, the salutary thoughts, the gentler emotions of the morning came back again, and he asked himself "What am I that I should be so hard, so unforgiving? Have I not borne——what? oh! never *hatred*—but *anger*, long enough? and now when I have reason to think that I *was* mistaken, after all, why not acknowledge my fault, and know again the calm delight of friendship —*friendship*"—he repeated, and he smiled; "how oddly the word sounds in that connection. Friendship!—ay! what more could I expect? Even that would be far beyond my deserts. Then suppose not even that were given me—suppose I were regarded still as worse than a stranger, and that the last spark of affection had died out in that heart, if it ever really loved me, as I once dared to hope—suppose my reappearance should only bring back unpleasant recollections, and disturb the even tenor of a calm and tranquil life—ah! if it proved so, how could I bear it?—how could I forgive myself for the folly of which I had been guilty? No! I will not do it—I will not run the risk of failure, where failure were so destructive of all my earthly peace, and probably the peace and happiness of my children. I am quiet now, if not happy, and I will endeavor to rest content."

At that moment, a ray of sunshine broke through the clouds westward, and, as if by magic, the sea was covered with a golden glory, the tall, bare masts of the ships in harbor, and their sailless rigging were tinted with the richest crimson, and the city itself was all a-glow with the flush of sunset. "Ha!" said Malvili, still soliloquizing, "Heaven itself clears up my doubts—I will take that splendid flash of sunlight as a favorable augury, and I will hope all things—all! even *my* life may have its flash of sunlight before its evening darkens into the night of age. *Courage, mon cœur, courage!*" The sunset was still gilding the dome of the Turkish mosque and all its taper minarets, and resting lovingly on the spires of the Christian temples, when the lonely watcher by the sea turned his steps homewards, a new hope, a new energy suddenly alive within him, sending the life-blood quicker through his veins, and flushing his cheek again with the long-vanished hues of youth. The darkness and the storm were over.

\* \* \* \* \* \*

That night old Nancy had been entertaining the young people in the old house by the Boyne with some of her old-time stories; to Maddalena they were all new, and Maddalena, simple child, loving the marvellous, was more than all delighted. Then for the first time, she heard of the fairies, their gay revels on the velvet sward, their moonlight rides and the gallant show they make winding on their way through the forest glades, and by the silvery streams, and along the green hill-sides of that old land of beauty and romance, the home of the Western Gael. Of the tricks they love to play on mortals, sometimes in sport, sometimes in malice, and the wonders of their enchanted halls at times revealed to mortal ken. Of divers midwives and nurses Maddalena heard with amazement, who had been carried off bodily to minister in their respective capacities to the wives and children of fairy-land. This was the hardest trial of all to Maddalena's credulity, but Nancy assured her that "the good people" did require midwives and nurses, for had not such and such a one of her acquaintance been "taken away" for the very purpose, and the Italian girl was fain to believe her, wondering much the while how such things could be. Of the leprachaun and the wild phooka she heard, and the banshee, and many other sprites of greater and lesser renown amongst the tribes of fairydom, and Maddalena began to think that people in Ireland were singularly favored in living amongst such delightful creatures as the fairies, with a chance of obtaining admission, now and then, to their gorgeous palaces within the ancient raths, and of hearing their charmed music in the stillness of the night. Then the gifts they gave to their favorites amongst mortals! the wedding presents and christening presents, rewards of industry, and all the rest! Who would not wish to be the recipient of fairy bounty? So Maddalena said; and Rose laughed, and Giacomo and Miss Ackland smiled at her simple earnestness. She, at least, had none of those "wretched doubtings" which the poet pathetically accuses of having "banished

All the graceful spirit people, children of the earth and sea,
  Whom in days now dim and olden, when the world was fresh
    and golden,
Every mortal could behold in haunted rath, and tower, and
    tree."*

"Well!" said Rose, regaining her composure, "I like the fairies, too, Maddalena—that is, to hear of them, you know; for, of course, one never expects to see them."

"Then you don't expect to see them?"

"Why, no, child!" and Rose laughed again; "I might when I was very young——"

"And how long ago may that be?" interrupted Giacomo gravely.

"Oh! I don't know—it is a long time ago now; but, Maddalena, you wouldn't like to see a ghost, would you?"

"A ghost!—oh! dear me, no!"

"The Lord save us, Miss Rose!" cried Nancy, "what makes you say the like o' that?" And the old woman shuddered as she looked back over her shoulder, and all around. "Mockin's catchin', you know!"

"Very true, Nancy!" said Giacomo without pausing to consider what he was saying—"who knows but that Captain Melville might be showing himself. This is just the night for a sailor's ghost to appear."

A simultaneous sign from Rose and Nancy admonished him of his error, and he remembered at once how the old woman had warned him not to speak of

* D. F. McCarthy's "Alice and Una."

the ghost in Miss Ackland's presence; but too late, one and the other—too late to avoid wounding the heart that had loved Ralph Melville, and loved his memory still. A mortal paleness overspread Miss Ackland's face, and she sank back in her chair almost fainting, as Rose had seen her once before when she delivered Mabel's message. Rose and Maddalena flew to her assistance; she smiled faintly and gently motioned them away, but by a sudden impulse, she caught Maddalena's hand, and the girl, sorrowing and amazed, knelt beside her, when she fixed a long and wistful look on her face, then sighed heavily, and her eyes filled with tears. Giacomo sent Nancy for a glass of water, and when Miss Ackland had taken a little she revived and sat up again smiling at her own weakness. Giacomo commenced to apologize, but she stopped him, saying—

"Pray don't mention it, Giacomo! It is I that should rather apologize for having so alarmed you and Maddalena. I am ashamed of my weakness which yet I cannot overcome.'

"An' still you weren't a bit daunted when you seen *him*, Miss Lyddy!" said Nancy with the respectful familiarity of long service and tried fidelity—"Mister Jacomy, she isn't the least bit afraid of ghosts!"

A severe look from Miss Ackland silenced her, and she soon after made her retreat to the kitchen, having been summoned to the sitting-room at Rose's request expressly to entertain Maddalena with her stories.

Much did Giacomo and his sister desire to know

who and what the Captain Melville had been who was so fondly remembered by Miss Ackland years after his death. They looked at Rose and Rose looked at them; she read their thoughts, and would gladly have given the information they so much desired, but she knew that neither then nor after was it allowable for her to make any allusion to that subject. Her aunt, moreover, warned her by a look, and she was glad to turn the conversation to something else.

Maddalena, however, could not help thinking of what she had heard concerning the ghost, and when she and Rose retired for the night, she asked with some hesitation where it was that Miss Ackland had seen the ghost. "Was it in this house?"

"Not exactly," said Rose, "it was out on the esplanade."

"On the esplanade! Oh! I will never go there again in the evening."

"And why?"

"Why, only think! if the *Signor Capitano* should appear to me. *O cielo!*"

"But, my dear Maddalena! why should he appear to you?"

"And why should he appear to your aunt?"

"Oh! because my aunt knew him when he was alive. He used to be a visitor here a great while ago."

"You tell me so?" said Maddalena with a shudder—"oh! I wish I had not come."

Rose did not like the subject for that particular time and place, but she tried to conceal her own fears in order to reason Maddalena out of hers; reasoning failed, however, and then Rose tried raillery, which she found more effective. She began to laugh and make a jest of the whole affair, going so far as to say that her aunt might only have imagined that she saw the ghost, and after a little she got Maddalena to laugh, too, and then Rose found, to her surprise, that her own secret fears had all but vanished, and she actually felt the courage she but feigned before. So much for the power of self-control, and the blissful elasticity of youth. When sleep came down on the eyelids of those two fair friends, it brought no dreams of terror.

Not so calm was Miss Ackland's sleep; fierce gusts of wind still shook the old walls at times, and howled around the casements, and Lydia Ackland was ever wakeful when the winds were abroad. Visions of terror and affright then filled her mind; the cries of drowning men were in her ears, mingling with the shrieks of the blast, and one voice she ever seemed to hear above all the rest, one face but too familiar her fancy still distinguished, turning ever on her a sad reproachful glance ere it vanished in the deep dark waters. Then it was that self-reproach was torture, and one trifling fault was magnified by conscience into a grievous sin. Then she wept and prayed, oh! how fervently, for that soul so suddenly called to its account; it was only when the winds were at length hushed, and the stillness of night brought calm to the troubled mind, that her weary eyelids closed in sleep, and past and present were alike forgotten.

On the following day, Giacomo came early to ask the ladies to go out for a drive in the afternoon; Miss Ackland declined going, saying that she felt rather indisposed, suggesting that the others should call for Mrs. Hamilton, a widow lady of her acquaintance who was in delicate health, and rather low in circumstances. She was very amiable and very intelligent, and altogether Miss Ackland felt much interested in her, having known her when the prospects of both were brighter, and Mrs. Hamilton a happy wife.

Rose caught eagerly at the proposition; Mrs. Hamilton was one of her favorites, too, and, as she said—"It will do the poor thing good; she cannot often have a drive."

Giacomo looked as though he would willingly have dispensed with the fair widow's company on the occasion, but of course he took care not to say so, and the matter was arranged accordingly.

The afternoon came, school was dismissed, and our young trio set out in the best possible spirits,—Rose telling her aunt to take care of herself as she laughingly kissed her hand to her when they drove off; Miss Ackland had gone down to the gate with them. Maddalena had petitioned to be allowed to remain with Miss Ackland, but her offer was gratefully declined, and she was reluctantly obliged to go with the others.

They had been gone an hour or so when a ring came to the door; and Miss Ackland, reading in the back parlor, was surprised by the entrance of a gentleman in uniform whom she instantly recognized as Major Melville. It was not without a certain degree of embarrassment that she returned his bow, and requested him to be seated. There was a momentary pause, and then it was the gentleman who spoke.

"Miss Ackland must be rather surprised to see me here, and I confess I feel rather awkward myself all things considered."

"I certainly did not expect the honor of a visit from Major Melville," the lady replied somewhat stiffly.

"And yet I have visited your house before, if not yourself."

"So I have heard, Major Melville, and with some surprise. I am at a loss to understand why you should visit my house, or myself either."

"Am I not welcome, then?"

"Yes, undoubtedly, if you come as a friend." Her voice trembled as she added—"Ralph Melville's brother cannot but be welcome under this roof."

"I thank you, Miss Ackland—for *his* sake, if not for my own," and the Major bowed with stately grace. "There was a time, I will frankly tell you, when I thought it was beyond the range of possibility that I should cross the threshold of your home."

"That was not strange," said Miss Ackland in a voice barely audible. "You thought you owed me no good will, and from your point of view you certainly did not."

"And from yours?" he abruptly asked.

"Sympathy—affection," she promptly answered.

"That I cannot admit," said the Major, shaking his head gravely. "What did I—what did we owe you of sympathy or affection?"

"I will tell you," said Miss Ackland, her pale cheek suffused with a crimson blush, and the light of her departed youth flashing from her eyes usually so mild —"I may tell *you* now what I never told your brother:—if the warmest and truest love for *him* in life, and the most enduring sorrow for him in death—ay! sorrow that blighted my life's bloom, and left me old ere youth was past—if these gave me any claim on your sympathy and compassion—then I tell you, Guy Melville! I deserved both!"

She covered her face with her hands, and the tears trickled from between her slender fingers. When she withdrew her hands, and hastily wiped the tears from her eyes, she found the Major standing before her, regarding her with a look which she could not understand, earnest, wistful, yet irresolute, as though a struggle were going on within.

"Then you regretted your treatment of my brother?" he said, in a husky voice.

"Regretted it!—oh! how much I did regret it!— I have been very wretched!"

"No doubt; remorse is hard to bear, when once it takes possession of the soul."

"Remorse, Major Melville, is too strong a word for *my* regret; to feel remorse, one must have done some grievous wrong."

"And did not you do a grievous wrong, when you wantonly sported with a heart so noble as was that of Ralph, and finally cast it from you as a worthless thing?"

Miss Ackland felt that a searching glance was bent upon her, but she did not shrink from its scrutiny. She raised her eyes and looked full in the face of her interlocutor.

"Pardon me, Major Melville," she said somewhat haughtily, "I cannot plead guilty to that extent. I repaid your brother's love with love equal to his own, and I meant nothing less than to sport with his affection; his own precipitancy in wresting a wrong meaning from my words was the first cause of our fatal separation, my annoyance at his want of penetration and his unkind suspicion, the second. But had I known at the moment that he really took my equivocating answer as a final one, I would undoubtedly have undeceived him."

Guy Melville looked at her a moment, and a smile curved his lip and brightened his grave countenance; he took her hand and said in a kindly tone—"I believe you, Miss Ackland! and if Ralph were in my place he would believe you—and be happy in believing  I shall hope to see you again."

He then took his leave, and Miss Ackland, though much surprised, felt all the better and happier for his visit.

## CHAPTER XVIII.

Some ten days after Major Melville's visit, Giacomo being about to return home, Miss Ackland said on the Friday evening that there was one place neither he nor Maddalena had yet seen, and which they must see before Giacomo left. Rose asked what place it was.

"Oh! never mind," said her aunt, "you will know it when we get there. I kept this for our last excursion, Giacomo, as the place is a favorite resort of mine, and I think you and Maddalena will find it interesting. So if to-morrow is fine we shall go in the forenoon and take our dinner with us."

"And the company?" said Giacomo.

"None—for this once!—we will go *en quartette*."

"I am very glad; so near my departure, I should much prefer having only ourselves."

"Oh! you selfish mort I!" cried Rose, with a sudden burst of gaity that seemed spasmodic, "you don't want others to share your enjoyment!"

"Yes! I do—but not too many, or my enjoyment would be none at all. One—or two—or even three may be company, -that is to say if they be those whose companionship is pleasant and agreeable—to yond that one finds the crowd, and companionship is lost."

"He is like my father in that," said Maddalena, "my father cannot bear much people about him."

"Oh! your father is a regular hermit," said Rose, "as I understand him."

"Almost—not quite," replied Giacomo smiling, as he rose to depart; "my father has *his* company, I fancy, in his own thoughts, and then he has a miniature, in a shagreen case, which he never shows to any one, keeping it always carefully locked up. But *I* have seen him when he did not think I saw him, as wrapped up in the contemplation of that picture as though it were some old and dear friend. And I think it is, too!—You know, Maddalena!"

"Yes, I know!"

"Dear me!" said Rose, much interested in the mystery, "I wonder is it the likeness of a man or a woman?—Has either of you ever seen it?"

"I once got a glimpse—barely a glimpse of it," said Giacomo, "but it is so very long ago that I can scarcely remember anything more about it than that it was a lady young and fair; childlike, I told my mother of it, at the time, and it seemed to trouble her, so I never spoke of it to any one after. I think it was only of late years, however, that my father began to look at the picture again; it seems to me now that he had put it away from his sight all the years of his married life."

Miss Ackland began to think that Signor Malvili

was a more interesting person than she had supposed him to be, but she did not think it necessary to say so, and the conversation ended. Giacomo said "good night" at last, and hurried away, as it was wearing late.

The sun shone out next day warm and bright for the season; early in the forenoon came Giacomo, but, early as it was, Tom Connor was at the gate with his car, and the girls were sitting on the bench in the porch shawled and bonneted. Nancy was just mounting the steps, after placing a well-filled basket in the well of the car.* She whispered to Giacomo as she passed him in the ascent—" Did Miss Ackland tell you that Major Melville was here while you were all out drivin' that day?" "Yes! she just mentioned that he had called, but said no more about it." "I thought maybe she didn't tell you, at all. You see I was right enough." She passed on, but her words did not pass from Giacomo's mind, and they rang in his ears for hours after.

Miss Ackland had been watching his approach from the parlor window, and she quickly made her appearance equipped for the ride. The morning salutation being exchanged, and the beauty of the day noted, the party descended to the gate, and took their seats on the car.

* Those who have never seen an "Irish jaunting-car" may require to be informed that the *well* is that part of the car situate between the backs of the two seats which occupy the sides. The well is a great convenience for stowing away spare r. uffling, baskets, and such like appurtenances of travelling.

"Where to, Miss Ackland?" inquired Tom Connor, as he mounted the driver's seat. Her answer was only heard by Tom himself, who nodded intelligently, smacked his whip, gave the reins a shake, encouraged his horse with a "Step out, Johnny!" and away they went at a brisk trot through the narrow streets right across the old town to the West Gate, then along the smooth turnpike road to the quiet village of Tullyallen, passing through which they came to the beautiful demesne of Townley Hall, and Rose, turning round to her aunt,—she and Maddalena sat on the opposite side together—she said—

"Oh! then, it is to Townley Hall we are going, Aunt Lydia!"

"There, and a little farther, my dear!"

"A little farther—oh! I know now—I am so glad!"

The woods around Townley Hall were rich in their many hued autumnal garb, green and gold and brown and crimson, and very tempting were the glimpses caught of the noble avenue sweeping through the demense to the door of the stately mansion. But it did not suit Miss Ackland's purpose to visit those sylvan scenes just then, so Townley Hall and its pleasant shades were passed, and a less inviting road taken which diverged from the high road, and ran for a considerable distance along the brow of a bleak and barren hill than which nothing could present a greater contrast to the smiling scenes just left behind.

Giacomo could not help saying—"What a cheerless road this is!—how different from anything we have seen before! Have we much more of this kind of scenery to pass through?" Miss Ackland smiled and said—"Not much," and they passed on.

They had reached the highest ground on the hillside, when Giacomo asked—

"What ruins are those?" pointing to the tops of some shattered edifices which had just become visible in a deep hollow on the left hand side of the road.

"You shall know presently," said Miss Ackland, "when you see them better. Look yonder," pointing over a bleak common to the right, "and you will see some other ruins with what is perhaps still more interesting to you, one of those famous round towers of which so many exist in various parts of Ireland."

"And what place may that be?"

"That is Monasterboice, an abbey of some note in early times."

"Are we going there?"

"No, you must be content with what you see of Monasterboice from here. But do you see that wooded hill there right before you, rising so grandly from the level country around?"

"Yes, I was just admiring it, with the lofty tower on its summit."

"Well! that is the hill of Slane, a place very famous in Irish annals. It was there that St. Patrick may be said to have commenced his mission; on that hill, on an Easter Saturday evening, he kindled the fire which has since illumined not only this country but many other parts of the earth. I will show all this to Maddalena by and by. Now, Tom," to the driver, " you can remain here with the car while we go forward on foot."

Our little party then alighted, and having descended the hill, came to the bank of a little river which there poured its limpid waters into a sort of fissure in the rocks. Following the course of the stream, they came to a large rock projecting forward till within a few yards of the river; the space between the rock and the stream had been once occupied by a gate-tower with an embattled wall connecting it with the rock; of this tower some remains were still visible, and through an arch, which was probably a fortified entrance in ancient times, a view was obtained which drew an exclamation of wonder from both the brother and sister. Nestling in the depth of the quiet, sequestered valley on the banks of the little stream, lay the stattered remains of several buildings, evidently dating from very ancient times; the sun not yet at the zenith was shining full upon the ruins, some of which were throwing their shadows westward over the long grass that grew green and rank in the shelter of the ancient walls. Immediately in front, about the centre of the valley, stood what had once been an octagonal building of some architectural pretensions, and of considerable beauty still even in its ruined state; adjoining that was another oblong building with its side towards the entrance from the tower, and the shattered interior of an upper story, with a belfry tower at the front end still in some preservation. Many other buildings, in a still more advanced stage of ruin and decay, lay scattered around, and the place would have seemed the very abode of silence and contemplation had not the charm been rudely, harshly broken by an unsightly flour mill, which you could not help wishing some Irish Aladdin would remove to some other locality where more of the busy living world was seen, and less of the dead and silent.

"My dear Miss Ackland," said Giacomo, after he had taken a hasty survey of the surroundings, "I never saw anything more solemn, more striking!— What do you call this charming place?"

"This is Mellifont!—the Melrose of Ireland I know you have been reading Scott's 'Lay of the Last Minstrel,' and, therefore, know what I mean by applying the term to Mellifont."

"What a strange place!" said Maddalena, "those ghosts of houses make one think of many sad things!"

"Are those ruins ecclesiastical, or what?" said Giacomo, whose eyes still wandered admiringly over the solemn features of the scene.

"Monastic rather. Those broken walls and arches are all that now remain of a stately Cistercian Abbey, founded here by monks sent from Clairvaux by St. Bernard himself. It was considered one of the great abbeys of Ireland, and certainly none of them is more interesting in a historical point of view. This octagonal building you see here was the baptistry, that one of oblong shape was St. Bernard's Chapel, a crypt, as you see, the floor being considerably lower than the surrounding earth, and this gaping aperture at the end was once a beautiful doorway, considered one of the finest in Ireland; there are people living who remember to have seen the zig-zag moulding which adorned the arch."

"And what place was that above the chapel?"

"I really cannot say; it appears to have been used as a dwelling, as the fireplace and recessed closets are still to be seen."

"Indeed?" said Maddalena; "oh! I should much like to go up and see it. Could one go?"

Miss Ackland smiled: "Yes, if one is not very much afraid of breaking their bones. If you were willing to venture you could manage to climb that flight of stone steps at the angle of the wall."

"Would *you* go up?" said Maddalena to Rose, after glancing at the dilapidated steps.

"Yes, I would; I have been up more than once."

"Will you go now?" said Giacomo. "If you do, I will undertake to bring you and Maddalena safe down again."

"Humph!" said Rose, "do you think I could not go alone?" And, without a moment's hesitation, she began to climb the steps, seeing which her aunt uttered an exclamation of terror, Maddalena screamed, and Giacomo bounded up after her, as it seemed to the imminent peril of both. But they reached the top in safety, and Rose, all flushed and breathless, turning to Giacomo, asked him why he had not staid below to assist Maddalena.

"You see I didn't require your aid," said she.

"But do you think I could leave you alone exposed to danger?"

"I think you *might*, at all events! One person in danger is better than two. Besides, I was in no danger, though it might seem to you I was. Well! Maddalena, will you come up now?"

Maddalena, somewhat encouraged, said she thought she would venture.

"In that case," said her brother, "I will go down for you." And he immediately began to descend, Rose, from the top, charging him to be careful, for that the descent was worse than the ascent.

"I will be careful," was the reply, "when you wish it."

When he reached the bottom, he took his sister by the hand, and held her fast till she, half laughing, half crying, ascended the first steps, but as two could not mount abreast, he could only keep close behind her the remainder of the way; Rose from above, and Miss Ackland below, warning them to mind well their steps, for that some of the stones might be loose. Giacomo laughed, and said "Never fear," but Maddalena became only the more fearful and the more agitated. Her nervous trepidation came near to be fatal to both, for when they had reached the middle of the ascent she fairly lost her presence of mind, and, overcome by her fears, turned and clutched her brother by the arm; at the same moment a stone on which she had just set her foot gave way, and she fell, dragging Giacomo with her. A wild scream burst simultaneously from Rose and Miss Ackland; but just then a gentleman stepped forward, and catching Maddalena in his arms, so broke the fall for Giacomo, too, that he alighted on his feet. Another gentleman now advanced to the assistance of the first, and as they seated Maddalena, pale and trembling, on a large stone, with her back resting against the front wall of the chapel, Miss Ackland and Giacomo exclaimed together—

"Major Melville!—is it possible!" "Possible and true, thanks to Providence!"

Yes! it was, indeed, Major Melville, who, having driven out that day to Mellifont with a young brother officer,—the same Captain Cornell who had been his companion when Miss Ackland and Rose first met him,—little expecting to meet any acquaintances there, had reached that particular spot just in time to save Maddalena and perhaps her brother from serious injury, at least.

"Thank God! thank God!" ejaculated Miss Ackland, her eyes filled with tears of joy and gratitude, "and you, Major!" extending her hand, which he took respectfully, "and you who came so opportunely to the rescue!"

"And you will please accept *my* thanks, Major Melville!" said Giacomo with manly frankness, shaking his hand; "how *can* I thank you?"

"By saying nothing about it," said the Major curtly "I hope you are nothing the worse for your fall?"

"Nothing whatever; and I am still more thankful that my sister escaped unhurt. It would almost be the death of my father if anything had befel *her*."

The Major turned at the words and fixed his keen glance on Maddalena where she still sat, with her head leaning on Miss Ackland's shoulder, a faint smile lighting up her pallid face, to which the delicate rose tints were gradually returning As he gazed a softened look stole over his face, he approached her, and said in a hesitating way—

"I hope you are not much hurt, Signora?"

She started at the sound of his voice, raised herself, and looked up in his face with a strange bewilderment, at which he smiled, and merely repeated his question.

"I do not feel hurt, at all," the girl replied, in her sweet, foreign accent; "the Madonna reward you, sir! For me, I cannot thank you as I would wish— but my brother will thank you, and, some day, perhaps, my father!"

"Suddenly her eyes fell, and her cheek flushed, and Major Melville turning to ascertain the cause perceived that Captain Cornell was leaning on a broken pillar near, watching the fair Italian girl with a look of intense admiration. "Come along, Cornell!" said he, "we have all to see here yet, and the day is passing."

"But where is Rose?" said Miss Ackland, all at once; "And where is Giacomo "

"Has any one a smelling-' ottle?" said the latter from above, ' Miss Rose has fainted, I believe."

Miss Ackland, much alarmed, took from her pocket a bottle of *sal volati'e*, but the difficulty was how to get it up. Captain Cornell, however, offered his services, and ascending the steps half way or so, succeeded in reaching the bottle to Giacomo.

"Shall I go up to assist you?" said the Captain.

"Thank you, it is quite unnecessary."

There was breathless silence below during the very few minutes that elapsed before Giacomo called to Miss Ackland that Miss Rose was recovering; the aunt raised her eyes to heaven in silent thanksgiving, then begged Major Melville and his friend to delay no longer on their account, but commence their exploration of the ruins.

"Have you gone all through?" said the Major.

"Oh! my niece and I have been here more than once before—it was only for the sake of our young friends that we came now, and I am sorry to say they have not seen much of the valley or the ruins yet. Do you think you would be able to go any farther, Maddalena?"

Somehow Maddalena's eyes met Captain Cornell's just then, and there was such a look of entreaty in them that she blushed as she answered—"Oh yes! I feel quite strong now—it was only the fright that made me feel faint. I know my brother would be much disappointed if we did not stay to see all."

"Very well, my dear, if Rose is not able to walk she can sit here till we return."

"In that case," said the Major, "we shall make the *tour* of the valley together—if *you* have no objection, ladies.!"

"Certainly not,' said Miss Ackland, "it will afford us pleasure to have your company, Major, and that of your friend, to me all the more, as from my familiarity with the place I may be of some service as a *cicerona*."

Whilst this short colloquy was going on below, another of a far different kind might have been heard above had any o.e been sufficiently near. When Rose opened her eyes and found her head resting on Giacomo's arm, a faint blush stole over her face, and she made a motion as if to raise herself, but the effort was beyond her strength, and her head sank heavily on the arm that so tenderly supported her.

"Thank Heaven, you are again conscious!" said Giacomo in a voice trembling with emotion. "Oh! Rose! how you frightened me—I mean us!"

"Not so much," she found voice to say, "as you frightened me. Oh! that moment!" She closed her eyes as if to shut out the sight, and a visible shudder ran through her frame.

"You are not hurt?" said Rose, opening her eyes with a start, and fixing them on the face that hung over her.

"No," said Giacomo—it was all he could say.
"Nor Maddalena?"
"Nor Maddalena."
"God be praised!" There was little in the words, but much in the voice, and Giacomo's heart thrilled. He said nothing, however, and Rose, feeling the silence awkward, and being now somewhat stronger raised herself, and gently put away his arm. Then she said, with a timid look at his flushed and agitated face—
"Had we not better go down now, Signor?"
"Do you feel able?" Giacomo asked in a low voice
"Oh! yes, I am sure I am able, and you know my aunt will be anxious till she sees me safe. Come, Signor, give me your hand; I am not strong enough, you see, to rise without help!" and she smiled with something of her wonted archness.

Instead of replying, Giacomo said passionately—
"*Signor!* you call me *Signor!*—Rose Ackland, this must not, shall not continue!—I love you more than my own life, yet you treat me as though I were almost a stranger!—When is this to end?—or shall it ever?"

Rose's face was crimson in a moment, then pale as death; she trembled, and seemed as though unable to utter a word.

'Rose! will you not speak to me?" said Giacomo beseechingly; he was standing full in front of her with his eyes fixed on her face. "I asked you are we always—always to be to each other as we are now?'

"You ask me a question which I cannot answer," said Rose without looking up."

"You cannot?"

"Not now, at least; I cannot stay here longer," she was going to say *Signor*, then checked herself, and said, "*Giacomo!*—I want to see my aunt and Maddalena," holding out her hand at the same time, which he took and raised her up, then pressed the hand before he resigned it.

By this time, the rest of the party were waiting at the foot of the steps, and Rose, on advancing to the top with Giacomo, glanced down and drew back in surprise on seeing the strangers, who were not in uniform. Her aunt noticed the movement and said—

"Don't mind, my dear! it is only Major Melville and a brother officer who chanced to meet us here. But how are you going to get Rose down?" she added, addressing Giacomo.

"Oh! Aunt Lydia, I am quite able to go down myself," said Rose.

"I should not like to see you try," said Giacomo in an under tone.

"Suppose we try to procure a ladder in the neighborhood," suggested Captain Cornell; "it is impossible for the young lady to get down without one."

"Not quite impossible, sir," said Giacomo, and turning again to Rose, he said in the same low whisper, "will you trust yourself to me?"

"I will!" she answered firmly.

"Thanks!—now, then, permit me!" And, encircling her waist with his arm, he gently drew one arm of hers around his neck, and ejaculating a fervent prayer to God and the Blessed Virgin, he began to descend slowly and carefully, little heeding the exclamations of terror and apprehension from below, his every thought, his every sense absorbed in the one beloved creature, whose head lay helplessly on his shoulder, for Rose's courage had again failed her. She was perfectly conscious, however, and clung with convulsive energy to him whose strong arm seemed alone between her and death. No word passed between them during the perilous descent, but their hearts held close communion, they entered then on a new phase of existence, and both felt that the relations between them had changed forever— they could no more be as they had been, concealment was at an end, dissimulation and doubt alike impossible. That moment, with all its thrilling sense of danger, was looked back on by those two in after years as the happiest of their life.

But this change was perceptible to none save themselves; when Rose stood safe beside her aunt, and mutual felicitations were exchanged, the affair was treated as nothing more than an exciting episode and all went on as before. It was remarked, however, that Giacomo was seldom absent from the side of Rose, and that Rose leaned on his arm as she had never leaned before. Captain Cornell seemed, in like manner, to take Maddalena under his special care, seeing which Major Melville and Miss Ackland exchanged a smiling glance of intelligence, and the gentleman said as he offered his arm to the lady:

"Pairing off, I protest, in parliamentary style. See what it is to be young!"

Just then appeared on the scene a peasant woman with a stone pitcher in her hand, and the thought occurred to Miss Ackland that she might be made useful. Accosting her, therefore, as she passed, she asked where she was going to get water there.

"Down at St. Mary's Fountain, ma'am!" said the woman with the usual low curtsey, almost down to the ground.

"Why, I did not know there was a fountain here."

"No more there wasn't, ma'am," (another curtsey) " till here a few years agone. In coorse, it was here in the ould ancient times, for it was the one that kept the monks in wather long ago."

"I suppose," said the Major, "you know a great many stories about this old abbey."

"Oh then, it's myself that does, your honor, an' how could I miss of it, for sure wasn't I born there abroad within a stone's throw of it." She squatted herself on the ground on her haunches, with her pitcher beside her, as one who desired nothing better than a good long *shanachus*.

"Sure but there's many a quare thing seen an' hard," she began, "about these ould walls, for all they're so quiet now. There's them above ground," and she lowered her voice to a mysterious whisper, "that has seen the monks walkin' in procession here in the dead hour o' the night, for all the world as if they were alive, and the moon shinin' on the great silver cross that was carried before them, till the sight of it 'id dazzle a body's eyes. An' the hymns they'd be singin'—och! it's a folly to talk, man or mortal never hard the like, barrin' them that hard it here."

"Who *they* were, deponent saith not," whispered the Captain to the Major.

"And what about the Mass-bell?" said Miss Ackland.

"Oh! you've hard of that, ma'am?"

"Yes, but others of our party did not?"

"Well! I'll tell the quality how it was. You see, there was once upon a time, a wild fellow by the name of Larry Delany, a journeyman waver by trade, an' the sorra thing he did the whole Sunday over but ramble abroad in the fields, and go from place to place divartin' himself. He got in time that he never set his foot inside a church, an' cared no more about missin' Mass than if he was a brute baste, the Lord save us! Well! one Sunday mornin'—it was in the summer time, too, an' as beauty-ful a day as ever came from the heavens, an' my bowld Larry was on his tramp, to be sure, as usual, an' he thought he'd take a short cut through the valley here to where he was goin', wherever that was. So he was makin' the best of his speed along, and was jist about where we are now, about the time of last Mass, when he hears a bell ringin'—the sweetest bell he ever hard in all his days, an' it rung, an' rung jist as you'd hear it in the chapel comin' on the time of the Elevation. With that the hair began to rise on

Larry's head, an' his knees shook un ler him. 'Christ save us" says he to himself, 'sure there's ne'er a chapel hereabouts. What's this at all?'—So he cocks his ear to listen, an' he says again—' Oh Blessed Virgin' it's in the ould chapel it is!' With that he looks in, an' sure enough he seen a sight that made him trimble all over,—there was a priest at an altar under that end window sayin' Mass, an' ever so many monks an' some that wasn't monks, kneelin' in the chapel with their heads bent down; now, you see, Larry knew well enough that there never was an altar there since the memory of man or long before it, an' that what he seen was nothing earthly, an' the cowld sweat broke out all over his body; down he pops on his knees, an' bent his head like the rest, but a prayer he couldn't say, he was so much afeard. Presently, the bell rung again, an' poor Larry makes bowld to lift his head the laste little bit, an', my dears' there was the priest with his hands raised up high all as one as if he was elevatin' the Host, an' Larry couldn't keep in any longer, he cries out—'Oh Lord! have mercy on me a sinner!' an' down he falls flat on the ground How long he lay there he never could tell, but when he woke up it was the middle o' the day, he knew by the sun, an' there wasn't monk or altar, either, in the ould chapel, but everything was jist as he had always seen it. So Larry made the best of his way home, an' from that day till the day he died, he never missed Mass on Sunday or holyday. An' sure *he* wasn't the only one that hard the Mass-bell ringin' in Mellifont Abbey since it came to what you see it. Ochone! an' isn't it the black sight for the country round, for sure they say it was past credit what the blessed and holy monks used to give to the poor every day of their lives, for all they lived so poor themselves."

"But they were very rich, were they not?" said Captain Cornell, the only Protestant present.

"You might say that, your honor! I hard ould people tell that the monks of Mellifont had as much silver an' goold in a manner as the king himself."

At this the ladies laughed, and the woman waxed somewhat indignant. "You may laugh as much as you like, ladies!" said she, "but I'm tellin' you the truth, as I hard it from them that was oulder an' wiser than myself. An' more by token, they say there's a power of that same goold and silver buried here still."

"Why, how could that be?" said Giacomo; "why would the monks bury their gold and silver?"

"Bekase they were turned out at last by the—ahem! by the English, an' the house taken over their heads, an' they were afeard to take their treasures with them, for fear they'd be taken from them, so they buried them somewheres about the Abbey, thinkin' that some day or another they'd be back again. But, ochone! that day never came since!"

"But how do people know that the treasures are concealed here?" inquired Major Melville.

"Well! they don't know it for sartin, your honor

but it was always said so, an' sure some got the knowledge of it in drames."

"Indeed?"

"Indeed they did, your honor, an' people have come here in sarch of the same treasures, from the farthest parts of Ireland. It isn't very long since a man came from Connaught, all the ways."

"From Connaught? is it possible?"

"Ay, indeed, did he!—he dramed, it seems, that if he'd come to Mellifont Abbey, near Drogheda, on the county march between Louth an' Meath, an' dig down at a particular spot among the ruins, he'd find enough of goold an' silver to make him as rich as a lord. So he travelled on ever, till he made out Mellifont, an' got a pick-axe and shovel an' a crow-bar an' went by night to dig down at the spot he seen in his drame."

"Well!" said Giacomo, " did he find the treasure?"

"No, but he was very near findin' it; after diggin' a long time he came to a big broad stone, an' his heart jumped at the sight for he knew the treasure was right undher it, but jist as he put the crow-bar in undher the stone to lift it up, behowld you, something all in white, like a monk with a hood up on his head, comes an' stands right fornenst him on the other side o' the stone, an' its hand stretched out pointing to the road he came. The poor man was scared enough, you may be sure, an' he gathered up his tools an was going to make off as fast as ever he could, stealin' a look every now an' again at the great tall monk, but jist as he was turnin' to go away, he hears a voice sayin'—'Cover the stone again!' an' with that the sperit vanished, an' maybe the poor man didn't make haste to do what he was bid, an' do it well, too, so as that nobody 'id know that the place was dug up, at all!"

So that was the end of the Connaught man's dream!" said Miss Ackland smiling, "and so ends many another dream," she added, turning to the others; "the search for earthly treasures is sure to end in disappointment, and we may all learn from the experience of this unlucky treasure-seeker. Just when we have reached, as it were, the fulfilment of our cherished dream of life, comes some spectre from the unexplored regions of possibility to warn us thence, and cover up once and forever the treasure we had so coveted."

Her eyes filled with tears, and her voice trembled with emotion. Major Melville drew her arm within his, and led her away, but not before he had given the good woman a piece of silver, which example was followed by the other gentlemen, and thanking the dame for her very acceptable information, they left her to fill her pitcher at St. Mary's fountain and hurry home with her prize.

"Now, good people," said Miss Ackland, when they had made the circuit of the ruins, "it is about time to have dinner, or lunch, or whatever you may choose to call it—I see Tom has brought the baskets hither, as I told him, so let us choose our *salle-a-*

*manger*, and sit down. Gentlemen," to the two officers, "you will, I hope, favor us with your company?"

The gentlemen were only too happy to be asked, and a place was chosen on the bank of the little river, where the sward was fresh and green, in the shade of the projecting rock, and the ruined gate-tower of the ancient Abbey. The spot commanded a view of the entire valley, scattered all over with the mouldering, dilapidated relics of departed wealth and power, glorious mementoes of the faith, and piety, and charity of dead ages, and of generations passed away. A spell hung over the place; an air of religious peace, of deep solemnity, pervaded every object, and the sun shone there with a mellow, softened lustre that harmonized with the solemn aspect of the place; tenderly, caressingly, as it were, those yellow sunbeams fell on the ruined fane, and the broken Abbey-walls, and the graves of the sainted dead.

During the repast, the conversation turned, as was natural, on the ancient glories of the place; Major Melville was passably well acquainted with them, and told how richly Mellifont had been endowed by Irish princes and by Norman lords, in the ages following its first foundation; how the Abbots of Mellifont sat as lords in the Irish Parliament of those days, and ruled with salutary sway the broad domains given their Order for God's service and the poor's. Amongst other things he told how Hugh O'Neil, the great Earl of Tyrone, had within the walls of Mellifont Abbey surrendered his sword to Lord Mountjoy, Queen Eliza beth's successful general, and with his sword the last hope of that generation of Irish Catholics.

"And there is another sad memory connected with Mellifont," said Miss Ackland, "which Major Melville is probably forgetting, for he cannot but have heard or read it. You remember, Giacomo, the princess of Breffni, Dervorgilla, whose tragical history I gave you to read a few days since?"

"What! the wife of O'Rourke, your Irish Helen, who was carried off by Dermot—Dermot something?"

"Dermot MacMurragh—precisely. Well! it was here she spent her latter years, in rigorous penance, and died at a good old age, contrite and humble but full of hope in the mercy of God."

Giacomo hearing this was much interested, and Miss Ackland went on to tell how the same Dervorgilla in the days of her youth and innocence had presented a golden chalice for the high altar of the Abbey-church, with rare and costly vestments. "Who could have foreseen that day," she added, "that other when she should come to hide her shame beneath those venerable walls, and humbly seek admission amongst the pious sisterhood of whose company contrition and mortification could alone make her worthy. Two striking pictures of human life in the light of prosperity and the darkness of disgrace! Of course, Major Melville, you know Moore's beautiful 'Song of O'Rourke,' founded on this sad story?"

"Yes, I know it—who does not?"

"Perhaps you would be good enough to sing it for our young foreigners here, who have never heard it, I am sure?"

"With great pleasure, Miss Ackland!—such as my vocal powers are, they are at your service." And, without further preface, he sang one of the best known and most generally popular of all the melodies, that fine historical ballad, commencing, "The Valley Lay Smiling Before Me."

The song was well sung, and Giacoma and Maddalena were delighted, as was also Rose, for *Colleen dhas cruthia na mo*,* was one of the airs she had learned to love in her earliest childhood.

"*Apropos* to love," said Miss Ackland, "I will tell you a story, short it must be, as it is about time we were starting for home. It occurred here quite near the old Abbey. You and I, Rose, have read it in the *Dublin Penny Journal*. A young miller had been betrothed to a pretty young girl, 'a neighbor's child,' as the country people would say, but, sad to relate, the young man died before the marriage had taken place. The grief of his affianced bride is described as heart-rending. The night of the wake, she was suddenly missed from amongst her sympathizing relatives and friends; search was made everywhere, and at length the horrible suspicion came into the minds of some present that the girl had committed suicide. It was not till all hopes of finding her had been given up, that she was found dead and cold be-

* The Pretty Girl milking her Cow.

side her lover, where he was laid 'under board,' as the peasantry call it; unheeded, she had crept in by his side, and there laid her down to die."

This story drew tears from Maddalena, and Rose looked askance at Giacomo with a strange, sweet trouble in her eyes. He saw the glance and it made his heart thrill with joyful emotion. The repast was now ended, and it was not without reluctance that some, at least, of the party left the vale of Mellifont —happier, nevertheless, than when they entered its hallowed precincts.

## CHAPTER XIX.

ALTHOUGH Giacomo was to have left on the following day, it happened, whether by accident or design, that the vessel in which he was to have gone, sailed without him. Nor did he appear to apprehend any disagreeable consequences from the delay, although Maddalena made herself miserable over the prospect of her father's displeasure, dreading its effects for Giacomo. But the latter only smiled, and said he would trust to her mediation to obtain his forgiveness. And how much longer, she asked, did he intend to remain? Oh! of course, till the next opportunity, which might not be for a week or two. His *sang froid* surprised Miss Ackland and Rose, the more so as it contrasted so oddly with the fears he had formerly entertained of incurring his father's anger. "Either," said Miss Ackland to herself, "either his father is not so severe as he used to be, or our friend Giacomo is not quite so dutiful." And do as she would these thoughts would keep possession of her mind. As for Rose, she appeared neither to trouble herself much about the possible consequences, nor to reason on the propriety or impropriety of Giacomo's postponing his departure; she did, indeed, rally him on it, but in a way that showed whether she meant it or not, her entire satisfaction.

Its effect on the Brodigan sisters was very remarkable. Only a few days had passed after it became known that the vessel had sailed without him, when Miss Brodigan took the opportunity of informing Harry Cusack that the affair was all settled, meaning a match between the young Leghorner and Rose Ackland. Harry was a little disconcerted, at first, but Ann so far unbent from her usual *hauteur* as to condescend to entertain him, which she did to such good effect that Cusack began to think she might really suit him better than Rose Ackland. The reader may possibly think of Reynard and his sour grapes in this connection, and smile at the thought, but we will not say that honest Harry thought of any such analogy. He thought of one thing, however, which effectually urged him on over the threshold of destiny, and that was,—a luminous idea surely that by popping the question to Ann Brodigan, and obtaining her consent on which, although no coxcomb, he counted with some degree of certainty,—he should deprive the good people of his native town of the opportunity of laughing at his expense, as he had some reason to think they would if the supposition of Rose's possible engagement to Giacomo was once noised abroad. On these considerations, and as a sort of *dernier ressort*, Harry Cusack proposed for Miss Brodigan, senior, and was accepted with the best grace possible under the circumstances.

The news of the elder sister's engagement had scarcely set Dame Rumor's many voices talking, when all Drogheda was astounded by the still less expected tidings that the younger was also "engaged" to Mr. Tiernan, a business connection of her father's, and a man who, in the ordinary course of nature, might have been her father himself. This was the greatest puzzle of all for the gossips of the old borough, and any number of visits were paid with the intention whether expressed or understood, of discussing a piece of intelligence which was pretty generally set down as "strange - passing strange—wonderful!" At first it was doubted, but the public doubt soon gave place to private and individual certainty when it became known that the day was appointed, the same day for both sisters, and the wedding dresses actually in course of preparation. Well! after that the townspeople said, they should not wonder at anything; about Harry Cusack and Ann they would not so much mind, for, after all, Harry's attentions had been pretty fairly divided between her and Rose Ackland; but that Jane, the prettiest and youngest of the two, should consent to have Tiernan, that was almost incredible, and formed undoubtedly a nine days' wonder, the greatest of the season.

What was known and talked of all over the town could not fail to reach the quiet dwelling of the Acklands; indeed, Mr. Brodigan himself came, in the joy of his heart, and with his usual singleness of purpose, to inform Miss Ackland, in virtue of their long friendship, of the double marriage about to take place. Miss Ackland, in all sincerity, offered her congratulations, and expressed no surprise whatever. The young people barely waited till Mr. Brodigan was gone to make their own comments on what they had heard. Maddalena, who had seen Mr. Tiernan more than once, said it was "a sad pity for so pretty a girl as Signora Jane to marry a man so much older than herself; she was sure the Signor Tiernan was as old as her father."

"And not half so good-looking," put in Giacomo.

"No, indeed, *mio fratello*, I do not think him fine, at all, the Signor Tiernan."

The ladies smiled and Giacomo laughed—"You mean *handsome*, Maddalena."

The girl colored as she looked from one smiling face to the other. "And was it not the same I said?—is not *fine* the same as 'good-looking?'"

"Not exactly the same, my dear," said Miss Ackland, to whom she had addressed herself; "in your language it is, and also in the French, but in English the words have two distinct meanings. We never use the word *fine* in the way in which you used it just now. You should have said 'handsome' instead of 'fine.'"

During this brief colloquy Giacomo said to Rose in an under tone—"Can you guess why the two Miss Brodigans,—and Mr. Cusack, too, have so taken the whole town by surprise?"

"Not I—nor you, either, I think," she replied in the same tone.

"In that you are mistaken, Rose!"—he had taken to calling her so ever since the day of the visit to Mellifont;—"I think I *can* guess the reason."

"And pray what is it?"

Rose looked up at the moment, and reading the answer in his eyes, she colored to the temples and rose in some confusion, for the ostensible purpose of taking a book from the table, but in reality to hide her face from observation.

It was quite remarkable how subdued she had become all of a sudden, and how much less quick at *repartee*. Her aunt, during those days, complimented her occasionally on her good behavior, telling her that she began to have hopes of her, now that she was becoming more guarded in her speech, and more reserved in her demeanor. The faintest possible smile might have been detected playing about Rose's mouth, and her dark eyes twinkled with something of their sportive mischief, but she seemed to take the compliment in perfect good faith, and gravely expressed her satisfaction that her aunt found her improving.

The middle of October was past, and the trees were almost bare, the foliage that had been their beauty and their pride lay rotting in the dust, and the earth was gladsome no more. Cold winds whistled through chinks and crannies, doors and windows creaked, and freside pleasures were again in demand. Giacomo had not yet found another opportunity of returning home, and Maddalena's fears grew every day stronger, especially as they had not heard from their father for over two weeks. Otherwise she was well content, and began to feel very much at home. It is true, her fears had not at all subsided in regard to Captain Melville's ghost, and many a time she stole into the kitchen to have a talk with Nancy on that solemn and mysterious subject, which had all the more attractions for her simple, girlish mind because of its being so carefully excluded from the general conversation of the family.

It was one of those cold, gray evenings which the late autumn is wont to bring; the little circle were seated around the fire between day and dark, in that old back parlor so much endeared to Miss Ackland and Rose, and to Giacomo, too, by its sweet and tender associations. Rose had just left the piano, after singing that beautiful "Evening Hymn of the Calabrian Shepherds;" Miss Ackland repeated the first stanzas, dwelling on their touching beauty and the tender piety that breathes in every line—

> "Darker and darker fall around
> The shadows from the pine,
> It is the hour with praise and prayer
> To gather round thy shrine.
>
> "Hear us, sweet Mother! thou hast known
> Our earthly hopes and fears,
> The bitterness of mortal toil,
> The tenderness of tears."

A knock was heard at the front door, and Nancy's slip-shod feet were heard in the hall as she went to open it. Rose, hoping it might be Mr. Brodigan and some of his family, opened the parlor door a little way and looked out, but drew back when she saw in the dim light a strange gentleman for whom Nancy had just opened the door. The next moment Nancy was heard to utter a loud scream, then ran into the parlor at full speed, and to the surprise of every one caught Miss Ackland by the arm, and gasping for breath, tried to speak, but could not, her eyes starting from their sockets, fixed wildly on the door.

"Dear me! Nancy, what is the matter?" said Miss Ackland; "is there anything wrong?"

"What have you seen?" cried Rose, who, with Maddalena, was almost as frightened as Nancy herself.

"I will go and see what it is," said Giacomo, but just then a wild scream burst from Nancy's ashy lips, and, pointing to the door, she cried—

"There—there he is!" and she crouched in a corner behind her mistress, unheeded by any one, for all eyes were turned towards the open door, where a man of gentlemanly appearance and of middle age stood regarding the astonished group with a smiling countenance.

"My father!" cried Giacomo and Maddalena in a breath.

"Your father?" cried Miss Ackland; "good God! it is Ralph Melville!" Her head swam, her brain burned and she would have fallen senseless and motionless to the floor had not Rose been near enough to catch her in her arms. Hastily disengaging himself from Maddalena's fond embrace, the Signor Melville, as we shall yet call him, approached, and, taking Miss Ackland in his arms, laid her gently on a sofa, then watched her with tender interest, while Rose and Maddalena applied restoratives.

Meanwhile Nancy rose, and, with the lightness of twenty years before, darted up to the new arrival, and, taking him by the arm, looked up in his face, every feature of her own working convulsively.

"So you're not dead, after all, Captain dear? It isn't your ghost, at all, that's in it?"

"No, Nancy, my old acquaintance! I am not dead, nor is it my ghost you see, any more than I see yours. But let us attend to your mistress."

"Mushin' thank God she's beginnin' to come to," said Nancy; "ah! poor Miss Lyddy! sure if joy 'id kill any one she'd never come to, at all! The Lord be praised! the Lord be praised! An' me sayin' the Rosary for his soul every night of my life, sure!"

When Miss Ackland, heaving a deep sigh, at last opened her eyes, the first object on which they fell was Ralph Melville, the lover of her youth, the mourned of her riper years, the dream of her life, kneeling on one knee beside her, holding her hand in his, and watching with eager anxiety the gradual return of life and consciousness to her languid frame. She looked at him a moment, at him only, then closed her eyes again without an effort to speak, as though fearing that the blissful vision might vanish, as so many others had done before. But the sound of her name, spoken in the old familiar tones that had haunted her heart all those dreary years like a funeral dirge, and the pressure of the hand that she had never hoped to feel again, assured her that now, at least, her imagination had not deceived her, that she saw, and heard, and felt Ralph Melville, his very self, a creature of flesh and blood, though how he came to be still in the flesh was yet a mystery. He had risen and now stood looking down on her with his own old smile.

Bending down, he touched her forehead with his lips, " for the first time, Lydia!" he said in a tremulous voice, " but you will pardon it now, will you not?" She smiled, as he whispered, "Are you now convinced?" He turned then to embrace his children, holding Maddalena longest in his arms, and holding up her face to see whether she was changed.

Rose had timidly withdrawn herself from the little circle around the sofa, and stood with Nancy contemplating the group with tearful eyes. Nancy was in ecstacies, making all sorts of odd gesticulations, occasionally giving vent to her overflowing delight in a manner peculiar to herself—" Oh! the darlin' the darlin'! isn't it new life to see him again! Look at him now! didn't I often tell you what he was, Miss Rosey dear?"

" But you weren't quite so glad to see him when he

came to the door!" Rose said, smiling through her tears; she, too, was watching Ralph Melville with admiring eyes, her heart glowing with sympathetic joy. She kept looking from him to her aunt, and from her aunt to him, scarcely daring to credit the evidence of her senses that they were again together in life and health as she saw them then. But she was not left long to her own thoughts, for Mr. Melville cast his eyes around as if seeking some one else, and Giacomo taking her hand drew her forward, smiling and blushing as she was.

"Father!" said the young man "you have forgotten Rose—*our* Rose!" and he glanced at Maddalena, who said in her eager, childish way—

"Yes, indeed, brother! *our* Rose—our own, own Rose!" And she laughingly pushed Rose into her father's arms, saying—"There, *il mio padre*, there is another child for you."

Mr. Melville looked at Giacomo and smiled. "With all my heart!" said he, "had she nothing but her name to recommend her, she would be thrice welcome to me—but she is more than an Ackland, she is *worthy* of the name,—as I know from the hold she has gained on the hearts of my children. She is handsome, Lydia!" he said, turning to Miss Ackland, "but not at all like you."

"No, half so handsome!" put in Rose, regarding her aunt with a look of proud affection, at which Ralph Melville smiled; he was probably of the same opinion. Miss Ackland, now quite recovered, yet still pale with wonder, sat motionless, with her eyes fixed on him who really seemed to her as one risen from the dead.

"Can it be possible, Ralph," she said at length, "that after all the long years during which you were mourned as dead, I see you still alive? It seems hard to realize it."

"An' us prayin' for him, Miss Lyddy! an' doin' everything we could for his poor sowl!"

At this every one laughed, and Mr. Melville said—"My poor soul had need of your prayers, Nancy! even though it was still in the body, and I hope it benefitted by them, too! But you must have been sadly discouraged, I fear, to find my poor soul still wandering on earth after you had been full twenty years praying for its repose."

"No, I wasn't discouraged," said Nancy stoutly, "I only prayed the harder."

"But how was it, father," said Giacomo very seriously, "that Miss Ackland really saw, or supposed she saw you, several weeks ago, on the esplanade in front of the hall-door? Were you here, then?"

"Certainly not; this is the first time in three-and-twenty years that I set foot about this house, or in the town of Drogheda."

"It must have been your fetch, then," said Miss Ackland gravely, "for I see you no plainer now than I saw you then."

"What it was, Lydia, that took my shape and form, I cannot say,' he replied; "I only know that I was not here in person—though in spirit I well might have been," he added in a tone meant only for her own ear.

"Oh Lord!" groaned Nancy from her corner, "if I had only known—if I had only *known* that the poor dear Captain wasn't dead, at all, wouldn't it have given me an aisy mind, anyhow?"

"So, father," said Giacomo, "I can now understand the strange attraction I found in Miss Ackland."

"How do you mean, my son?"

"Why it always seemed to me as if I had seen or known her a long time ago; now I know that it was because I had seen her portrait in your private desk when I was a little child."

"You saw it, then?" said his father with a start.

"Yes, father, I may now confess it, and the face haunted me ever after, hence, as I suppose, the before unaccountable feeling of curiosity, with which I used to regard Miss Ackland, wondering, as it were, why I did so."

"My dear Giacomo," said Miss Ackland, "I am glad to find that we were mutually interested in each other. I had never seen your portrait nor was it your features that reminded me of one whom I supposed long dead," and she glanced at his father, "but there was that in your voice and in your smile that brought him constantly before me. Even Mabel noticed the resemblance there. You remember Mabel Ralph?"

"Indeed I do'—poor Mabel! is she still alive?"

"I can barely say she is; her race is almost run. But it will give her new life to see you once again before she dies, and to see us together as of old."

"Shall we not go soon to see her—you and I?"

"To-morrow as early as you will."

"Then you were not born in Italy, father?" said Maddalena.

"No, my child, I was born here in Ireland. Miss Ackland can tell you why I left it."

"But our name is an Italian one, surely!" said Giacomo, hesitatingly.

"An Italianized French one," replied his father with a grave smile—" Melville, you know, is a purely French name — one of those brought into these islands by our Norman ancestors; it was easy changing it into the Italian Malvili when one desired to change their identity."

"And you desired to change yours," said Miss Ackland with strong emotion, "in order to punish one whom you supposed had wronged you."

"No, no, not to punish, Lydia! surely not to punish, for I had no reason to suppose that my appearance or disappearance was of any importance whatever to the person in question."

"And now?"

Mr. Melville paused a moment, during which he and Miss Ackland regarded each other in silence; then he replied—" That I am now of a somewhat different opinion is, I think, sufficiently manifest from the fact of my being here."

"Who enlightened you on that head?"

"My brother!"

"What, Guy!—Major Melville?"

"Precisely."

An exclamation of surprise here burst simultaneously from Giacomo and Maddalena, "Major Melville our uncle!"—"Is it possible?"

Rose only smiled, which Giacomo noticing, said—"This news does not seem to surprise you, Rose, as it does us."

"Certainly not; I have known for some time that Major Melville was the brother of the Captain Melville whom my aunt had known in her younger days——"

"And of whose perturbed spirit you and Nancy were so much afraid."

"And Maddalena, too, Aunt Lydia!—were you not afraid of the ghost, Maddalena?"

Maddalena blushed, looked at her father and hung her head, but made no answer. Her father tapped her glowing cheek with his finger, and said—"Never mind, *mia carissima*, you did not suppose it was your father's ghost, else, I am sure, you would not have been so much afraid of it."

Nancy was here dispatched to the kitchen to commence preparations for supper, a meal seldom taken in that house, at least for many years past. "Miss Rose shall go by and by to assist you," Miss Ackland whispered, "but go now,—you shall have time enough to look at Captain Melville." Nancy betook herself to her task with such alacrity as she had not shown for many a long year past.

"Dear me!" said Maddalena, "only to think that it was Major Melville who caught us the other day at Mellifont when we fell from those old steps. Was not that strange?"

"I was just thinking so," replied Miss Ackland; "if the Major knew who you were, how delighted he must have been."

"Oh! he knew me, I am sure, for I was quite ashamed to see how he looked at me. I thought it was very strange."

"But I did not," Miss Ackland said, "although I noticed it at the time. No one who had ever seen your father could fail to be struck by your likeness to him. Did you know, Ralph, that your daughter resembled you so much?"

"Oh yes! I have been often told so, and I was inclined to suspect them of flattery who said so, but since *you* have discovered the likeness I am to suppose that it exists. Giacomo resembles his mother," he added after a pause, "not in disposition, though, for in that respect," and he smiled—"I believe he is more like me, whereas Maddalena is her mother in all save her Irish face."

"Then her mother must have been a dear, sweet, creature," said Miss Ackland, patting Maddalena's hand which rested on the arm of her chair.

"She was so," said Mr. Melville, with perfect composure, "she was very amiable, and deserving of all affection."

"More than you had to give her," said Giacomo to himself, and a cloud gathered on his brow as he thought of the strange dislike his mother had for Drogheda, a place she never saw. That dislike was not without some foundation, as the young man now understood, but how his mother came to suspect any former attachment on the part of her husband, or what her reasons were, was what he could not comprehend. It never occurred to him, what was really the case, that his father was, at that period of his life, given to talking in his sleep, and that it was, consequently, from his own lips she had learned a secret which had much disturbed her placid mind, till the salutary counsels of her spiritual director, and the supernatural grace drawn from the frequent reception of the Sacraments, had gradually restored her equanimity by raising her thoughts and her affections far above the creatures of earth. But all this being known only to the good father Rinolfi was never to be heard by mortal ear, and was as dead to her little world as the gentle Laura herself.

"I see you are surprised at all this, my dear children," said Mr. Melville, "and long to know how it happened that I first went to reside in Leghorn, how I came to change my name, and leave those who had known me in earlier life under the impression that I was dead. Will you pardon me when I say that I do not feel disposed at present to enter upon details very painful in the recollection?"

"My dear father," said Giacoma, "I have no desire, and I am sure neither has my sister, to hear anything from you that it would give you pain to tell." Maddalena's loving eyes said the same, and more, too, and their father, evidently much relieved, glanced from one to the other with a look of such tender affection that they felt amply repaid for whatever self-denial they had practised.

A few minutes after Rose all of a sudden started up, and asked Maddalena to go with her to the schoolroom to arrange something there for the morning. Giacoma offered his services, too, and the three young people left the room together.

It was then that Ralph Melville first gave expression to the joy that filled his heart on meeting again, after so many years of separation, her whom he had loved with the heart's first pure and warm affection.

"I know all, Lydia!" said he, "Guy has written it all to me, and I find it hard to forgive myself for all I have unwittingly made you suffer. Nothing but the strong assurance I received of your continued remembrance of me could have induced me to make my existence known to you."

Tears were now flowing from Miss Ackland's downcast eyes; she was silent, and when Mr. Melville seated himself beside her, and took her hand in his, he felt it cold and trembling.

"I fear you are growing faint again," he said tenderly.

"No, no, I am quite strong."

He looked at her pale and agitated features, and smiled. "Will you forgive me, then?" he asked.

"Yes, I will, Ralph!" Miss Ackland said in a faint voice; "if you left me all those dark years in ignorance of your existence, I am to suppose that it was because you thought me indifferent as to your fate. But oh! if you only knew what I suffered from remorse of conscience whilst imagining that my silly pride and petulance in withholding an explanation had been the cause of your destruction! Oh Ralph! when I think of that!"

"Poor Lydia! the story is written here all too plainly," and he laid his hand on her head, where the silver hairs not of age but of care and sorrow were already mingling with the golden brown of other days. "How can I ever make amends for all you have suffered on my account?'

"I am more than repaid by the joy of seeing you, of hearing your voice, when I had so long believed you dead, and indirectly, if not directly, through my fault. But you have not told me, Ralph, how you escaped—or were you really on board when your ship went down?"

"I was," he replied with a sudden change of manner; "I was on board."

"And how were you saved?"

"When all except myself had been washed away

from the deck, or drowned below in the water that filled every part of the sinking ship, I gave myself up for lost, and began to pray, with such fervor as I never prayed before; I particularly invoked the Blessed Virgin, beseeching her to save me."

"You did?" said Miss Ackland, catching his arm, and looking anxiously into his face. "And what followed? Go on, Ralph, go on!"

"Just at that moment the black clouds opened above my head, and a star, a bright, glittering star appeared in its lonely beauty; I hailed it as the Star of the Sea,—and I said from my heart—*Ave Maris Stella, ora pro me!* Strengthened as it were by a new hope, I lashed myself to a spar, and finding the vessel sinking, in the name of MARY I committed myself to the deep."

"My God! what a fearful alternative!"

"I had no other. I knew the day would soon dawn, and trusted to our blessed Mother to send some vessel that way in time to save me."

"And it happened so?"

"Yes, I had been some two hours floating on the surface of the sea, now gradually becoming calm,—for the storm had subsided,—when a vessel came so near that I was seen from the deck, and a boat being immediately sent out, I was rescued from my perilous position, just as my strength and consciousness were both beginning to fail."

"So it was the Blessed Virgin who saved you?" cried Miss Ackland, radiant with joy; "and your prayers and mine were not in vain. Do you know, Ralph, when I heard of your having sailed that sad day, I specially recommended you to her powerful protection, and you see you were inspired to do the same. Oh Ralph! how much do we owe that tender Mother!—shall we not love and serve her always?"

"I have endeavored to do so ever since then," said Melville, deeply touched by this new proof of the affection he had once so blindly, so fatally doubted. "But how little I knew, while buffeting the waves that night, that you were praying for me—that your loving solicitude followed me. Oh! Lydia, had I but known—had some consoling spirit revea'ed it to me then, how many years of sorrow and suffering it would have saved us both—from what bitterness of heart, what misanthropic feeling towards my fellow-creatures it would have saved me!"

"Well! we must not murmur against the will of God!—those dark days of trial and of tribulation were for us days of grace, and out of their blackness has broken the sun of our present happiness."

"But you do not ask me," said Melville after a pause, during which he had been regarding her with a look of ineffable affection, "you do not ask me how I came to——"

"To forget me!"

"No, not exactly that; I never forgot you in the ordinary sense of the word, although the feelings with which I did remember you were certainly of too b tter and resentful a kind to be painful to my wife did she but know of them. The vessel which had picked me up was from London, happily bound for Civita Vecchia, and thence I proceeded immediately to Leghorn. I resolved to give up the nautical profession, and quietly settle down to the pursuit of commerce. My mother had died, as you know, some time before, my sister was in her novitiate with the Sisters of Mercy in Dublin, and there was only my brother Guy to occupy my thoughts. So I wrote to him an account of my providential escape, informing him at the same time that I did not wish to have it known, least of all to your family. I asked him what I could do to serve him, and he stated in his answer that if I could obtain him a commission he would like the profession of arms better than anything else. So I managed to purchase the commission for him; he came to Leghorn to see me before joining his regiment, which was then stationed at Gibraltar, and we spent some pleasant weeks together, at least as pleasant as I could have in my then frame of mind. I soon after obtained a junior partnership in an old and respectable firm, and under the name of Malvili embarked on a new career. One of the partners, Signor Salvati, had a young and handsome daughter, Laura by name, who being an only child and heiress to her father's large fortune, was, of course, much sought after."

"The old story," said Miss Ackland with a melancholy smile :

> "My father lived beside the Tyne,
>   A wealthy lord was he,
> And all his wealth was mark'd as mine,
>   He had but only me."

"And, of course,
> "Among the rest young Edwin bow'd."

And *she* bowed to Melville with something like the sportive grace that had first charmed his heart.

Ralph Melville smiled, his own old radiant smile, as he replied—"There you are mistaken, Lydia! I, at least, bowed not there, nor yet 'spoke of love.'"

"How, then, did you win your rich and lovely bride?"

"That I cannot tell you; unless it were because I did not pay my court to her."

"I do not quite understand you; pray explain yourself."

"I will, since you desire it, though I had rather not. You must know, then, Lydia, that the Signor Salvati himself proposed to me the union with his daughter"

"Indeed?"

"Yes, indeed, and his motive will surprise you. He broadly hinted, too broadly as I thought, that his child, his Laura——"

"Loved you?"

"That was what he intimated, and so plainly that I could not choose but understand him. The old man seemed to suppose that I, too, had been making love to Laura. Astounded as I was what could I say? what could I do?"

"What *did* you say and do?"

"For a moment I scarce knew what to say, but presently came the recollection of your supposed heartlessness; then I reflected that whilst you had rejected all the earthly love I had to offer, Laura Salvati had given me hers unasked, unsought; I knew she was good, gentle, pious, and I resolved to make her my wife, trusting that the love I could not feel then would come in time."

There was a quick decision about his way of telling all this, a business-like sort of dispatch that no other but Lydia Ackland could have understood. It told her plainer than words could have done that his heart was not interested in the matter of which he spoke, only his reason and his judgment.

"Oh Ralph!" she could not help saying, and she bowed her head on her hands. Melville was silent for a few moments, then he said:

"Lydia! I speak of what is long past; hear me patiently, I have little more to tell." He went on in the same quick way: "I married Laura; we lived with her father till the old man's death, some five years after our marriage, when Giacomo was four years old, and Maddalena two. Soon after that, my gentle wife began to droop and fade away like a blighted flower, and so she drooped and faded till she died, although that was not for some four or five years later. During all that long time her health was broken, her frame enfeebled, and nothing could rouse her from the languor that had gradually benumbed her faculties. She had never been lively or animated, but always rather inclined to melancholy, and for the last years of her life a veil seemed to be drawn between her and this nether world, husband, children, all, included; she devoted herself to God, in Him lived, and so died, admired, respected, revered even by those most nearly connected with her in life, but leaving no aching void in the heart such as a more variable and impulsive nature, made up of cloud and sunshine, is wont to leave behind it when it bids farewell to earth. I had nothing to reproach myself with in regard to my poor Laura; I had endeavored to forget, whilst she was my wife, that I had loved another earlier and dearer, one that could have been to me what she could never be,—harsh word of mine, nor angry look, had never wounded her gentle heart,—so I said to myself in thankfulness to Heaven when I laid her in her father's grave. I then devoted myself to the education of my children and the care of my affairs, till, with Heaven's good aid, I was enabled to retire from business about two years since, and enjoy the repose that is so sweet after years of assiduous and unremitting application.'

He paused, but Miss Ackland remaining silent, he resumed: " Little remains for me to tell, though, perhaps, the most important of all--to myself, at least. You must imagine, for I shall not attempt to describe the feelings with which I heard of the strange chance that had thrown my dear son on your kindness and charity; of all you did for him; how I marked the grateful affection he cherished towards you. Shall I tell you that it rather displeased me at the time, and that I could not feel towards you the same gratitude I would have felt towards any other in similar circumstances?"

"I do not wonder at that now, Ralph!" said Miss Ackland gently, "although I did then, for I saw it plainly at the time, and was disposed to regard you as a reasonably cold-hearted man."

Melville smiled, took her hand in his, and went on: "It were superfluous to tell you the little minute circumstances that, related by Giacomo from time to time, awoke in my mind the idea that I, or you, might, after all, have been mistaken—that you did love me. Certainty came at length, after Guy's interview with you; you may remember that it was very soon after that, Maddalena came to you. I wished to make her love you, as her brother already loved you, and knowing now that both my children love you, I have come myself to ask you to be my wife, and their mother. I *know* you love me, my heart tells me that you do; how I love you, I need not tell you. It is true, the summer of our life is past, but shall we not spend the tranquil autumn together, and, if God so wills it, the winter of our age, consoling, strengthening each other, bearing each other's burdens, and walking hand in hand to the tomb, then only to part that we may meet again before the throne of God to inhabit forever the eternal mansions? Say, Lydia! shall it not be so?"

Miss Ackland laid her hand in his, and said with that smile which had been, and was even now, the sunshine of Melville's heart:

"I am old now to be a bride," said she, "but if *you* are content to take me as I am, then surely *I* may be. But I can hardly realize it to myself that you are here beside me in very deed, that I am still to be your wife! Oh Ralph! how can I believe it?"

It is possible that Mr. Melville succeeded in convincing her, for when they joined the young people at supper a few minutes after, they all declared that she looked ten years younger, and Rose, in her arch way, complimented "the dear Captain, as Nancy used to call him," on the wonderful faculty he possessed of conjuring up smiles and blushes.

"I am happy to know, then, that the *faculty* is hereditary," said Melville smiling, and glancing at his son in a way that covered Rose's face with blushes. "Ha! ha! Miss Rose, I see you understand me!— Will you pardon me if I quote an old proverb to you, viz., that *those who live in houses of glass should not throw stones.* Now for supper, Lydia!"

Next day Miss Ackland and Mr. Melville went to pay their proposed visit to Mabel. Overjoyed as the old woman was to see "the Captain," she was not so surprised as might have been expected. In the strange hallucinations to which her mind was subject, she had long cherished a dreamy sort of half conviction that he was alive, and would some day return;

she had, from the first, associated Giacomo and him in her mind, and not seldom confounded one with the other. But the joy was too much for her worn-out frame; that night she died, thanking "God and the Blessed Virgin Mary that she had lived to see Miss Lyddy happy."

The astonishment of those who had known Captain Melville, and lamented his supposed death, may well be imagined. Major Melville was one of Miss Ackland's first visitors on the following day; he came with his brother who had paid him an early visit at Millmount that morning. Guy was very sincere in his congratulations, for, during his short acquaintance with Miss Ackland, he had learned to love her "It was well for me," he added, with a smile, "that *I* knew Ralph was still alive, although *you* did not; else I might have loved you too well for my own peace. Now I can truly say that I already love you as a sister, and shall be happy to see you the wife of my dear, my only brother. But unless I am much mistaken we shall have some other weddings in or about the same time." And he looked at Giacomo and Rose, to the great confusion of the latter.

"I assure you it will not be my fault, uncle, if you do not," said Giacomo, "that is if my father, Miss Ackland, and one other will consent."

Of course his father and Miss Ackland were but too happy to consent, and the *one other* made no very great objection. So then and there the matter was arranged, only Rose, from some fancy of her own, would have it postponed till the early Spring.

The second week of November saw the quiet but happy union of Ralph Melville and Lydia Ackland solemnized by Father O'Regan; the school had been given up from the very day after the arrival of the former. They went on a short tour and returned in a few days, as they were all to remain in Drogheda till after Rose's marriage, then go all together to reside in Leghorn, at least for a while. By the time appointed for the union of Giacomo and Rose, Captain Cornell had persuaded Maddalena to give him her hand at the same time and in the same place. Early in the winter, the two Brodigan sisters " were led to the altar," as the newspapers phrase it, by Cusack and Ternan, and who can doubt that they were all very happy. At least, if they were not, that you and I may, (courteous readers,) as the old story-tellers have it!

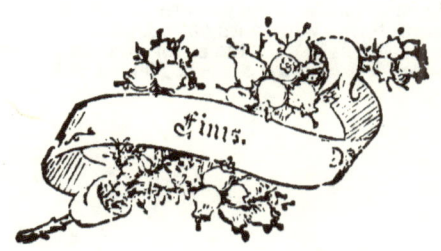

# PUBLICATIONS OF P. J. KENEDY,

## EXCELSIOR

### Catholic Publishing House,

**5 BARCLAY ST., Near Broadway,**

Opposite the Astor House,      NEW YORK.

---

| | |
|---|---:|
| All for the Sacred Heart of Jesus. Dedicated to associates of League of Sacred Heart. Net, | 50 |
| Adelmar the Templar, a Tale of the Crusades | .40 |
| Adventures and Daring Deeds of Michael Dwyer | 1.00 |
| All about Knock. Complete account of Cures, etc. | 1.00 |
| Apparitions and Miracles at Knock, paper cover | .25 |
| Atala. By Chateaubriand. Doré's Illustrations, 4to gilt. | 3.00 |
| Battle of Ventry Harbor, paper cover | .20 |
| Bible, Douay Octavo, large print. Vellum cloth | 2.50 |
|    The same, American Morocco, gilt edges., | 5.00 |
|    The same, Turkey Morocco, antique, gilt edges.... | 10.00 |
| Bible, Haydock's, Style G. Fr. Morocco paneled, 2 clasps. | 18.00 |
|    The same, Style H., Turkey Morocco beveled | 25.00 |
| Blanche, or the great evils of Pride. | .40 |
| Blind Agnese, Little Spouse of the Blessed Sacrament. | .60 |
| British Catholic Poets, red line, gilt edges | 1.25 |
| Brooks (Senator) and Hughes (Archbishop) Controversy. | .75 |
| Burke's Lectures and Sermons 1st series, cloth | 2.00 |
|    The same, full gilt side and edges, | 3.00 |
| Burke's Lectures and Sermons, 2d series cloth | 2.00 |
|    The same, full gilt side and edges | 3.00 |
| Burke's Lectures and Sermons in Ireland, cloth | 2.50 |
|    The same, full gilt side and edges | 3.00 |
| Burke's Lectures—The set complete, 3 vols, plain | 6.00 |
|    The same gilt | 9.00 |
| Burke's Reply to Froude, Ireland's case stated | 1.00 |
| Cannon's Poems and Dramas. Red line, gilt edges... | 1.25 |

*Catholic Prayer-Books*, 25c., 50c., *up to* **12 00**

☞ Any of above books sent free by mail on receipt of price. Agents wanted everywhere to sell above books, to whom liberal terms will be given. Address

**P. J. KENEDY,** Excelsior Catholic Publishing House, *5 Barclay Street, New York.*

## Publications of P. J. Kenedy, 5 Barclay St. N. Y.

| | |
|---|---|
| Canon Schmid's Exquisite Tales, 6 vols, Illustrated | 3 00 |
| Cannon's Practical Spelling Book | 5 |
| Captain of the Club, a Story for Boys | 5 |
| Carroll O'Donoghue. By Christine Faber | 1.25 |
| Carpenter's Speller and Definer | .25 |
| Catechism Third Plenary Council, large, No. 2, paper, per 100 net | 2.50 |
| The same, abridged No. 1, paper per 100 net | 1.50 |
| The same, No. 2, cloth flexible, per 100 net | 5.00 |
| The same, No 1, " " " " " | 3.50 |
| Catechism, General, National Council, paper per 100 net | 2.00 |
| The same, abridged paper cover, per 100 net | 1.50 |
| Catechism, Butler's large, paper per 100 net | 2.50 |
| The same, abridged, paper per 100 net | 1.50 |
| The same, cloth, Illustrated Mass Prayers | .30 |
| Catechism, The, or Short abridgment, New York, per 100 net | 2.00 |
| Catechism, Boston. Prayers at Mass, etc., paper per 100 net | 2.00 |
| Catechism, Keenan's Doctrinal, cloth | 50 |
| Catechism, Poor Man's, large and thick | 40 |
| Catechism, Spanish, Ripalda, paper cover | .12 |
| Catechism, Spanish, Astete, paper cover | .15 |
| Catechism, Spanish, Nuevo Caton, paper cover | .15 |
| Catholic Christian Instructed, paper .20, cloth | .30 |
| Catholic Excelsior Library, 6 vols, per set | 4.50 |
| Catholic Faith and Morals, By L'Homond | 1.00 |
| Catholic Fireside Library, 10 vols, per set | 7.50 |
| Catholic Flowers from Protestant Gardens, gilt | 1.25 |
| Catholic Home Library, 8 vols, per set | 4.00 |
| Catholic Juvenile Library, 6 vols, per set | 2.40 |
| Catholic Keepsake Library, 6 vols, per set | 4.50 |
| Catholic Missions and Missionaries. By Shea | 2.50 |
| Catholic Offering or Gift Book. By Abp. Walsh | 1.00 |
| Catholic Piety, (Prayer Book). Prices range upwards from | .60 |
| Catholic School Book | .25 |
| Chambers' English Literature, 2 vols, Octavo | 5.00 |

Catholic Prayer-Books, 25c., 50c., up to **12 00**

☛ Any of above books sent free by mail on receipt of price. Agents wanted everywhere to sell above books, to whom liberal terms will be given. Address

**P. J. KENEDY**, Excelsior Catholic Publishing House, *5 Barclay Street, New York.*

## Publications of F. J. Kenedy, 5 Barclay St. N. Y.

| | |
|---|---|
| Chancellor and his Daughter. Sir Thos. More | 1.25 |
| Christian Etiquette For Ladies and Gentlemen | 1.25 |
| Christian Maiden's Love. By Louis Veuillot | .75 |
| Christian's Rule of Life. By St. Liguori | .50 |
| Christian Virtues. By St. Liguori | 1.00 |
| Christopher Columbus. Illustrated, 4to gilt | 3.00 |
| Chivalrous Deed. By Christine Faber | 1.25 |
| Clifton Tracts Library of Controversy, 4 vols | 3.00 |
| Collins' Poem. Red line, gilt edge | 1.25 |
| Converted Jew. M. A. Ratisbonne | .50 |
| Countess of Glosswood | 5 |
| Crown of Jesus (Prayer Book). Prices range upwards from | 1.00 |
| Daily Companion (Prayer Book). Prices upwards from | .25 |
| Daily Piety, (Prayer Book). Prices upwards from | .30 |
| Dalaradia. By William Collins | .75 |
| Davis' Poems and Essays, complete | 1.50 |
| Devout Manual, 18mo, (Prayer Book). Prices upwards from | 75 |
| Devout Manual, 32mo, (Prayer Book). Prices upwards from | .35 |
| Dick Massey, a Story of Irish Evictions | 1.00 |
| Diploma of Children of Mary Society, per 100 net | 8.00 |
| Doctrinal Catechism. By Rev. Stephen Keenan | .50 |
| Dove of the Tabernacle. By Rev. T. H. Kinane | 75 |
| Drops of Honey. By Father Zelus Animarum | .75 |
| Drops of Honey Library—9 volumes, per set | 6.75 |
| Elevation of the soul to God | .75 |
| Empire and Papacy. The Money God | 1.25 |
| Epistles and Gospels, 24mo. Good Type | .20 |
| Erin go Bragh, Songster. Paper cover | .25 |
| Evenings at School. New edition Net | 1.00 |
| Exercises of the Way of the Cross, paper cover | .05 |
| Faber's (Christine) Works, 4 vols, large, 12mo. per set | 5.00 |
| Fair France during the Second Empire | 1.00 |
| Fair Maid of Connaught. By Mrs. Hughes | 75 |
| Faugh a Ballagh Songster. Paper cover | .25 |
| Feasts and Fasts. By Rev. Alban Butler | 1.25 |

*Catholic Prayer-Books,* 25c., 50c., *up to* **12 00**

☞ Any of above books sent free by mail on receipt of price. Agents wanted everywhere to sell above books, to whom liberal terms will be given. Address

**F. J. KENEDY,** Excelsior Catholic Publishing House, *5 Barclay Street, New York.*

**Publications of P. J. Kenedy, 5 Barclay St. N. Y.**

| | |
|---|---|
| Feast of Flowers and The Stoneleighs | .75 |
| Fifty Reasons why the R. C. Religion, etc | .25 |
| Flowers of Piety (Prayer Book). Prices upwards from | .35 |
| Following of Christ. A Kempis, 1.25, 1.00 and | .40 |
| Foster Sisters. By Agnes M. Stewart | 1.25 |
| From Error to Truth, or the Deacon's Daughters | .75 |
| Furniss' Tracts for Spiritual Reading | 1.00 |
| Gems of Prayer, (Prayer Book). Prices upwards from | .25 |
| Glimpse of Glory and other Poems. E. C. Kane | .50 |
| Glories of Mary. By St. Liguori. Large, 12mo | 1.25 |
| Golden Book of the Confraternities | .50 |
| Golden Hour Library, 6 vols, red edges. per set | 3.00 |
| Good Reading For Young Girls | .75 |
| Gordon Lodge, or Retribution | 1.25 |
| Grace O'Halloran. By Agnes M. Stewart | .75 |
| Green Shores of Erin. Drama, net | .25 |
| Grounds of the Catholic Doctrine | .25 |
| Guardian's Mystery. By Christine Faber | 1.25 |
| Handy Andy. By Lover. Large edition | 1.25 |
| Hay on Miracles Explanation, etc | 1.00 |
| History of the Catholic Church in the U. S. J. G. Shea | 2.00 |
| History of Ireland. By Moore, 2 volumes | 3.00 |
| History of Modern Europe. By J. G. Shea | 1.25 |
| History of the United States. By Frost | 1.25 |
| Hours with the Sacred Heart | .50 |
| Irish Fireside Library, 6 vols, 16mo | 6.00 |
| Irish Fireside Stories, Tales and Legends | 1.25 |
| Irish National Songster. Comic and Sentimental | 1.00 |
| Irish Patriot's Library, 6 vols, 12mo | 7.50 |
| Irish Race in the Past and Present | 2.50 |
| Irish Rebels in English Prisons | 1.50 |
| Irish Scholars of the Penal Days | 1.00 |
| Jesus in the Tabernacle. New Meditations | .50 |
| Keenan's Doctrinal Catechism | .50 |
| Keeper of the Lazaretto. By Souvestre | .40 |
| Key of Heaven, 18mo, (Prayer Book). Large. Prices up from | .75 |

*Catholic Prayer-Books,* 25c., 50c., up to **12 00**

☞ Any of above books sent free by mail on receipt of price. Agents wanted everywhere to sell above books, to whom liberal terms will be given. Address

**P. J. KENEDY,** Excelsior Catholic Publishing House, *5 Barclay Street, New York.*

**Publications of P. J Kenedy, 5 Barclay St. N. Y.**

| | |
|---|---|
| Key of Heaven, 24mo, (Prayer Book). Medium. Prices up from | .60 |
| Key of Heaven, 32mo, (Prayer Book) Small. Prices up from | .50 |
| Kirwan Unmasked. Paper cover. By Abp. Hughes.. | .12 |
| La Fontaine's Fables. Red line, gilt edge | 1.25 |
| Last of the Catholic O'Malleys | .75 |
| L'Ange Conducteur, (French Prayer Book) | .75 |
| Latin Classics, Expurgated. Volume 1. Net. | .40 |
| Latin Classics, Expurgated. Volume 2. Net | .50 |
| Legends and Fairy Tales of Ireland | 2.00 |
| Library of American Catholic History, 3 vols. set | 6.00 |
| Library of Catholic Novels, 6 vols. per set.. | 7.50 |
| Library of Catholic Stories, 6 vols " | 7.50 |
| Library of Controversy. Clifton Tracts, 4 vols " | 3.00 |
| Life of Archbishop Mac Hale. Paper .25, Cloth gilt.... | 1.00 |
| Life of Christ. By St. Bonaventure | 1.25 |
| The same, gilt edges | 1.50 |
| Life of Pope Pius IX. By Monsignor B. O'Reilly.... | 2.50 |
| Life of Robert Emmett. By Madden | 1.50 |
| Life of St. Bridget. Paper cover | .10 |
| Life of St. Ignatius, 2 vols. By Bartoli | 3.00 |
| Life of St. Liguori. By Mullock | .50 |
| Life of St. Louis, King of France | .40 |
| Life of St. Mary of Egypt | .60 |
| Life of St. Patrick. By O'Leary, 16mo | 1.00 |
| Life of St. Winefride, 18mo. Cloth | .60 |
| Life Stories of Dying Penitents | .75 |
| Lily of Israel, Life of the Blessed Virgin Mary | .75 |
| Little Flowers of Piety, (Prayer Book), 1.75-1.25 and.. | .75 |
| Little Follower of Jesus. By Rev. A. M. Grussi | .75 |
| Little Lace Maker or Eva O'Beirne | .75 |
| Little Lives of the Great Saints. By John O'Kane Murray | 1.00 |
| Little Man'l Bl. Trinity, (Prayer Book). Prices up from | .75 |
| Little Office of the Immaculate Conception. Per 100 net | 2.50 |
| Lives of St. Ignatius and his Companions. | .75 |

*Catholic Prayer-Books*, 25c., 50., *up to* **12 00**

☞ Any of above books sent free by mail on receipt of price. Agents wanted everywhere to sell above books, to whom liberal terms will be given. Address
**P. J. KENEDY.** Excelsior Catholic Publishing House, *5 Barclay Street, New York.*

**Publications of P. J. Kenedy, 5 Barclay St. N. Y.**

| | |
|---|---|
| Lives of the Japanese Martyrs. Spinola, etc. | .75 |
| Louisa Kirkbride. By Rev. A. J. Thébaud, S. J. | 1.50 |
| Love of Christ. By St. Liguori | .50 |
| Maidens of Hallowed Names. By Rev. Chas. Piccirillo S. J. | .05 |
| Maltese Cross and a Painting and its Mission | .40 |
| Manual of the Bl. Trinity, (Prayer Book). Prices upwards from | 1.00 |
| Manual of Catholic Prayers. (Prayer Book). Prices upwards from | .37 |
| Manual of the Children of Mary. 448 pages | .50 |
| The same, for Pupils of the Sacred Heart | .25 |
| Manual of the Crucifixion, (Prayer Book). Prices upwards from | .63 |
| May Brooke. By Anna H. Dorsey. New edition | 1.25 |
| Meditations on the Incarnation. St. Liguori | .75 |
| Merchant of Antwerp. By Hendrik Conscience | 1.25 |
| Mirror of True Womanhood. By Rev. B. O'Reilly | 2.50 |
| The same, gilt side and edges | 3.00 |
| "Mirror" and "True Men"—2 vols. in one, gilt | 3.50 |
| Mission Book, 18mo, (Prayer Book). Prices upwards from | .75 |
| Mission Book, 24mo, (Prayer Book). Prices upwards from | .50 |
| Mission Cross and Convent at St. Mary's | .75 |
| Mission and Duties of Young Women. By Rev. C. I. White, D.D. | .60 |
| Monsieur le Curé. Drama. Net | .25 |
| Month of Mary. By D. Roberto | .50 |
| Moore's Poetical Works, Complete. Octavo gilt | 3.00 |
| Mother Goose Melodies. For Children | .20 |
| Mother's Sacrifice. By Christine Faber | 1.25 |
| Mysteries of the Living Rosary. Per hundred Sheets net | 2.50 |
| Nannette's Marriage. Translated from the French | .75 |
| Nelligan's Speeches and Writings | 1.25 |
| New Ireland By A. M. Sullivan | 1.25 |

*Catholic Prayer-Books,* 25c., 50c., *up to* **12 00**

☞ Any of above books sent free by mail on receipt of price. Agents wanted everywhere to sell above books, to whom liberal terms will be given. Address

**P. J. KENEDY,** Excelsior Catholic Publishing House, *5 Barclay Street, New York.*

**Publications of P. J. Kenedy, 5 Barclay St. N. Y.**

| | |
|---|---:|
| New Seraphic Manual, (Prayer Book). For use of members of third order St. Francis. Cloth, red edge | .75 |
| New Testament, 18mo. Small edition, good type | .50 |
| New Testament, Octavo. Large type, vellum cloth | 1.50 |
| New Testament in Spanish. El Nuevo Testamento | 1.50 |
| Nobleman of '89. By M. A. Quinton | 1.50 |
| Oramaika. A Catholic Indian Story | .75 |
| Our Country, History of the U. S. By John G. Shea | .50 |
| Pastor's Visit to the Science of Salvation | .60 |
| Pearl in Dark Waters | .75 |
| Pocket Key of Heaven, (Prayer Book). Prices range upwards from | .25 |
| Poor Man's Catechism. By Rev. Mannock, O. S. B. | .40 |
| Prairie Boy. A Story for Boys | .75 |
| Prayer, the Great Means of Salvation. By St. Liguori. | .50 |
| Priests' Blessing, or Destiny | 1.25 |
| Procter's Poems. Red line, gilt edge. | 1.25 |
| Procter's Poems. Presentation edition. Octavo | 4.00 |
| Purgatory Opened. Month of November | .40 |
| Queen's Confession. By Raoul de Navery | .75 |
| Religion and Science. By Father Ronayne, S. J. | 1.25 |
| Rival Mail Carriers. Drama. Net | .25 |
| Rodriguez Christian Perfection, 3 vols | 4.00 |
| Rome, its Churches, Charities and Schools | 1.00 |
| Rosario, a Tale of the Sixteenth Century | .75 |
| Rosary Book. Illustrated. Paper Cover | .10 |
| Rose of St. Germains, or Florence O'Neill | 1.25 |
| Rose of Venice. A Story of Hatred and Remorse | .75 |
| Sacred History. By Bishop Challoner | .50 |
| Scapular Book, approved by Abp. of New York | .10 |
| Seraphic Staff—3d Order St. Francis | .25 |
| Seven of Us. Stories for Boys and Girls | .75 |
| Silvia, a Drama by John Savage. Net | .90 |
| Sixteen Names of Ancient Ireland. O'Leary | .50 |
| Solitary Island. By Rev. John Talbot Smith | 1.25 |
| Sophie's Troubles. By Comtesse de Segur | .75 |
| Southern Catholic Story. Minnie Mary Lee | 1.25 |

*Catholic Prayer-Books,* 25c., 50c., up to **12 00**

☞ Any of above books sent free by mail on receipt of price. Agents wanted everywhere to sell above books, to whom liberal terms will be given. Address

**P. J. KENEDY,** Excelsior Catholic Publishing House, *5 Barclay Street, New York.*

## Publications of P. J. Kenedy, 5 Barclay St. N. Y.

| | |
|---|---|
| Speeches from the Dock, Emmett, Wolfe Tone, etc.. | 1.25 |
| Spirit of St. Liguori. Visits to Blessed Sacrament... | 75 |
| St. John's Manual, (Prayer Book). Prices upwards from.................. | 1.50 |
| Stations of the Cross. By Rev. G. J. Misdziol. Paper. | .10 |
| Stories for Catholic Children. Rev. Grussi............ | 1.00 |
| Story of Italy, or Lionello. By Bresciani............ | 1.25 |
| Strayed from the Fold. Minnie Mary Lee......  ...... | 1.25 |
| Sunday School Teacher's Class Book. Per doz. net.... | 1.20 |
| Sybil, a Drama. By John Savage. Net................ | .50 |
| Sure Way to find out the True Religion. Rev. Baddeley. | .25 |
| Tales of Flemish Life. By Hendrik Conscience... ... | 1.25 |
| Talks about Ireland. By James Redpath. Paper.... | .30 |
| Think Well On't. By Bishop Challoner................ | .40 |
| Three Kings of Cologne. Rev. Titus Joslin .. ...... | .30 |
| Tracts for the Young—1st and 2d Series. Each....... | .50 |
| True Men as we need Them. Rev. B. O'Reilly....... | 2.50 |
| Turf Fire Stories and Fairy Tales of Ireland.......... | 1.25 |
| Two Cottages. By Lady Fullerton.................... | .50 |
| Two Brides. By Rev. Bernard O'Reilly............. | 1.50 |
| Universal Irish Songster. Profusely Illustrated...... | 1.50 |
| Ursuline Manual, (Prayer Book). Prices upwards from | 75 |
| Vision of Old Andrew the Weaver............  .... | 50 |
| Visits to the Blessed Sacrament. Red edges........ |  |
| Vultures of Erin. A Tale of the Penal Laws. ...... |  |
| Waiting for the Train. Drama. Net ........... | .25 |
| Western Missions and Missionaries. De Smet..... | 2.00 |
| Wild Irish Girl. Lady Morgan.... ...........  ...... | 1.00 |
| Willy Reilly. Large edition. 12 full page illustrations. | 1.25 |
| Within and Without the Fold...................... | 1.25 |
| Year with the Saints, 12mo. Red edges. Net. ....... | 1.50 |
| Young Captives. St. Augustine, etc................. | 40 |
| Young Poachers. Drama. Net.... .......... . | 25 |
| Youth's Director. Familiar Instructions.... ....... |  |
| Zozimus Papers. Blind Story Teller of Dublin...... . | .75 |

Catholic Prayer-Books, 25c., 50c., up to **12 00**

☞ Any of above books sent free by mail on receipt of price. Agents wanted everywhere to sell above books. To whom liberal terms will be given. Address
**P. J. KENEDY,** Excelsior Catholic Publ'n House, 5 Barclay Street, New York.

www.ingramcontent.com/pod-product-compliance
Lightning Source LLC
Chambersburg PA
CBHW030407230426
43664CB00007BB/787